MW00659323

Mysterious New Mexico

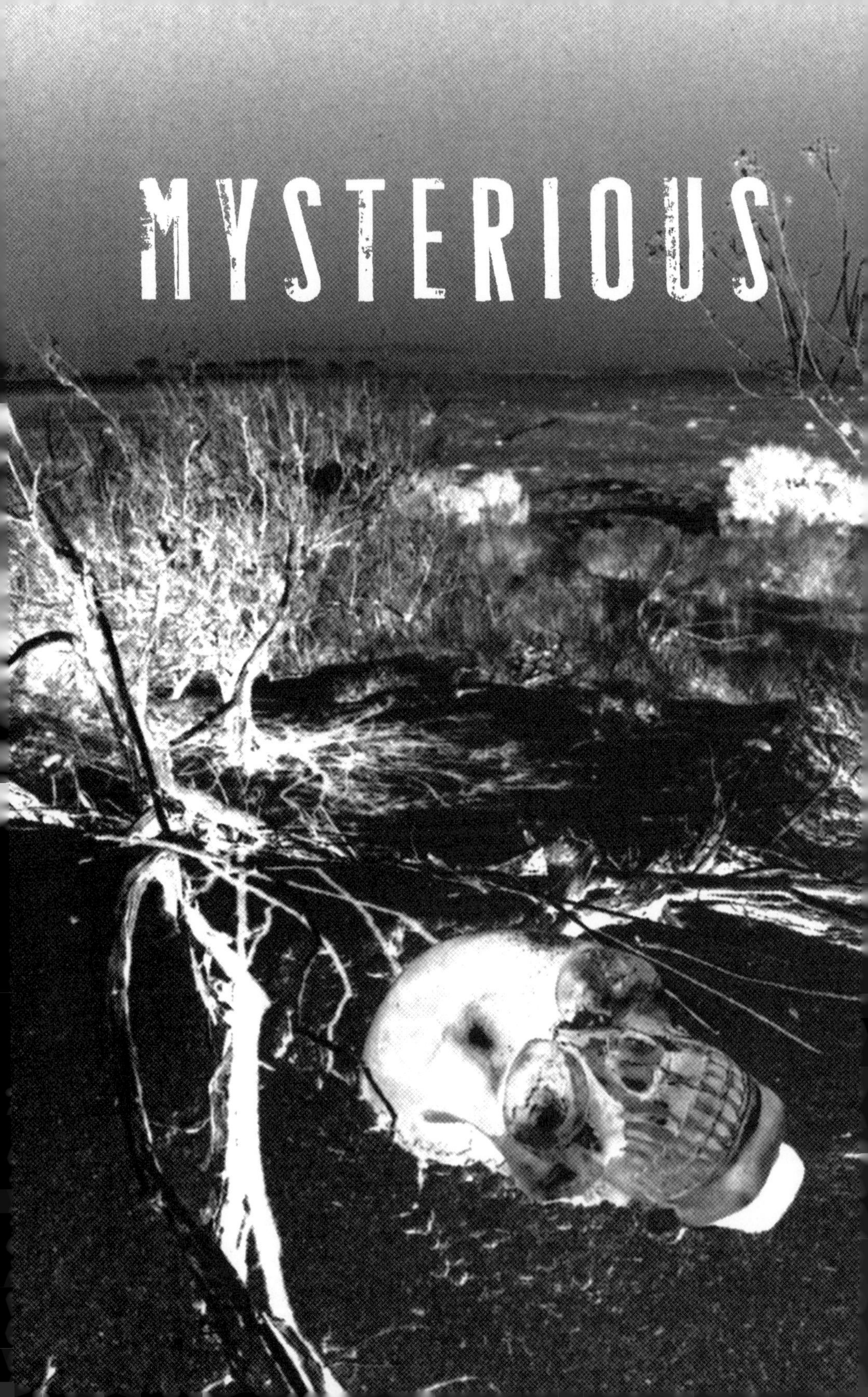
MYSTERIOUS

NEW MEXICO

MIRACLES, MAGIC, AND MONSTERS IN THE LAND OF ENCHANTMENT

BENJAMIN RADFORD

University of New Mexico Press ‡ Albuquerque

Printed in the United States of America
21 20 19 18 17 16 2 3 4 5 6 7

LIBRARY OF CONGRESS CATALOGING-IN-PUBLICATION DATA

Radford, Benjamin, 1970–
Mysterious New Mexico : miracles, magic, and monsters in the land of enchantment / Benjamin Radford. — First [edition].
pages cm
Includes bibliographical references and index.
ISBN 978-0-8263-5450-1 (pbk. : alk. paper) — ISBN 978-0-8263-5452-5 (electronic)
1. Haunted places—New Mexico. 2. Occultism—New Mexico.
3. Parapsychology—New Mexico. I. Title.
BF1472.U6R325 2014
001.9409789—dc23
2014001546

Designed by Lila Sanchez
Set in Sabon 10/13; Display type is Asphaltum and Copperplate Gothic

For *Armando Cordoba*,
and my greatest champion, *Martha Cushing*

CONTENTS

ACKNOWLEDGMENTS

In addition to those mentioned in the text, I am grateful for the support and assistance of many people, including Larry Barker, Robert Bartholomew, Dorion Cable, Matt Crowley, Rachel Duecaster, Ken and Ruth Frazier, Susan Gerbic, Sharon Hill, Lorie Hebler, Laura Aten Olshak, Amy Squish Stoker, Rob and Laurie Tarr, Dave Thomas, and Clark Whitehorn.

INTRODUCTION

New Mexico has a well-earned reputation for the mysterious and the bizarre. It is a land of contradictions and stark contrasts, a place where the exceptional and the commonplace, the rational and the mystical, seem to mix freely.

Beyond the black-ribboned highways and the bustling cities lies the surreal New Mexico, where ancient riddles lurk amid the sunbaked desert. Sometimes the strangeness is well known—even world famous—such as the 1947 Roswell crash. Other stories of ghosts, monsters, miracles, and magic are told regionally in hushed whispers.

It is no accident that the forty-seventh state is dubbed the Land of Enchantment. Mystics, artists, outlaws, dreamers, explorers, and scientists have been drawn to New Mexico for centuries. Spanish conquistadores, the first Europeans to meet Native Americans, searched for seven mythical cities of gold; many died in that pursuit. Later, outlaws such as Billy the Kid and Jesse James were lured here by New Mexico's reputation for lawlessness. Artists such as Georgia O'Keeffe sought out this part of the Southwest for its unique landscapes, natural beauty, and unusual light. Tens of thousands of New Agers and mystics have flocked to New Mexico, seeking the desert's wisdom and earth energies. And, of course, countless UFO and alien buffs visit the most famous UFO crash site in the world at Roswell.

Yet while New Mexico is steeped in the strange and supernatural, science has played a big role in the state's history. The world's top scientists came to New Mexico in the mid-1940s, developing (and then exploding) the world's first atomic bomb here. The New Mexican desert is also home to a huge array of radio astronomy dishes, studying the heavens and searching the skies for signs of intelligent alien life. A spaceport—the first of its kind—is being built in southern New Mexico, which will one day be used to take travelers into space. In many ways, New Mexico is truly a portal to other worlds.

Mysterious New Mexico is the first book to blend these two parallel traditions, using science and scientific methods to explore the mysterious and the bizarre. As a boy growing up in New Mexico not far from the Rio Grande, I was always fascinated by the world's mysteries, especially those in my home state: local ghost stories, monster sightings, and UFO crashes; stories of miracles and mysteries, strange and wondrous events that seem to defy explanation.

My interest is in exploring these mysteries and, when possible, solving them. Everyone loves a good mystery—who doesn't like to be intrigued and tantalized by the lure of the unknown? I certainly do.

But as Mark Twain said, "Supposing is good, but finding out is better." A story or legend may be fun and interesting, but is it also true? With this book I try to find out, to separate truth from myth where possible. Most authors who write about the mysterious and unexplained are content to merely repeat and rehash stories; I have taken a different approach. I have tried to bring an unprecedented level of research and scholarship—augmented with personal investigative experience—to these mysteries. I take them seriously and investigate them thoroughly because I believe that they deserve such attention. We can't plausibly deem these strange events "unexplained" until we have tried our best to explain them.

I've investigated mysterious phenomena in sixteen countries on four continents, traveling the world in search of answers. With *Mysterious New Mexico*, I return to my home state to tackle some of its weird phenomena, including haunted hotels, healing waters, witchcraft, alien visits—and, of course, many legends of miracles and mayhem.

In nearly all the cases, I have done original research and firsthand field investigation. Other writers may give their readers an overview or analysis, but few can tell readers what it's like to actually investigate these mysteries, to be there personally, because they research their books by going to the library (or, these days, by surfing the Internet).

I do that too—there's nothing wrong with scholarly and academic research—but to me that's just the first step in investigating these mysteries, not the last step. Doing real investigation is not easy; it is time consuming, difficult, laborious, and often tedious. It's much easier to read some articles and books, visit a few websites, and write it up than it is to dig a little deeper for real answers. I have never been content to repeat other people's stories, to credulously accept other people's word for what happened. I want to investigate; I want to interview eyewitnesses, go to the locations, see for myself what happened, and try to piece the mystery together.

Unlike most other books on mysteries in the Southwest and New Mexico, I have actually *solved* many of the mysteries, and this book is the first to publish the explanations. I give background information on the topics, drawing on folklore, sociology, history, and even forensic science investigation, while guiding the reader through truths and myths about each topic. So join me as I reexamine some old mysteries—and unearth some new ones—in the Land of Enchantment.

CHAPTER 1

PHANTOM PERFORMANCES AT THE HAUNTED KIMO THEATER

Haunted theaters are nothing new; ghosts have long been said to tread the boards right along with accomplished actors and struggling playwrights. Many of these stories are mere thespian superstition, of course. But one haunted theater in New Mexico's largest city is not only reputedly home to a ghost but the location of one of the greatest poltergeist cases in history.

The KiMo Theater in Albuquerque is a remarkable building. It was built in 1926 (the same year Harry Houdini died) and opened its doors on September 19, 1927. Located downtown at 421 Central Avenue, it has a unique architecture that combines art deco with Native American motifs, creating one of the city's best-known landmarks. The KiMo's early years were successful as the venue hosted the big stars of the era, including Tom Mix, Ginger Rogers, and Vivian Vance (of *I Love Lucy* fame).

The KiMo is the best-known haunted theater in New Mexico, if not the entire American Southwest. The KiMo's ghost has been the subject of dozens of newspaper and magazine articles, book chapters, and even a few investigations by local ghost hunter groups. It's a rare Halloween in Albuquerque that one or more news outlets don't carry some mention of the KiMo haunting. The KiMo ghost has also been featured on national television.

Figure 1.1. *Albuquerque's KiMo Theater, said to be one of the most haunted theaters in New Mexico and throughout the American Southwest. Photo by the author.*

TRAGEDY AT THE KIMO

The theater was successful for its first quarter century, hosting everything from vaudeville to Hollywood films. But tragedy waited in the wings, striking just before four o'clock on a Thursday afternoon, August 2, 1951. About a thousand people were in the theater to see the Abbott and Costello film *Comin' Round the Mountain* when a water heater supplying the concession stand exploded into the lobby. Chunks of plaster, scalding steam, and glass shot into the air. When the dust and chaos had settled, eight people were injured; several were treated for fractured arms and legs. One man, Corporal Mike Tullio, had severe cuts and abrasions covering his body that "resembled shotgun wounds." His face was heavily lacerated, and the blast cost him his right eye, although fortunately his twelve-year-old daughter escaped injury.

Frank Ellis, eighteen at the time, described the explosion: "I was sitting about four rows from the back. [The film] had just started. All of a sudden I heard a boom. After that people were getting up and

Figure 1.2. *Dennis Potter, the longtime technical director at the KiMo Theater, shows the author where the explosion occurred. Photo by Mike Smith.*

running. Some were screaming. After that some men came running in the theater yelling 'Quiet!' I did the same. A lady was lying on the floor, she must have had a broken leg. 'Am I dead?' 'Am I dead?' she kept saying. I tried to calm her down, then some men came over and took care of her" (Giannettino and Bennett 1951).

Tragically, the most seriously injured was Robert (Bobby) Darnall Jr., a six-year-old boy. Bobby had gone to the theater with two friends, eleven-year-old Lou Ellen and seven-year-old Ronald Ross. The trio sat in the balcony watching *This Is America: They Fly with the Fleet*, a sixteen-minute short documentary about U.S. naval aviation training in Pensacola, Florida. Bobby became frightened by a sudden loud siren in the film and ran from the balcony, Lou Ellen in pursuit. As it turned out, the boy's head start may have saved Lou Ellen's life, because the boiler under the stairs exploded just as Bobby entered the lobby. According to the August 3 account by the *Albuquerque Journal*, "The child's head and face were crushed as the blast hurled him into a wall."

A defective thermostat was eventually blamed for the explosion.

Although the blast was powerful, it did far more damage to the filmgoers than to the theater itself. Manager George Tucker estimated that damage to the building was only "several hundred dollars." As they say in theater, the show must go on. Repairs were made, wounds were bandaged, and the KiMo soon reopened. Funeral services were held for Bobby on August 4, and he was buried in Albuquerque's Fairview Park Cemetery. Injuries healed and life went on for the city. No one thought much more about Bobby or the explosion that took his life until a few decades later—when Bobby returned.

LITTLE BOBBY RETURNS FROM THE GRAVE

One typical account of Bobby's return from the grave comes from Jewel Sanchez, who spent fourteen years working at the KiMo beginning in 1979. In an interview by Antonio Garcez for his book *Adobe Angels: The Ghosts of Albuquerque*, Sanchez told of a tradition of leaving doughnuts for Bobby's ghost. Another source, HauntedHouses.com, states that "in 1988, someone unseen helped itself to some doughnuts which were left untouched by the living on a table in the stage area. Bite marks made by a little mouth could be seen on some of the doughnuts. To pamper their little ghost, crew members started to hang doughnuts on the water pipe that runs along the back wall of the theater behind the stage." The New Mexico Tourism Department's website offers its own version of the story: "To appease the spirit, the cast hangs doughnuts on the water pipe that runs along the back wall of the theater behind the stage. Often, the treats are gone the next morning. Of those that are left, bite marks made by a little mouth can sometimes be seen."

Apparently, little Bobby Darnall returned in a most spectacular fashion. According to Sanchez,

> one Christmas Day in 1974 there was a performance of some sort, and a member of the crew who was unaware of the doughnut tradition saw the collection of sweets hanging on the water pipe and, apparently disgusted with the sight, removed them and placed them in the trash. I was told that as soon as they were removed all sorts of weird and negative stuff began to happen. Anything that could go wrong, did go wrong. Props which had been well-anchored to the floor toppled over, as if intentionally pushed by invisible hands. Electrical cables blew up in a storm of sparks and flashes. . . . While going through the live

> performance, [the actors] tripped and fell over an invisible object. Some actors stated that their fall felt as if it was caused by a pair of invisible hands that quickly but firmly pushed them to the floor.

Dan Mayfield, a reporter for the *Albuquerque Journal*, described the consequences: "The entire cast forgot to show up. Stage lights were popping. Once they got there, actors forgot lines, and doors and windows were flying open" (Mayfield 2004). Once the doughnuts were replaced (and Bobby was presumably appeased), the incidents miraculously stopped! This is typical of what many think of as poltergeist activity, the terrifying kind often seen in horror movies, featuring cabinet doors opening and closing on their own or dishes crashing around a kitchen late at night.

The KiMo ghost story includes one of the world's most famous cases of public poltergeist activity. Alleged ghostly activity is usually very minor (missing keys, odd lights or sounds, etc.) and experienced by only one person; to have a whole theater community witness the mysterious phenomena is very rare indeed. In this case the activity happened in front of hundreds of eyewitnesses. Not only did the cast and crew see these inexplicable ghostly activities, but so did the entire audience! One of the best-documented poltergeist cases in history apparently happened in downtown Albuquerque.

What do we make of this account of the invisible hands and mysterious disasters? Is this ghost story fiction or a real event? Unfortunately, Antonio Garcez did little or no investigation for his book *Adobe Angels* to sort fact from fiction. He simply passed along what he had been told as fact. This is a common problem with books containing "true accounts" of ghosts: with very rare exceptions, authors are content to simply record and publish the stories without doing even the most basic research to find out if they are true or not. There's nothing wrong with collections of fictional ghost stories; folklore provides a wonderful and fascinating look at different cultures. But it is problematic to call such stories "true" without confirmation through independent research. It is dishonest and inaccurate to call a fictional story or novel a "true story."

Rather than rely on thirdhand information about the ghostly encounter, I visited the KiMo with a coinvestigator, Mike Smith, to check for ourselves. Sanchez is long gone, but the theater's current technical manager, Dennis Potter, has almost singlehandedly kept the story of Bobby alive. Potter has seen his share of strangeness in his more than twenty years at the KiMo.

To be honest, I was skeptical about the story. There are countless ghost and haunted house cases in which a little investigation quickly reveals that the whole story is completely made up; there are no eyewitnesses to the events because they didn't happen.

Thus I was (pleasantly) surprised when I spoke to Potter, a friendly, balding, and bespectacled man with an easy smile and the gift of gab (figure 1.3). The disastrous performance could not be dismissed as a mere fabrication. Not only did Potter confirm the basic details of the story, but he was there that night and witnessed the whole thing! "It was just before Christmas, and the New Mexico Repertory Theater Company did *A Christmas Carol*," Potter (2008a) explained. The director, Andrew Shea, noticed the doughnuts strung up against the brick wall at the back of the stage: "He saw a large collection of doughnuts. They had just sort of accumulated there." According to Potter, Shea had a fit about the doughnuts and ordered them removed. The doughnuts came off the walls and were thrown into the garbage. This, according to legend, is what spawned the story of the KiMo ghost.

Figure 1.3. *The author and KiMo technician Dennis Potter on the stage, where a poltergeist is said to have ruined a performance. Photo by John Thompson of the* Albuquerque Journal. *Reprinted by permission.*

THE POLTERGEIST APPEARS

The next day was a Saturday, with two scheduled performances. The problems began almost immediately. The cast and crew began arriving for the two o'clock show, and someone soon realized that none of the child performers who played Bob Cratchit's children were there. They had gone to see the new *Star Trek* film, and volunteers were dispatched to local theaters to round up the children. They arrived with mere minutes to spare before the scheduled show time, and the production started fifteen minutes late.

"About ten or fifteen minutes into the show, weird things started going wrong," Potter remembers. "People were forgetting their lines, people were tripping and falling on stage, odd pieces of equipment would fall from the ceiling, light bulbs exploded. Electrical cables fell down . . . light gels came off and fluttered down during dramatic moments. They were having trouble getting through the show. Windows and doors on the set were either not opening, or were opening when they weren't supposed to. It was just really weird. They almost literally didn't get through the show, there were so many disruptions." It sounds like a spooky scene from *Poltergeist*, *The Amityville Horror*, or *The Exorcist*!

Finally, somehow, the show managed to wrap up, and the cascade of mysterious disasters came to an end. The cast and crew, stunned by their ordeal, blamed the director for discarding the doughnuts and rousing the ire of Bobby's ghost. According to Potter, the director apologized to everyone for removing the doughnuts, then spent fifty dollars on two cases of doughnuts and strung them up all over the building, including the lobby. This tasty offering apparently appeased Bobby, for the eight o'clock show went without a hitch. From then on, doughnuts were left out for Bobby, although some years ago they were moved to a small shrine near the dressing rooms (figure 1.4). A collection of offerings for Bobby, ranging from toys to theater tickets to ballerina shoes, continue to be left for the boy ghost. (The doughnuts are mostly a thing of the past, for sanitary reasons.)

Some say that Bobby continues to haunt the KiMo and has ruined other performances since that time when he was first denied his doughnuts. Writer Scott Johnson claims, "For a period of time, it seemed that not one performance went off without some type of disaster. Between actors locked in their dressing rooms and tripping while making their entrances, many of which were accompanied by child-like laughter, it seemed the little boy was bent on wrecking the business." In fact, according to Johnson, "Bobby is still frequently sighted. . . . Sightings of Bobby are continuous, year round" (Johnson 2007).

Another source, HauntedHouses.com, states, "This scenario has happened many times. As long as treats are hung on the water pipe, everything works fine, goes smoothly, and the child ghost is happy. If his treats are taken down and not replaced, disaster happens with the technical effects. Calm is restored immediately after hanging new treats on the pipe!" I was excited to hear this, because it meant that I might be able to experience Bobby's ghostly wrath myself. Perhaps if I attended enough shows, or we took down some of the items from his shrine, Bobby would show himself. Additionally, there would be not hundreds, but potentially thousands of eyewitnesses who had experienced similar supernatural events at different performances over the years. Maybe someone in the audience had even recorded such events. The prospect that this could be a world-class, rock-solid case for ghosts excited me, and I was eager to dig deeper into the mystery.

OTHER GHOSTLY ENCOUNTERS

A few other people have reported seeing what might be Bobby's ghost. In one case a woman who happened to be standing across the street from the theater claimed to see a boy waving at her from the (apparently vacant) third floor. Jewel Sanchez, on another occasion, says that she saw a young boy wearing a striped shirt and jeans running up and down the stairs, who then disappeared before her eyes. There are a few other stories from the theater, none with a clear connection to Bobby. For example, one person claims to have heard footsteps when no one was there; on another occasion a child's laughter was heard; still another time a woman claimed that some play props were mysteriously moved. Unfortunately, such reports were never investigated and are little more than third- and fourth-hand stories. The fact is that there are virtually no other verifiable reports of Bobby; the story of the KiMo ghost rests almost entirely on the doomed performance of *A Christmas Carol.*

ENTER THE GHOST HUNTERS

The story of the KiMo theater has all the elements of a classic ghost story, including the tragic death of a young boy and mysterious and unexplained events that occur thereafter. Yet all the reports—true or

Figure 1.4. *A shrine backstage at the KiMo Theater, where offerings are left for Bobby Darnall's ghost. Photo by the author.*

not, without further investigation—are simply stories, not the hard evidence science would need to verify a ghost. Ghost stories (as fun and entertaining as they may be) are not evidence.

There are a few people who claim to have found evidence of Bobby's ghost in the decorated halls of the KiMo. They include Albuquerque ghost hunters Ron and Sherri Andree and their (now-defunct) ghost group, New Mexico Paranormal Investigations (NMPI). The NMPI team appeared on television several times with regard to the KiMo haunting, including on KRQE Channel 13 in an award-winning feature segment broadcast on Halloween 2007.

The NMPI team conducted a one-night investigation, searching for evidence of Bobby or other spirits in the theater. They used cameras, electromagnetic field (EMF) detectors, dowsing rods, thermometers, and other equipment (for a scientific analysis of these devices and methods, see Radford 2010, chapter 4). Sherri Andree stated, "We thought about what a six-year-old from the 1950s would like to play with so when we did our investigation we brought him a baseball and some Silly Putty." It's a quaint thought, although it's not clear how a disembodied spirit without human hands would play with a baseball or Silly Putty. During their investigation, the Andrees reported finding "anomalous EMF energy," a "wisp of energy," and so on, as well as taking photographs they claim are of Bobby's ghost.

Cody Polston, the founder of another Albuquerque-based ghost hunting group, the Southwest Ghost Hunters Association, also looked into the KiMo ghost story. In his book *Haunted New Mexico*, he gives a few accounts of Bobby, "who has been seen playing on the stairs leading to the balcony. He is described as having brown hair, wearing a stripped [*sic*] shirt and jeans" (Polston 2004, 35). The team investigated the KiMo on several occasions, including in February 2007 and March 2008.*

* Prior to my investigation, the Southwest Ghost Hunters Association suggested that they had found evidence of Bobby Darnall's ghost and that the KiMo Theater was indeed haunted. After my investigation was made public around 2008, their website was updated with the following information: "We do not believe that the Kimo [*sic*] theater is haunted based on the following data collected from these investigations." The site goes on to list information revealed for the first time in work I published in my own investigations, although the ghost hunters' statement carefully neglects to specify whose "historical research" found these facts. I'm pleased that Polston's ghost-hunting group endorses my KiMo research and agrees with its conclusions.

. . . BUT IS IT TRUE?

At first glance, the evidence that Bobby Darnall haunts the KiMo Theater seems impressive. Hundreds of eyewitnesses saw unexplained phenomena during the ruined Christmas production; and at least two teams of ghost experts "confirmed" the existence of *something* strange—possibly supernatural—at the KiMo, complete with "anomalous" photos and instrument readings. All in all, the KiMo ghost story seems pretty solid. It's only on closer inspection that one realizes that things are not always as they appear. As they say, "The devil is in the details." In this case, the ghost is in the details—or not.

The account of the disastrous production is an important key to understanding the KiMo ghost story, for several reasons. It is the first time that the ghost of Bobby Darnall was linked to mysterious occurrences at the KiMo. Perhaps more importantly, it is something tangible, something that can be verified. Most "evidence" for ghosts consists of odd feelings, ambiguous photos, and occasional sightings—information that can't really be examined or tested. But the unexplained phenomena of exploding lights, mysterious falls, and objects moving on their own—witnessed by thousands of people on several occasions—is much closer to hard evidence.

Something—whether Bobby's ghost or some other mysterious force—ruined the production of *A Christmas Carol* on Christmas Day 1974.

Or did it?

THE DOOMED CHRISTMAS CAROL

The first step in unraveling the mystery was verifying the date. According to several sources, including Antonio Garcez in *Adobe Angels*, the doomed production was held on December 25, 1974. Yet, as researcher Mike Smith discovered in newspaper archives, it is very unlikely that *A Christmas Carol*—or any other play—was in production at the KiMo that day, for on Christmas Day 1974 the theater was advertised as "the Notorious KiMo, the plushest adult theater in New Mexico." Instead of a family-friendly production of *A Christmas Carol*, KiMo patrons saw a film called *Teenage Fantasies* (with the tagline, "If *Deep Throat* made you tingle, this will make you twitch!"). If Bobby's ghost were present that day, the big-screen early-1970s porn was probably more disturbing to the boy ghost than the lack of doughnuts.

So that detail wasn't true. Potter told me that the infamous performance occurred some time in the late 1980s or early 1990s. He wasn't sure of the date—or even the decade—which seemed odd for such a memorable event; I thought to myself that if I'd seen more than an hour of supernatural activity, I'd probably remember exactly when it had occurred. He also corrected another piece of common misinformation about the KiMo ghost: there was only one supernaturally disastrous show, not several, and they certainly have not been occurring to the present day, despite the claims of some ill-informed writers. I was disappointed to realize that I wouldn't be able to interview a pool of thousands of eyewitnesses, but at least I knew that one audience was there.

But what year was it? Using the *Star Trek* film that Potter said the child actors attended before the show as a clue (specifically, *Star Trek IV: The Voyage Home*), Mike and I narrowed down the month and year to December 1986. We then could identify which performance it was and interview other people involved with that production of *A Christmas Carol*. I was eager to hear other stories of the poltergeist activity; maybe some attendees had seen other ghostly phenomena.

I first tracked down Steve Schwartz, the actor who played Bob Cratchit, and asked him what he remembered about that fateful night.

"It went great, it was a wonderful performance," he said.

I was puzzled. *A wonderful performance?* With all the unexplained problems, the exploding lights, actors tripping on the set, and everything else? How could he have failed to mention experiencing a terrifying poltergeist firsthand? I elaborated, hoping to jog his memory: "The story goes that there was a performance of *A Christmas Carol*—in fact it was one of the ones you played in—that was ruined by mysterious phenomena: the actors forgot their lines, there were exploding lights, missing props, basically everything that could go wrong went wrong."

Schwartz was silent for a moment, incredulous. Finally he asked, "One of *our* performances?"

"Yes, that's the story," I replied.

"That sounds like good copy, but I can't corroborate any of that. I don't remember any problems like that, or any problems with the show."

We spoke further about the show; he remembered it well and described it in some detail. There was no mention of anything strange at all. Just so there was no mistake, I asked one more time: "As far as you know, are any of the accounts of that night true?"

"Not that I know of," Schwartz replied, "unless the events were so catastrophic that I blocked them out of my memory!" I ran out of different ways to ask the same question and hung up the phone, trying to understand why the lighting tech and a lead actor in the same play had two completely opposite memories of the show. Of course, people's memories change over time, and although Schwartz didn't recall problems with the play, someone else might.

To get a third eyewitness account, Mike interviewed Andrew Shea, who directed the play and whose dismissive doughnut disposal had allegedly led to the ruined performance. Shea spent eight years directing plays at the KiMo Theater, from 1984 to 1991, and is now a successful film director.

Shea also disputed Potter's recollection of that night: "I don't remember it being a disaster in any way," he said. He agreed with Potter that some of the child actors were late for the show but stated that they arrived in time for their on-stage appearances. Asked if he recalled any of the incidents described by Potter and repeated by others—the exploding lights, the falling actors, the props moved by unseen hands, and so on—he said no. "In terms of that day that Dennis is talking about, no. All I remember is the kids not showing up [on time]."

Furthermore, Shea said, the story of him taking down the doughnuts and then replacing them after the disastrous performance is a fabrication. In fact, Shea had never heard the story of Bobby the KiMo ghost until I told him, so he certainly hadn't been leaving doughnuts for any ghost children. "I didn't even know that people connected that one particular performance with the doughnuts and the ghost stuff." Shea's account makes sense: if there was no ruined performance, then there would be no reason to put the doughnuts back up. He also discredits other stories about ongoing strange occurrences at the KiMo, due to Bobby or any other ghost: "There were no events during my eight years there that didn't have mundane explanations. . . . I don't recall anything supernatural or out of the ordinary happening."

So one of the play's main actors and the director both discredit the ghost story. But could we find any audience members who were there? There was no real way to determine who was in the audience at the time, but it's possible that a critic from a local newspaper attended the play—surely such a mysterious and infamously disastrous performance would have been noted at least in passing in the *Albuquerque Journal* or the *Albuquerque Tribune*.

The mystery deepened: there was nothing. The reviews were positive, and not one mentioned actors falling or tripping, or exploding lights, or any ghostly activities. Just to be sure, Mike contacted Ollie Reed Jr., who had been the drama critic for the *Albuquerque Tribune* in 1986. Reed said, "I do not recall any stories about any unusual events related to that production." Other people we interviewed who were there at the time said the same thing. All the evidence points to one inescapable conclusion: the ruination of the play—the very genesis of the KiMo ghost story—simply did not occur; it is but folklore and fiction.

SPAWNING THE STORY

Where does this leave Dennis Potter and the countless ghostly stories his tale spawned? I don't believe that Potter is a liar or that he's crazy; he simply did something we all do from time to time: he misremembered. Voluminous psychological research has shown that human memory is remarkably fallible. The brain is not, as many suppose, a sort of tape recorder that accurately preserves what we experience. Instead, memories change over time. As memoirist William Maxwell noted in his book *So Long, See You Tomorrow*, "What we refer to confidently as memory . . . is really a form of storytelling that goes on continually in the mind and often changes with the telling."

Psychologist Tom Gilovich, in his book *How We Know What Isn't So*, explains how memories change over time and become distorted. "When people are given a message to relay to someone else, they rarely convey the message verbatim. The limits of human memory and the implicit demand that the listener not be burdened with too many details constrain the amount and kind of information that is transmitted. . . . Secondhand accounts often become simpler and 'cleaner' stories that are not encumbered by minor inconsistencies or ambiguous details" (58).

During the 2008 presidential campaign, Senator Hillary Clinton recalled landing in Bosnia via helicopter in 1996 under sniper fire. Yet news footage of the occasion showed that her group did not arrive under attack. Clinton's critics accused her of deception, but psychologists know it is more likely that she simply and honestly misremembered her experience, as many of us unknowingly do when telling stories of our personal experiences. A comforting, kindly mist enshrouds our holy past, and unless we are confronted with evidence to the contrary, we will continue to confidently believe our own memories. (For a much fuller discussion of memory errors and how false memories can be created, see the work of Elizabeth Loftus and Richard Ofshe.)

GHOST STORIES AS FACT

Psychology helps explain how Potter's faulty memory could create a ghost story. But thousands of sources, from Antonio Garcez to Albuquerque ghost hunters to local television reports and websites, repeated the story of Bobby and the doomed show. How could so many accounts have gotten it wrong? The simple answer is that Dennis Potter is the source of virtually all the information, and the journalists, writers, and investigators repeated his stories, never bothering to independently verify his account.

One difficulty with information on the KiMo ghost is the tendency of many writers on the subject to simply copy information from one source to another without checking any facts. The problems range from shockingly sloppy research to outright plagiarism. To give just one example, Cody Polston heavily plagiarized a book chapter on the KiMo ghost. Nearly half of a two-page entry on the KiMo ghost from Ellen Robson and Dianne Halicki's *Haunted Highway: The Spirits of Route 66* (1999, 116–18) is lifted verbatim (and uncredited) in Polston's own *Haunted New Mexico*. With so many authors simply copying each other's work instead of doing any actual research, it's little wonder that errors are repeated and myths taken as fact. If they fail to do their own research, such authors certainly can't be trusted to complete a credible investigation. With rare exceptions, such writers provide no references or notes for their information, making follow-up research difficult or impossible. If one makes a statement without citing a source, readers can't determine whether that statement is factual or just made up on the spot.*

THE BOY ON THE STAIRS AND IN THE WINDOW

Jewel Sanchez, who claimed to have seen a boy on the KiMo stairs, is the only eyewitness to Bobby's ghost. It's impossible to know what, if anything, she saw, but other information she provided turned out to be wrong. Furthermore, Dennis Potter himself is less than impressed by her credibility: "I wouldn't believe anything she had to say," he stated flatly.

* Compare Polston, *Haunted New Mexico*, 32–34, with Robson and Halicki, *Haunted Highway*, 116–17. The plagiarism is obvious and unmistakable; Polston simply took other writers' words and claimed them as his own.

The only other alleged Bobby sighting is that of a boy in the third-floor window of the KiMo. According to an article in the *Albuquerque Journal*,

> It was early one morning about two years ago at the KiMo Theatre. All the performers and staff had left for the night. But there, trapped on the third floor of the Downtown theater, was a boy. He was waving at the office across the street, grinning. 'It was morning, and I had somebody call me,' said Craig Rivera, the KiMo's manager. 'He's waving at us,' the people in the office told Rivera in a panic. 'So what happens is, I see the door is locked. There's no kid in there,' Rivera said. 'At that point I said, 'You may be the first person I know that's seen Bobby.' (Mayfield 2004)

Without more information, it's hard to know what to make of this report. Who was the woman? What exactly did she see? Could she simply have been mistaken? Did anyone else see it? There also seems to be a contradiction in the account: it supposedly occurred early one morning after the "staff had left for the night," which would be some time past midnight. Why was a woman in an office building across the street, looking up at the third floor of the KiMo at that hour? And from that distance in the night's darkness, even with street lamps, could she really have seen details such as a boy's grin? Did the anonymous woman call Rivera that night, or wait until the next morning (as he suggested) to call him "in a panic"? There's good reason to suspect that this story is false, or at least exaggerated.

Note also that it was Rivera who first (perhaps jokingly) identified the boy as Bobby, and this assumption became part of the KiMo ghost story. Perhaps the best explanation comes from folklorist Jan Brunvand, who states, "I would link the 'ghost in the window' to the 'image on glass' theme in traditional legends. . . . A folklorist named Barbara Allen . . . showed that in the early days of photography people thought that a lightning flash (like the flash power used to make photos) might cause an image to appear in a glass pane (like the glass plates used in cameras then), and that this general idea might have led to the various permutations of the motif in folklore" (Brunvand 2008; Allen 1982). Indeed, the "face in the window" is a common theme in folkloric ghost stories; for example, in an 1876 incident in Carrollton, Alabama, a man's face appeared in a window near where he was killed (Durm 1999).

DOUGHNUTS

The revelation that the doomed performance was in fact quite ordinary answers one mystery but raises another: if the doughnuts weren't left to appease Bobby after the botched play, where did the doughnut tradition come from?

Potter says that the doughnut tradition started with an employee getting coffee and doughnuts for the cast and crew, as happens in many workplaces across the country. "Usually an extra cup of coffee or doughnut would be left at the end of the day," Potter explained. "Nobody wanted to be a pig and eat the last doughnut, so usually there'd be one left in the box. The next morning, sometimes the doughnut would be gone, or half gone, or have a bite out of it. It was a back-of-the-mind curiosity: Who ate the doughnut? As a joke . . . we'd take the doughnut and tie it up on the electrical conduit on the back wall. After a while we had a pretty amazing collection of doughnuts!"

Potter told me that the doughnuts did not begin as an offering to Bobby's ghost: "No, it was a souvenir collection, an oddball history of the building," not unlike a pub adorned with sports memorabilia or photographs of its famous patrons. It was a joke, a running gag among colleagues, not a ghostly offering.

In a classic case of legend making, there's the added "spooky" detail of the "child-size" bites in the doughnuts. But what does that even mean? Did someone actually measure the size of the bites? And would anyone but a forensic dental specialist really be able to distinguish a child's bite mark from that of a petite woman, or anyone just wanting a nibble? Besides that, do ghosts have teeth, or even need to eat food? They can supposedly pass through walls, yet are their teeth sufficiently solid to take a bite out of a doughnut?

With the application of some critical thinking, the disappearing doughnut becomes a nonmystery. The most likely explanation is that one of the last people to leave the theater either threw the (by then staling) doughnut away, or ate part or all of it. If half-eaten office doughnuts are a true mystery and evidence of ghosts, then perhaps Bobby is also haunting hundreds of thousands of offices across the country!

As for Shea's removal of the doughnuts, "We told [the director] it was a bad idea," Potter said—not because it would anger Bobby, since few in the cast and crew had heard of him, but because it was "messing with the theater tradition . . . discarding the history of the building."

The doughnuts went from an inside joke to a souvenir collection to the basis for a ghost story.

So how did Bobby Darnall become part of the KiMo ghost story?

Potter noted that almost all theaters have some ghost tradition or superstition: "It's always easier to blame it on the ghost. Theater people are generally superstitious anyway. . . . We figured the theater had some sort of spirit in the building. We already knew that little boy had been killed here in the building, so it was just a natural assumption that if someone were playing April Fool's jokes, it was probably Bobby."

Potter (as it turns out, wrongly) believed that bad things happened after the doughnuts were removed. In addition to the children being late, there may have been a few normal, minor problems with the show that Potter misremembered as a string of disasters. (The same thing happens when a person is having a bad day—the negative, difficult things stand out in the person's mind, and he or she will focus on those instead of any positive things.)

This is common in superstitious thinking; the same principle occurs when, for example, professional athletes, after a big win, eat exactly the same meals and stay in the same rooms at the same hotels at future contests at that same location. They think that their success must have something to do with circumstances beyond their playing ability. Poker players will wear the same "lucky" shirt they were wearing when they hit it big, and so on. This logical fallacy is known in Latin as *post hoc ergo propter hoc* (after this, therefore because of it), also known as faulty causation. The human brain seeks patterns and causes and will often find them even when they don't exist; an observer at the KiMo might reason, "We took down the doughnuts, then something bad happened. We put them back up, and things were okay, so taking down the doughnuts must have caused the bad things to happen." But such reasoning is often misleading; a simple and cogent test of Bobby's curse would be to simply remove the doughnuts (without the cast and crew's knowledge) and see if a string of disastrous performances follow.

As Potter himself noted, minor mishaps, problems, and glitches are not uncommon in theater. Putting on a stage production is a difficult and complex task involving dozens of people, props, lights, sounds, and so on. The only reason the events were mysterious was because he remembered them all happening at about the same time. "The events of that particular afternoon, if they had been spread over a month it wouldn't have been a big deal," Potter said. "But the fact that they literally happened within about two hours of each other was not typical."

But if the handful of random accidents and annoyances and events that Potter remembers as having happened in one afternoon actually occurred over the course of days, weeks, or even months, then the mystery vanishes. There would be no cluster of unusual or mysterious incidents, thus no need to invoke a ghostly or supernatural explanation.

All roads lead back to Dennis Potter as having (however unwittingly) created the KiMo ghost and its story. It wasn't Andrew Shea or Steven Schwartz, as they either didn't know about Bobby or heard about him only later. It was Dennis Potter (or one of his colleagues at the KiMo) who first connected various minor mishaps to the death of Bobby Darnall thirty-five years earlier.

GHOSTLY EVIDENCE

With some diligent research, the story of Bobby Darnall's ghost collapses like a haunted house of cards. With virtually the entire story of the KiMo ghost discredited, a curious question arises: What about the ghost hunters who claimed to find evidence of Bobby's ghost? What phenomena at the KiMo did they interpret as evidence of the paranormal?

To answer this, some background on ghosts and ghost hunting is helpful. First, there is no definitive proof that ghosts exist. Despite centuries of speculation, no one has yet found hard evidence of life after death or spectral visits. As a result, ghost hunters accept a far lower standard of evidence than scientists and skeptical investigators do. To many self-styled ghost hunters, virtually anything that appears odd to them for any reason may be considered evidence of ghosts (see Radford 2010). For example, some ghost hunters claim to be psychic "sensitives," and if they feel uneasy, have negative impressions, or simply get frightened while in a supposedly haunted place, they will attribute that to a ghost's presence. One member of the New Mexico Paranormal Investigations team "felt a huge sense of sadness, darkness, and meanness" while at the KiMo Theater.

Is this evidence of a ghost? Or is there another explanation? The problem is of course that these feelings and sensations cannot be independently or scientifically verified. There's no test for a "sense of sadness, darkness, and meanness." They can, however, be explained by psychology and the power of suggestion: just because a person has a panic attack doesn't mean that the perceived threat is real. (A friend of mine with an anxiety disorder had panic attacks when he crossed bridges; his fear, perspiration, and racing heart were real, but the perceived threat was all in his mind.) In the same way, if a ghost hunter is convinced that he or she is in a room with a scary, angry ghost, that person will likely have experiences similar to those the NMPI staff described—even if no ghost is there. It's not necessarily a hallucination, but people can be very suggestible, especially in places they consider scary.

Most ghost hunters realize that their personal feelings are neither good science nor good evidence, and therefore they use more reliable tools and equipment. On the face of it, this is a step in the right direction, from subjective feelings to objective measures. But the problem is that the science and methodology doesn't necessarily improve with better gear. For example, many ghost hunters (including the NMPI) use dowsing rods and pendulums when searching for ghosts, conveniently ignoring the fact that neither dowsing rods nor pendulums have ever been proven to find ghosts. They, along with the Southwest Ghost Hunters Association, also use higher-tech gear such as digital thermometers, digital cameras, and EMF detectors. While this impresses many laypeople as being very scientific, it is in fact exactly the opposite; it is pseudoscience.

The problem is that, given the lack of hard evidence for the existence of ghosts, it cannot therefore be assumed that they generate EMFs (or, for that matter, change the room temperature, appear in photographs, etc.). So when an investigator is seen on television with a beeping, flashing EMF meter, it impresses the public, who assume that they are detecting ghosts, when in fact they are simply detecting electromagnetic fields, which are given off by many things including cell phones, radios, and anything with an electrical current running through it (figure 1.5).

Many ghost hunters seem unaware of this fact, or willfully ignore it. As with the story of the doomed play, the "ghostly evidence" evaporates under a little critical thinking and close examination. Almost every part of the ghost hunters' investigation is scientifically invalid and/or factually wrong.

ORBS

One of the NMPI's favorite pieces of evidence for ghosts is something called an orb. These are "unexplained" round or oval white shapes that appear in photos. The problem is that orbs are not caused by ghosts. There is not a single cause for orbs; many things can create the phenomena including insects, reflected flashes, and dust. Orbs may seem otherworldly because they appear only in photographs and are usually invisible to the naked eye at the actual scene of the photo. It is only later while examining the photograph that the presence of a ghostly, unnatural, glowing object is discovered, sometimes appearing above or next to an unsuspecting person. To those unaware of alternative explanations, it is no wonder that orbs appear spooky.*

The ghost hunters made another serious mistake. The NMPI website posted a short write-up of their investigation, and one photograph showed an orb at the top of the KiMo's stairs (seen in figure 1.2); the caption read, "Note orb at location of Bobby's death." A second photo, also showing an orb, read: "Orbs photographed from the staircase location of Bobby's death." To an amateur ghost hunter this might seem like strong corroborating evidence: a "ghostly" image right where little Bobby took his last breath. It's a perfect place to find a spirit.

Unfortunately for their theory, Bobby Darnall did not die on the stairs, as the NMPI investigators claim. A close inspection of photos and newspaper accounts reveals that the stairwell and railing were intact and undamaged in the explosion. According to a photo and caption in the August 3, 1951, *Albuquerque Journal*, "Balcony stairs directly over the heaters were undamaged but panel boards and plastering of the wall beside it were blown in all directions, peppering everyone in the hall, and those in the back theater seats." Since the stairs above the heater were "undamaged," Bobby could not have been on the stairs (much less on the landing where the "ghost orb" appeared) when the explosion occurred. A closer analysis of the blast trajectory shows that Bobby was in the lobby near the boiler room. Had Bobby been on the stairs, the concrete stairs themselves would have actually shielded him from the blast underneath.

The ghost hunters are even wrong on a more basic point: not only didn't Bobby Darnall die on the staircase where his "ghost" appeared, he didn't even die at the KiMo Theater! According to the August 2, 1951, *Albuquerque Journal*, Bobby Darnall was not killed in the blast but was alive when he left the KiMo: "Police said the boy had a faint pulse when picked up in the theater lobby, but he was dead on arrival at St. Joseph's Hospital." So Bobby actually died in an ambulance somewhere on the streets of downtown Albuquerque.

This is an important detail, because the ghost hunters claimed that Bobby's ghost (in the form of an orb) appears right where he died, which would be impossible unless they were able to track down the ambulance

* For more on orbs, see Radford 2010 and Biddle 2007.

where he finally succumbed to his injuries. Any credibility the ghost hunters may have hoped for evaporates under the mountain of basic errors, mistaken assumptions, poor research, and unchecked facts. Perhaps most troubling, both ghost hunting organizations that looked into the KiMo case portrayed themselves as authorities in the investigation of paranormal activity. They sell books, give lectures, and charge money for seminars, supposedly teaching clients how to conduct ghost investigations.

MYSTERIOUS EMFS

Most of the evidence the ghost hunters found was in the form of personal intuition and photographs of "orbs"—nothing that comes close to being scientific or conclusive. But there was one piece of apparently compelling evidence that the NMPI team found—and even captured on film. They recorded what they interpreted as mysterious electromagnetic fields. In a KRQE-TV segment that aired on Halloween 2007, the Andrees took reporter Annie McCormick along on their ghost hunt. The audience watches as Ron and Sherri search for ghosts with an EMF detector, which beeps and flashes dramatically when detecting electromagnetic fields. Sherri walks around a darkened room in the theater, and as she nears the center of the room it starts beeping and flashing—slowly at first, then faster and more urgently. Sherri gets very excited about the high reading: "It's just going off!" she exclaims, clearly astounded and amazed. "This is just crazy!"

Indeed it is. The readings seem mysterious because Sherri is in the middle of the room and presumably not near any devices that might generate electromagnetic fields (such as a computer, or a fan, or even a cell phone). Sherri clearly takes this as evidence of a ghost—what else could it be?—but there is a simple, logical explanation.

The ghost hunter doesn't realize that the electromagnetic field she's picking up is being generated by the large television camera she's being filmed with, only about two feet away. The cameras have small motors (driving the autofocus lenses, videotape spools, and other mechanisms) and battery packs about the size of a brick. (I tested this myself with the cameras used by that television station; before an interview I asked the cameraman to turn on the camera, and I used my own EMF meter. Sure enough, it registered the camera's electromagnetic field from several feet away; figure 1.5.)

Figure 1.5. *The author demonstrating for local news station KRQE how ordinary electrical outlets can be mistaken for a ghostly presence by ghost hunters. Photo by Larry Barker.*

BOBBY AND THE KIMO

Just as I don't believe that Dennis Potter intentionally created the story of the KiMo ghost, I don't think the NMPI ghost hunters intended to hoax or mislead anyone. The evidence they thought they found was simply the result of a series of errors and mistaken assumptions. To be fair, the low level of scientific and investigative expertise exhibited by the NMPI is typical of amateur ghost hunter groups. They are staffed by sincere people who have good intentions but a very poor understanding of investigative, research, and scientific methods.

Moreover, there are other logical problems with the KiMo ghost story that may not be obvious at first glance. For example, there's the curious thirty-five-year delay between Bobby's death in 1951 and his alleged reappearance in 1986. According to Potter, Bobby's ghost was never seen, believed to exist, or even thought of until after the doomed play in 1986, when a theater tradition (regarding leftover doughnuts) was transformed into a ghostly tradition. There are no reports of ghostly goings-on for three and a half decades. If the spirit of Bobby Darnall were real and haunting the KiMo unnoticed for a third of a century, why would it suddenly decide to ruin a single performance of *A Christmas Carol*, then (with one or two possible exceptions) disappear, never to be seen again?

Longtime KiMo manager Craig Rivera is a skeptic, and, typical theater superstition notwithstanding, it's hard to find other KiMo folks who take the story seriously or who have encountered the supposed ghost. When facts are checked and mistakes are corrected, the inescapable conclusion is that there is simply no evidence of a ghost at the KiMo Theater. All the evidence contradicts the story, and not a shred supports it.

Ultimately, the KiMo ghost story is not a lie, nor a hoax—but nor is it true. It is nothing more than a collection of myths, mistaken memories, and misunderstandings. There are no villains in this story, no conspiring bad guys for Fred, Daphne, and Velma to unmask at the end. The only deception in this mystery is self-deception. Overactive imaginations, factual errors, and mistakes combined with standard theater ghost lore and some misguided ghostbusters to create the KiMo ghost. The story spread, was told and retold, was hashed and rehashed, each iteration adding or omitting details without anyone bothering to check the facts.*

The KiMo ghost was the subject of local lore for at least a decade and remains unexplained in many books that have touched on the topic. While some may mourn the passing of a good ghost story, no harm can come from finding out the truth. In fact, it may be a good thing that I solved this mystery. It's easy to forget that Bobby Darnall

* In response to this investigation, Dennis Potter (2008b) contacted the *Weekly Alibi* newspaper (where a version of this piece appeared) and stated, "There may or may not be physical evidence of ghosts and I would certainly be skeptical, but I will just as certainly assert that the KiMo Theatre has its own energy and 'spirit.' Much the same as the tangible difference in feelings you get when sitting at your favorite table in your favorite restaurant with all your best friends, or walking alone down a cold hospital corridor. If the authors of this story wish to discount that spirit I can only mention that on that specific afternoon in 1986 I was at the KiMo and they were not." Potter is correct that neither Mike nor I were there (believe me, I wish I had been); however, the fact remains that, out of the scores or hundreds of people who witnessed the purported poltergeist-plagued play, not a single one has corroborated his ghost story.

was a real boy and that he has a family. The myth of Bobby as the KiMo ghost has pestered and haunted the Darnall family for decades. When Mike and I tracked down Bobby's brother and sister, we found them living in Florida. They had little to say to us, except that they feel exploited by the story and do not appreciate the claims that their beloved brother is continuing to eat stale doughnuts and ruin performances at the KiMo Theater.*

Only when the KiMo story is related as fiction, not fact, can the memory of little Bobby Darnall truly rest.

ACKNOWLEDGMENTS

I would like to thank Mike Smith for his excellent research and collaboration in investigating this mystery, as well as Dennis Potter, Larry Barker, Mark Corey, and Carl Peterson of the *Weekly Alibi*.

REFERENCES

Albuquerque Journal. 1951a. "Theater Blast Kills Boy; 7 Hurt." August 3, A1–2.

———. 1951b. "Blast in Theater Blamed on Valve and Thermostat." August 4, A1–2.

———. 1974. "The Notorious KiMo." December 25, C4.

Albuquerque Tribune. 1951. "Blast Laid to Heater Defect." August 3, A1–2.

Allen, Barbara. 1982. "The 'Image on Glass': Technology, Tradition, and the Emergence of Folklore." *Western Folklore* 41, no. 2 (April): 85–103.

Andree, Sherri, and Ron Andree. 2008. Interview by Benjamin Radford and Mike Smith, June 29.

Biddle, Kenny. 2007. *Orbs or Dust? A Practical Guide to False-Positive Evidence.* N.p.: Paranormal Investigators and Research Association.

Brunvand, Jan H. 2008. Personal correspondence, August 31.

* In late 2013 I received an e-mail from a woman whose last name was Darnall and who claimed to be (and likely was) the niece of Robert Darnall Jr.; she wrote, "My father was the brother of Robert Darnall. He was never called Bobbie [but instead Rob]." As for those who have perpetuated the ghost story, "Get the names right and remember that it might be a selling item for you but for us, it's something that affected my family. . . . Everyone [should] leave my uncle's memory alone and let everyone rest in peace." I expressed my condolences and explained that, as the KiMo's ghost story has many factual errors, it would not surprise me if his name was among them. I offered her a chance to correct any other misinformation about this tragedy, but she refused any further comment.

Durm, Mark. 1999. *Stripped of Their Sheets: The Truth About Alabama's Most Famous Ghost Tales*. Birmingham, AL: Seacoast Publishing.

Garcez, Antonio R. 1994. *Adobe Angels: The Ghosts of Albuquerque*. Truth or Consequences, NM: Red Rabbit Press.

Garcia, Stephanie, and Tim McGivern. 2004. "Newscity." *Weekly Alibi* (Albuquerque) 13, no. 11 (March 11–17).

Giannettino, Pete, and Don Bennett. 1951. "Tragedy Sidelights." *Albuquerque Tribune*, August 3, A1–2.

Gilovich, Thomas. 1991. *How We Know What Isn't So: The Fallibility of Human Reason in Everyday Life*. New York: Free Press.

Hauck, Dennis William. 2002. *Haunted Places: The National Directory*. New York: Penguin Books.

Johnson, Scott. 2007. "KiMo Theater." Dread Central Media. http://www.dreadcentral.com/story/kimo-theater.

Krenich, Stephanie Garcia. 2007. "Albuquerque's KiMo Theater Celebrates Its 80th Anniversary." *Albuquerque Tribune*, October 1.

Mayfield, Dan. 2004. "KiMo Keeps Its Ghost Happy with Treats, Trinkets." *Albuquerque Journal*, May 30.

McCormick, Annie. 2007. "The Haunted KiMo." KRQE-TV, broadcast, October 31.

New Mexico Paranormal Investigations. 2007. "Investigation of the KiMo Theater."

New Mexico Tourism Department. 2008. "KiMo Theater." www.newmexico.org/western/experience/kimo.php.

Polston, Cody. 2004. *Haunted New Mexico: The Ghosts of Albuquerque*. N.p.: PublishAmerica.

Potter, Dennis. 2008a. Interview by Benjamin Radford and Mike Smith.

———. 2008b. "The 'Spirit' Is Still Here!" Alibi.com, November 4. http://alibi.com/feature/25111/The-Definitive-KiMo-Ghost.html.

Radford, Benjamin. 2010. *Scientific Paranormal Investigation: How to Solve Unexplained Mysteries*. Corrales, NM: Rhombus Publishing.

Robson, Ellen, and Dianne Halicki. 1999. *Haunted Highway: The Spirits of Route 66*. Phoenix: Golden West Publishers.

Rule, Leslie. 2001. *Coast to Coast Ghosts: True Stories of Hauntings Across America*. New York: Andrews McMeel.

Schwartz, Steven. 2008. Interview by Benjamin Radford, June 3.

Shea, Andrew. 2008. Interview by Benjamin Radford, May 12.

CHAPTER 2

RESURRECTION AND SACRED SOIL

MIRACLES AT CHIMAYO

For many pilgrims, the path to the blessed place is a march of pain, as the accompanying sounds make clear. A low whoosh is followed by a crackle, a sharp snap, and sometimes a spatter of blood.

Some of the bare-chested men whipping their own backs crimson grimace in pain, but most simply endure the cleansing agony and plod forward toward healing and salvation. The pain, you see, is helping them atone for their sins. Such beliefs have been around for centuries; in medieval Europe the penitents' ideological forefathers whipped and flogged themselves to appease a wrathful God who'd visited the terrible black plague on them. They believed that if their collective pain was great enough, God would absolve mankind of its sins and remove the curse.

Some of the pilgrims even submit to crucifixion, allowing stakes or nails to be driven through their palms in a pale reenactment of Jesus's suffering. Indeed, the more pain the better: "Members of the procession that accompanied the cross bearers lashed themselves with cactus-studded whips; women stuffed their shoes with cactus for the long, painful march" up the hill (Kutz 1988, 45).

It's Good Friday, the day that commemorates the Passion and crucifixion of Jesus, and the faithful are on their way to the small shrine of Chimayo, in the town of the same name half an hour's drive north of Santa Fe. Not everyone goes to extremes, of course; most visit in air-conditioned, flagellation-free cars and bear not whips but crucifixes and rosaries. For many, this is not their first trip, and Lord willing it won't be their last. Some have been doing it every year for decades—a sign of genuine devotion. "It's an expression of their faith to walk to Chimayo on Good Friday," said Archbishop Michael Sheehan. "It's a time for devotion and prayer, asking God's blessings and thanking him for graces received" (Roberts 2011).

Tens of thousands of pilgrims visit the Shrine of Our Lord of Esquipulas at El Santuario de Chimayo during Holy Week. Some come from down the dusty, winding streets of nearby towns; others come from Santa Fe, Albuquerque, and elsewhere around the Southwest and around the world. Most drive, but many walk—in some cases for days, along the side of the roads and highways. (Tragically, a few have been killed by careless or drunk drivers on their way to Chimayo.) Estimates of the number of pilgrims during Holy Week range from thirty thousand to fifty thousand people; the shrine is the most visited Catholic pilgrimage site in North America, with nearly a third of a million visitors each year.

Figure 2.1. *The church at Chimayo, "the Lourdes of New Mexico," the site of miraculous healings. Photo by the author.*

Similar gatherings occur elsewhere in New Mexico, including in Tomé at Tomé Hill.

Of course, prayers can be offered anywhere, and there are holy places all over the world where the faithful make pilgrimages. Some are grand churches and cathedrals; others are small shrines. Lourdes, France, holds perhaps the most famous (and most revered) healing shrine in the world. But Chimayo, the "Lourdes of America," nestled among the scrub-dotted tan hills of northern New Mexico, is also a place of miracle healings.

A booklet explains the site: "El Santuario de Chimayo was built between 1813 and 1816. The crucifix of Our Lord of Esquipulas was found in 1810. Don Bernardo Abeyta built a small shelter next to his home, at his own expense, in which to house the crucifix. . . . There is no written testimony concerning an apparition of Our Lord in the Chimayo area. What we have is tradition passed from one generation to another. Here are two such accounts, each 'true' depending on the story teller."

One story goes that on the night of Good Friday in 1810, a Penitente brother named don Bernardo Abeyta was atop one of the hills in prayer when

> suddenly he saw a light springing from one of the slopes of the hills near the Santa Cruz river. Don Bernardo went to the spot and noticed that the shining light was coming from the ground. . . . "It was in this way that we found the carving of our Lord Jesus Christ," Abeyta would later write. "Still we had not seen the Lord, but he was right in front of us. Just like in the light, He also shot up out of the darkness of the earth. My hands scraped against it. The sand was not very compact there. In a matter of seconds a dozen hands were scraping around the holy wood. That is how our Lord appeared to us: still nailed to the cross." (Gonzales 2009)

Abeyta and other Penitentes and townspeople unearthed a six-foot-tall cross and carried it to the parish church in the nearby town of Santa Cruz. The town was delighted to have been blessed with this relic, but soon they were in for a miraculous and mysterious surprise, for "the next morning the crucifix was gone, only to be found in its original location. A second procession was organized and the crucifix was returned to Santa Cruz, but once again it disappeared. The same thing happened a third time. By then, everybody understood that El Señor de Esquipulas wanted to remain in Chimayo, and so a small chapel was built" (Gonzales 2009).

Reverend Julio Gonzales, pastor of Holy Family Parish, which oversees the sanctuary, states that "so far there is not an accurate idea of how the crucifix came to be here at the santuario" (Uyttebrouck 2010). The best guess is that the Spanish brought it with them from Guatemala (the crucifix depicts Our Lord of Esquipulas, a tradition of Guatemalan origin) at some point. Along the way, a priest died here, in Chimayo, and the cross was buried with him—only to be discovered through erosion decades later by Abeyta.

THE MIRACLE DIRT

While the shrine is impressive on its own merits, Chimayo is most famous for its healing dirt. If the miraculous discovery of El Señor de Esquipulas was a blessing for Chimayo, it seems to have been a curse for don Abeyta, who was soon mysteriously struck down with a grave illness. Historian Alice Bullock offers two versions of his story and how he came to be healed:

> One version tells that Abeyta, gravely ill, saw the image of his patron saint shimmering the air across the acequia, and the saint beckoned him forward. Weakly he strove to obey; he fell exhausted on the ground where the vision had first appeared, and contact with the earth completely cured him.
>
> Another legend has it that Doña Abeyta stood under the cottonwood trees bordering the acequia, praying for her husband who was so close to death that it was feared the priest from Santa Cruz would not be able to arrive in time. The vision came. It bade her take the dirt from this spot to her husband. Obeying, she saw Don Abeyta rise from his deathbed completely cured. (Bullock 1972, 3)

Whichever legend you believe, "Word of the miracle of Don Abeyta's healing was carried by word of mouth up and down the valley and over the mountains. The stream of pilgrims to the spot began, and continues. . . . The faithful still kneel by the gaping hole, taking the soil with reverent hands, some mixing it with water and drinking it. Others rub the holy dirt on withered and shattered limbs or other diseased parts of the body for the cures they so confidently expect. Where the patient is too ill to make the journey, the dirt is carried to him."

According to Bullock's *Living Legends of the Santa Fe Country*, "[the shrine] has a tiny candle-lit room at the left of the altar centered with a hole of sacred soil. . . . The holy dirt from this hole in the ground has been carried away by the faithful for decades, yet the hole grows no larger—it is always miraculously replenished" (Bullock 1972, 1).

In fact, the magic is said to go beyond healing and to bring good fortune or prevent misfortune: "In far villages mothers keep minute quantities on hand to toss a few grains into the fireplace to allay a storm and allow a husband or son to make his way safely home from a distant pasture or a long trip" (Bullock 1972, 1).

Fame spread quickly; in a November 16, 1813, letter to the Episcopal See of Durango, Father Sebastian Alvarez of Santa Cruz noted that Chimayo had already begun attracting pilgrims seeking cures and healings. Don Abeyta died in 1856 and was laid to rest in the chapel by

Figure 2.2. *The author at the* posito *in Chimayo, examining the miracle dirt. Photo by Jennifer Lawrason.*

special permission of Archbishop Jean Baptiste Lamy (who also played a role in another famous New Mexican miracle mystery, Santa Fe's Loretto staircase; see chapter 6.)

Lupita Trujillo, a woman of nearly eighty from Ponderosa, spoke glowingly of the power of the miracle dirt: "If you believe it, really inside of you, the soil can do anything you pray for" (Dominguez-Lund 2007). So is the dirt miraculous? The church does not officially endorse the claims of miracle cures: "It all depends on how you understand a 'miracle,'" the official Chimayo booklet states. "For some a miracle is something supernatural, something above nature. Others demand something less, and for them anything out of the ordinary is a miracle. As far as extraordinary happenings at El Santuario, officially the Church has never investigated any of the claims" (Gonzales 2009).

ANALYZING THE MYSTERIES

There are many aspects to the miracles at Chimayo. Some—such as the original claims dating back to the 1800s about the mysteriously disappearing and reappearing cross—are almost certainly not true. Most people recognize the origin story as legend, not historical fact; if the cross were today moved to a different location, it would surely not supernaturally reappear in the Santuario de Chimayo the following morning, as it was said to have done three times in 1810.

And what of the never-ending supply of "miraculously replenished" healing soil that Chimayo is world famous for? Does the sand spontaneously multiply overnight through divine intervention?

Alas, this too is a myth. According to Erik Eckholm (2008) of the *New York Times*,

> Few leave without some of the reddish soil, scooped from the 18-inch-wide "posito," or well, that is continuously replenished—by a caretaker, Father Roca is quick to explain, despite rumors over the years that the pit was refilled by divine intervention. He pointed to a small building nearby where trucked-in dirt was stored. "I even have to buy clean dirt!," he complained. . . . Father Roca said, "I always tell people I have no faith in the dirt, I have faith in the Lord. But people can believe what they want. . . . I don't like to think about it. People come here not for the crucifix but for the dirt, and some people even sell it."

It seems that the fame and commercialism of the dirt have overshadowed the shrine's significance (it should be noted that the Chimayo gift shop sells little bags of the blessed dirt).

Much of the truth about Chimayo is shrouded in legend and pious mythmaking. But not all of it is; the modern-day miraculous healings are certainly claimed as real, as dozens of testimonials from the faithful attest. I examine two cases here.

THE MIRACLE HEALING OF DESEREE MARTINEZ

In 2011 a television show called *Miracle Detectives* featured a Colorado woman named Deseree Martinez, who had been diagnosed with cancer at the age of fifteen. She had more than twenty lesions around her body. She visited Chimayo during an eighth-grade field trip, and while there she rubbed some of the famed healing dirt on her lesions. She returned to Colorado to resume her chemotherapy treatments, and soon the scans and test results showed significant improvement. She and her family believe that she was healed by a miracle at Chimayo. Her cancer went into remission, and as of 2013 she's cautiously optimistic about the future.

Martinez's recovery is certainly inspiring and wonderful—but is it a miracle? Her doctor, Brian Greffe of the Children's Hospital in Denver, spoke (on *Miracle Detectives*) about Martinez's treatment and recovery. "For non-Hodgkin lymphoma in pediatrics our cure rates are quite high, but Deseree was in an unusual situation in that it was in many, many bones, over twenty different bones. That presented more of a challenge in terms of treatment" (Sullivan 2011). Of course, she was treated both before and after her visit to Chimayo. Dr. Greffe described how she responded to treatment at the hospital: "She did very well, in fact I remember once we started the chemotherapy she had significant bone pain. Within days she began feeling better, she was able to be more mobile and just overall felt much better than when she first came in."

Miracle Detectives cohost Indre Viskontas asked, "Was there anything in her recovery that surprised you?" After an awkward pause, Dr. Greffe replied, "I was pleased that she responded so quickly and I was very, very happy about that, and I think that brought a lot of relief to her family. I can say just from a personal point of view, she really was very positive about the whole thing, very close with her family, had a lot of family support, and that helps tremendously when you're dealing with a potentially life-threatening illness." Dr. Greffe tried to put the best face on it, but obviously he knew that he was being interviewed for a show about miracles and that Deseree Martinez was convinced that her recovery had been due to divine intervention instead of good medical care. He was clearly uncomfortable in his role as the naysaying medical authority having to explain that her recovery wasn't really all that unusual or miraculous. Viskontas summarized her own impression: "I was really hoping that there would be some part of her recovery that really surprised him. The fact that he didn't mention that doesn't necessarily mean that there isn't some supernatural involvement, but the scientific evidence has to come from somewhere else."

Unfortunately, that scientific evidence never emerged; there's no proof or reason to believe that Deseree was healed or cured by the dirt. She recovered, and her cancerous lesions went away—but it was only after a full course of treatments of the best medical care available. Was it the medical treatments at Children's Hospital in Denver? Was it the miracle dirt from the small, sand-filled posito in the Chimayo chapel? Or was it both, or neither? There's no way to know for certain, but only one of those treatments—chemotherapy—has been proven to treat non-Hodgkin lymphoma, in tens of thousands of patients.

Diagnostic factors for evaluating the survival rates for patients with non-Hodgkin lymphoma include age, the stage of the disease, where the lymphoma is found, and whether the patient is able to function normally. Deseree would have been placed in the low or low intermediate risk group (with one or two of the prognostic risk factors). This allows us to evaluate Deseree's likelihood of surviving her disease. By way of comparison, "In the studies used to develop the index, about 75% of people in the lowest risk group lived longer than 5 years, but only about 30% of people in the highest group lived at least 5 years" (American Cancer Society 2010).

Thus the majority of patients in Deseree's condition live at least five years (often much longer), and even if she had been in the worst possible risk category (over age sixty with stage four lymphoma all over the body, with difficulty moving, etc.), she would have a one in three chance of surviving. If she had only a one-in-a-thousand chance of surviving, her recovery might be quite remarkable, but a survival rate between 30 percent and 75 percent is hardly miraculous. Cancer that goes into remission following chemotherapy (as happened to Deseree) is certainly not rare; hundreds of thousands of cancer patients have survived what she did. The American Cancer Society estimates that there are about 66,360 new cases of non-Hodgkin lymphoma in the United States each year, and about 19,320 annual deaths from the disease. The disease is terrible, but the good news is that it's often treatable (especially if the patient is young, as Deseree was), and most people who get it survive.

Of course, these numbers don't matter to people like Deseree; she, quite understandably, is less interested in the statistics than in her own personal struggle and healing. What matters is *her* healing, *her* cancer remission—not whether her experience is typical or not. I'm sure if I'd gone through what she did, I'd feel the same way. But if the question is whether or not a miracle occurred, whether or not something unexplainable by science happened to her, that's another matter.

Randall Sullivan, cohost of *Miracle Detectives* and author of the book *The Miracle Detective*, perhaps best summarized the way most of the faithful feel. He acknowledged that the healing miracles at Chimayo were not scientifically proven by Deseree's experience. But, he says, "that's a truth on the surface. There's a deeper truth that is the one that Deseree embraced and I embrace it with her. She, in a moment of supreme faith, used the dirt to initiate a healing. To me that's a miracle that should go on the wall at Chimayo as testimony to the power of the place" (Sullivan 2010).

Although Deseree's healing turned out to be less than miraculous, I did get the chance to talk to another person who'd experienced the powers of Chimayo firsthand.

THE MIRACLE OF ARMANDO CORDOBA

In 2010 I got a phone call from a man named Armando Cordoba. He'd heard of my reputation as a science-based investigator. He'd seen my appearance as an expert investigator on a previous *Miracle Detectives* show, in which I'd researched miracles at a shrine outside of Cleveland.

He asked me if I'd be interested in talking to him, as he had been healed by the miraculous dirt of Chimayo many years earlier. Soon I visited his modest home in Albuquerque; he kindly invited me in, and we sat down at a small wooden table in his living room as he told me his story. About twenty minutes later, Cordoba's wife, Antonia, and one of their grandchildren came in carrying groceries. We had delicious enchiladas bathed in red chile sauce as we talked.

Armando was twenty-one years old at the time he was healed, nineteen days out of the navy. He was at his mother's house in Albuquerque, already with Antonia, who would become his wife of sixty years.

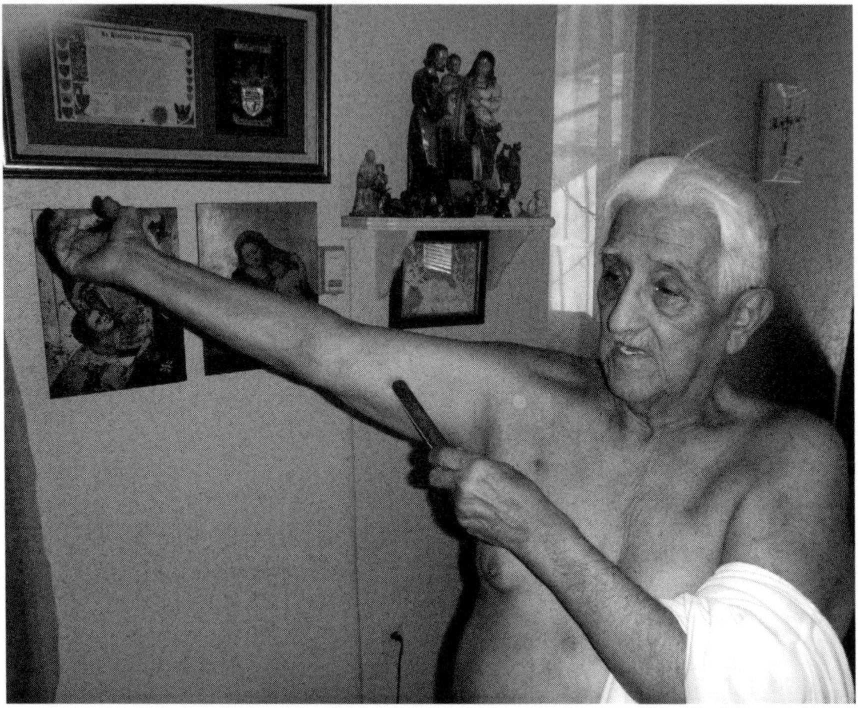

Figure 2.3. *New Mexico resident Armando Cordoba claims to have been miraculously healed by the dirt at Chimayo after a serious burn in 1954. Photo by the author.*

"In 1954 I was discharged from the navy around March 19. We lived at my mother's house on the west side, and two Sundays after I got home we were going to baptize my oldest son. She had a wood fireplace and I put the wood in there, and I put kerosene on the wood, and I lit it, and it blew up. It hit me, the fire came out at me, and I was burned from here up," he said, motioning to his waist. He showed me some scars on his arms and chest; the fire had also burned his face.

Antonia fleshed out some details: "We were getting the baby ready for confirmation, and Armando thought the room was kind of cold, it was in March. So he said, 'I think I'll light the fireplace.' So he did, then threw into the fire what he thought was kerosene but must have had gasoline, and that thing exploded. When it blew up, it somehow ignited the can, and he threw it. My mother-in-law had an old-fashioned overstuffed sofa, and it fell on that, and that was burning."

Armando added, "One thing that helped me a lot was that I ran onto the back porch, my mother-in-law came out with cold water and threw it on me." He then ran out of the house to his brother's house, about four blocks away. "I ran down there, my brother put me in the car, and he took me to Saint Joseph's [Hospital]. When I first got burned it hurt really bad."

Armando said that he was at Saint Joseph's for three days—not in the burn unit, but waiting to be seen. (It's hard to imagine a burn patient—even one with minor burns—waiting three full days before receiving medical attention, even back in the 1950s; it seemed that Armando's memory about some things was understandably fuzzy, fifty years after the fact. He also suggested that he'd spent a month in the hospital, although it's more likely it was between one and two weeks.*)

When he finally was seen at Saint Joseph's "they gave him first aid," Antonia explained. "And they bandaged him. We didn't have any money, so they said, 'Why don't you take him to Veteran's,' . . . so we did, and they took him and the gauze had stuck to the wounds, so they had to use acid to pull all that skin off."

It's not clear how long Armando was in the hospital, but on the Saturday before Easter he asked the doctors if he could go to Chimayo. "For Easter, I was getting better, and so I asked, 'Can I go home for Easter?' And they said, 'You're crazy!' They'd marked me down to get skin grafted. So I begged them again and they said okay and let me go. . . . The doctor bandaged me and said, 'Don't take these off,' and so my wife and my father came for me. . . . We got home Friday afternoon, and Saturday morning I said, 'I need to go to *santuario*.' My mother told me, 'You're crazy, you son of a bitch, you're going to die!'" Armando laughed.

"All I knew was that we had to go to Chimayo," Armando explained. "Instincts told me I had to be there. It was a strong feeling . . . it was like a magnet pulling me there. I didn't hear no voices, no visions, *nada*. It was within me, pulling me there. We got in the car and my father was going to drive, and I said no. For some reason I had to drive. I drove all the way to santuario wrapped up like a mummy! We got there and a lot of people saw me, wondering what this mummy was doing there. . . . We

* At one point Armando said that the accident occurred in March, although he later said it happened about two weeks after he was discharged from the navy on March 19, which would place the incident about April 3. If this is accurate, then two to three weeks elapsed between the time that Armando was burned and the time he visited Chimayo, on April 18, Easter Sunday.

went into the chapel, to the posito. I told Toni, 'Take all of this off of me!' 'No,' she said. 'What are you going to do?' she said, and I said, 'Don't worry about it, just put the dirt on me!' So she did. I left the dirt on and they wrapped me back up. They told me I was crazy. And maybe I was! But it was the faith in God."

I asked Antonia what she thought when her burned husband asked her to unwrap his bandages and put dirt on the red wounds. "I looked at him, and my first thought was that he shouldn't put dirt on it, but he was very determined."

"Weren't we made out of dirt?" Armando added. "God made us from dirt, and to dirt we'll go back." Armando's mission completed, they left Chimayo and headed back to Albuquerque. "Monday morning I went back to the hospital, and when we unwrapped the bandages, it was like a sunburn, a bad sunburn," Armando told me. "Then they checked me over, and they released me. There was nothing wrong with me. They looked at me and examined me, and got doctors to come in who'd seen me before. They asked, 'What did you put on your burns?' and I said, 'Dirt.' The doctors said I was crazy, but they released me, and I went home happy."

Curiously, in a situation that echoed that of Deseree Martinez, neither Armando nor Antonia reported that his doctors were surprised or shocked by the healing; if anything, they were more surprised to find dirt and sand underneath his bandages. Whether their doctors were impressed or not is irrelevant to Armando and his wife; they expected the wounds to be much worse, and since they weren't, it was a miracle.

"I think there's a lot more people that this has happened to," Antonia tells me. "I know they're looking to see what special qualities the dirt has, or whatever. I don't know what's there as far as the dirt, but I think it's your faith, I think that's it." Armando nodded in vigorous agreement: "Faith, yeah, I have faith. A miracle? By all means. But that miracle is because I have faith in God, that He would heal me. And if He hadn't healed me, I would still be able to accept His wishes . . . *His* wishes, not mine."

It was certainly a fascinating story, made all the more enjoyable and compelling by the delicious homemade enchiladas. I recorded the interview and took copious notes. I told Armando that in order to properly investigate this miracle I'd need some paperwork or documentation, something giving us a better idea of what Armando's condition was when he entered the hospital. A miracle healing or cure must have a before and after, even if it may not have a clear cause and effect.

The medical records would be the only evidence attesting to Armando's condition, treatment, and recovery. They would have doctors' and nurses' records of the severity of his burns (perhaps including photos)—but more importantly they would surely have a record of the sudden and miraculous healing. Any patient that badly burned who recovers so suddenly would surely be noted in the records.

I explained that since medical records are legally private information, I would need Armando to locate the records from that time. A written request by him from me wouldn't do; privacy laws are very strict, and he'd have to ask his doctor for a copy of them. Even then, it was a gamble, since the records we'd need dated back half a century. I doubted that information about a burn that Armando had suffered as a teenager would be kept in his current medical records, although if the burn had been serious it would likely still be there, because it might have implications for later treatments.

I contacted Armando again about a month later, partly to check up on him and partly to ask if he'd had a chance to inquire about getting a copy of his medical records. He sounded quite well on the phone, although wearier than he had been before. "No, *no hay*," he told me. "They destroyed all the old medical records." There was nothing there, he said, nothing earlier than the past ten or twenty years. Without the records, there would be no way to prove his case, and tracking down any hospital workers who might remember it would be problematic if not impossible.

I didn't doubt Armando's story—he was a very open, sincere man who certainly had no reason to lie or embellish. But at the end of the day, it was clear that he was rehashing a bit of family lore. Recollections change over half a century, and the sharpness of his memory (and that of his wife) was not going to be convincing enough to prove a miracle. (I investigated a similar case in 2009 when looking into what was called "the best case for psychic detectives" [Radford 2010]. Although two witnesses claimed that a psychic had given them accurate information about a serial killer in 1982, all the official records had been destroyed, and all three people involved had different memories about what had happened.)

Disappointed by this evidentiary dead end, I reviewed the case anew. The possibility of proof, one way or another, was long gone, but I still wanted to know more, to understand what might have happened all those years ago. Could there be another explanation?

I listened again to my interviews with Armando. I played back the details of his descriptions of the accident and found a clue. It wasn't what happened at Chimayo or the hospital, but what happened at his mother's house that fateful day in 1954.

From both Armando's and Antonia's descriptions of the accident, it's clear that he was burned in what's called a flash fire. He had thrown what he thought was kerosene onto a fire, but it turned out to be another fuel, probably gasoline. If it had been kerosene, the accident would have been even more curious, since kerosene has a higher ignition temperature.

According to Joseph E. Shepherd, professor of aeronautics and mechanical engineering at the California Institute of Technology in Pasadena, "Even with the development of better lamps and implementation of fire safety education, there remains the rather serious problem of fuel contamination. Kerosene is universally used to fuel lamps and stoves because of its intrinsic safety—the flash point of kerosene is greater than 38°C (100°F), and the vapor pressure is rather low at normal temperatures. This means that at normal temperatures and pressures, a pool of kerosene evaporates very slowly; the concentration of vapors above the pool is well below the lower flammability limit; and it is extremely difficult to ignite a pool of kerosene with a single match. In contrast, gasoline has an extremely low flash point and a high vapor pressure. A pool of gasoline will evaporate quickly, the vapors above the pool mix with air to form a flammable region of large extent, and the fuel-air cloud will ignite readily with a single match. Contaminating kerosene with even a small percentage of gasoline will cause a decrease in the flash point, will increase the vapor pressure, and will create a much more hazardous situation for the consumer overall. The problem of contamination is particularly serious when it is combined with a lack of fire safety awareness and carelessness in handling fuels" (Shepherd and Perez 2008).

So it seems certain that what Armando threw into the fire was either gasoline or kerosene that had been mixed (or contaminated) with gasoline. This assumption is supported by Antonia's observation that fumes from the can itself caught fire.

This is important because it helps us determine how severe his initial burns were. We have no photographs and no medical reports, only the recollections of the victim and his wife from fifty-one years ago. Through research and interviews with doctors, I learned more about flash fires like the one that had burned Armando. Although scary and painful, most burn injuries are not life threatening; 95 percent of hospitalized burn patients survive. One study of campfire-related burns examined 241 patients admitted to hospitals following open-fire burns; of those, only four died, and the average length of stay in the hospital was 8.6 days (Fraga et al. 2010). Severe burns can take several years to heal, whereas most minor burns often heal within a few weeks as long as they are cared for and kept from infection.

There are several different types of burns, including scalds (when the skin comes into contact with hot liquids such as water or oil); contact burns (when the skin comes into contact with hot objects such as metal or glass); and chemical burns (when the skin comes into contact with corrosive chemicals such as battery acid). The kind that Armando encountered is called a thermal burn, which entails injury by flames (for instance, coming too close to a burning log or flammable fumes). This is among the least damaging types of burns because of simple physics: "Conductivity of the specific skin tissue involved has a significant influence on the extent of burn injury. Heat transfer within skin is influenced by the thermal conductivity of the heated material, the area through which heat is transferred, and the temperature gradient within the material. . . . Because skin is a relatively poor conductor of heat, it provides an extensive barrier to heat injury" (Edlich 2010).

In other words, flames contain much less energy than, say, boiling water or a hot metal pot, and they therefore do less damage when their heat is transferred to human skin. This is especially true if the skin is only exposed to the flame for a split second, as happens in a flash fire. This does not mean that flash fires are not dangerous, because they certainly can be. But most people who are seriously injured or killed in flash fires succumb not to serious burns but instead to smoke inhalation or asphyxiation. Compared to other types of burns, the damage done to the skin in a flash fire is relatively superficial and minor.

Armando's description of his injury closely matches that of a first-degree burn: "In first-degree burns, minor epithelial damage of the epidermis exists. Redness, tenderness, and pain are the hallmarks of this injury. Blistering does not occur, and . . . healing takes place after several days without scarring. Because the epidermal barrier remains intact, metabolic response and risk of infection are minimal" (Edlich 2010).

Although Armando suggested that he had suffered second- and third-degree burns, this is medically very unlikely. Third-degree burns are "full-thickness burns that destroy both epidermis and dermis. The capillary network of the dermis is completely destroyed. Burned skin has a white or leathery appearance with underlying clotted vessels and is anesthetic. Skin grafting always is necessary to resurface the injured area." In second-degree-burns, "some portion of the skin appendages remains viable, allowing epithelial repair of the burn wound without skin grafting. These burns appear pink, moist, and soft and are exquisitely tender when touched by a gloved hand. They heal in approximately 2–3 weeks, usually without scarring."

From Armando's description, it's clear that his injuries were mostly first-degree burns. Indeed, the "most common causes of first-degree burns are flash burns and sunburns" (Edlich 2010). The fact that Armando was doused with cold water immediately after his burn played an important part in minimizing his injury and recovery time. "The beneficial effects of immediate cold water treatment of burned skin appear to be related to several factors. First, cold inhibits lactate production and acidosis, thereby promoting catecholamine function and cardiovascular homeostasis. Cold also inhibits burn wound histamine release, which in turn blocks local and remote histamine-mediated increases in vascular permeability" (Edlich 2010). In other words, the cold water cools the skin and prevents further damage to the skin cells and blood vessels.

It's highly unlikely that Armando's burns were as serious as he and his wife now remember. His wounds did not heal any faster than normal, and by the time he visited Chimayo they were already mostly healed anyway; they would have resembled "a bad sunburn" (as he described it) with or without the healing dirt. His wounds were much better than when they were first bandaged and had been healing slowly but surely under the bandages for weeks. Armando and Antonia would not necessarily have looked closely at his wounds when they put the Chimayo dirt on them since the room at the shrine is poorly lit, and they were surely more caught up in Armando's religious fervor than they were interested in closely examining his skin.

It's easy to unintentionally exaggerate or misremember the severity and details of an injury like that; it happens all the time. And this is especially true if one looks at an injury and its healing in the context of a miracle of faith. Acknowledging or remembering that the burn was very painful and scary (not to mention potentially disfiguring)—but not especially serious or life threatening—might diminish the importance of the Chimayo miracle.

At the end of the day, I can't prove for certain how serious Armando's burns were; I have absolutely no evidence other than Armando's and his wife's recollections, and medical knowledge about burns. I have to follow the best evidence, which is that Armando's recovery time (two to three weeks) is typical of most flash-fire burn victims, and therefore there's no evidence that Chimayo's dirt had any effect on him.

ANALYZING THE MIRACLE DIRT

So is there anything special or miraculous about the dirt? Apparently not. The dirt (actually it's mostly sand) is purchased from a gravel yard, which brings it in by the truckload from neighboring hills. It is blessed by the padre but has no particular special physical qualities, just as water blessed by a priest is physically identical to ordinary water. The benefit is spiritual and psychological, not physical or paranormal.

On *Miracle Detectives*, Indre Viskontas had samples of the Chimayo soil examined by a geoanalytical chemist, Dr. Mehdi Ali. He found that there was nothing unusual about the soil in terms of healing or curative powers, with one exception: it is high in calcium carbonate. In a bizarre quirk, calcium carbonate is a common ingredient in stomach remedies such as antacids, and this may explain why many people who have certain stomach conditions such as heartburn and indigestion might feel better after eating the dirt. This, of course, does not explain all of the claimed effects, but it might explain some of them.

Others of a more mystical or New Age bent attribute the healings not to the power of prayer but instead to healing energies or vibrations from the earth. Some claim that the Chimayo shrine was built on "ley lines," imaginary lines straddling the earth that supposedly connect mystical places and cosmic centers (such as the ruins at Machu Picchu in Peru or the Great Pyramid in Egypt; see Radford 2013). There's no scientific evidence for the existence of these lines—they cannot be measured or detected—but they remain popular in certain circles. On *Miracle Detectives*, a local shaman, Michelle Ama Wehali Rozbitsky, was filmed walking around Chimayo with copper dowsing rods, trying to find healing earth-energy lines. "They cross when you walk over like a particular strong place where their waters cross, which all sacred sites across the planet, or most of them, are built on, that's where the healing energy comes in, where they cross," she stated.

However, since dowsing has never been scientifically proven to work (and is claimed to find many other things including water, ghosts, and gold—see Radford 2011), it's not clear what, if anything, the shaman was finding. While Viskontas searched for scientific answers, her colleague, Randall Sullivan, interviewed a pair of dowsing rods, asking them whether or not the Chimayo dirt had miraculous healing powers. Although it made for entertaining television, it was not a highlight of scientific research.

FAITH HEALING AND THE PSYCHOLOGY OF MIRACLES

To be sure, these are only two of many stories of healings at Chimayo, and I could not possibly research all of them. Thoroughly investigating all the claims in depth would take years (and several books) to accomplish and is beyond the scope of this book. But research suggests that these two cases are typical of many faith-healing claims.

In an investigation of the miracle healings at Lourdes, the CBS newsmagazine *60 Minutes* researched claims of healings and concluded that while stories and personal anecdotes of healings and cures were plentiful, the evidence supporting them was not: "There are stories of the crippled who suddenly could walk, the blind who suddenly could see, the incurable cancers that were cured. But most of these remain undocumented stories, part of the mythology that gives other pilgrims hope" (quoted in Randi 1989, 21).

Indeed, "For something so popular, faith healing has a remarkably undocumented success rate. . . . Evidence to prove faith healing must be of good quality. No number of purely anecdotal accounts can suffice. Before-and-after medical evidence is absolutely essential, along with careful consideration of the possibility that any remission may be within the probable incidence of such occurrences and not remarkable in itself" (Randi 1989, 279). This is because it's well known that many diseases heal on their own, with or without treatment (medical or divine).

Even the Vatican has difficulty deciding whether or not a miracle cure has happened. In 2010 questions were raised about a miracle attributed to Pope John Paul II. Although John Paul was one of the most beloved spiritual leaders of modern times, in order for him to be eligible for sainthood there must be documented proof that he performed miracles.

Theoretically any miracle might do, from raising the dead to desalinating the Red Sea, but in practice the most common alleged miracles used to beatify popes are medical ones such as spontaneous cures and healings. These are also among the most difficult to verify, since diseases can be unpredictable and, as mentioned, often heal (or go into remission) on their own. If anyone—whether pope or plumber—visits enough sick people, some of them will get better, with or without divine intervention.

How can we be sure that a miracle truly occurred? The Vatican's guidelines say that a medical cure must be unexplainable, instantaneous, complete, and lasting. (These criteria seem fair; after all, a cancer that immediately disappears but returns within a few hours wouldn't be much of a miracle.)

But this is where things get complicated for those who support John Paul's bid for sainthood. A French nun named Simon-Pierre prayed to him for relief of her Parkinson's disease, and two months after John Paul died she woke up completely and inexplicably cured. As an Associated Press (2010) story noted, "While the nun's cure was by all indications instantaneous and complete, some would argue the world will have to wait her entire lifetime to determine whether it was lasting, in case the symptoms return. New questions were raised in recent weeks, after a Polish newspaper reported that doubts had been cast about whether Simon-Pierre had Parkinson's to begin with. The *Rzeczpospolita* daily, one of Poland's most respected and widely read newspapers, suggested that Simon-Pierre instead may have suffered from another neurological disease which has similar symptoms as Parkinson's but which can be cured."

Thus it's possible that the disease John Paul miraculously cured was never really incurable in the first place. If the nun was originally misdiagnosed, then her later recovery would not be any more remarkable than recovering from the flu or another relatively short-term illness.

Many pilgrims seeking healing will experience pain relief simply from the psychological experience, not from any mystical powers. Dr. Steven Novella, a clinical neurologist at Yale University, explains that "placebo effects (plural) are varied and complex, and mostly not what people assume: a biological response to the expectation of benefit. . . . There are real physiological effects resulting from the ritual of treatment. For example, treatment may involve relaxation, or simply taking a break from your otherwise hectic daily routine. Believing one is being treated may reduce anxiety about the illness or symptoms, which in turn may reduce sympathetic activity and reduce blood pressure and strain on the heart, as well as reduce the levels of stress hormones."

Novella (2010) points out, "The perception of pain in particular is subject to these non-specific effects, as an improved mood may reduce the perception of pain. In addition conditioning, expectation, and non-specific benefits may actually cause the release of natural endorphins which reduce pain transmission, or the release of dopamine in the reward centers of the brain." He also discussed the results of research done by Asbjørn Hróbjartsson and Peter Gøtzsche, which concluded that "in certain settings placebo interventions can influence patient-reported outcomes, especially pain and nausea, though it is difficult to distinguish patient-reported effects of placebo from biased reporting. The effect on pain varied, even among trials with low risk of bias, from negligible to clinically important." So it's not surprising that the placebo effect could account for at least some of the reported miracle cures.

What about the stories of healings, and the crutches on display? Although the dozens of crutches that line the walls at the shrine are dramatic and impressive (see figure 2.4), it's not clear what to make of them. Each of them might represent a true miracle, but they might not. There are no names or dates on any except a very few of them, and of course anyone can leave a crutch there. Just because someone went in with a crutch and left without one, from a scientific point of view, does not necessarily mean that a miracle occurred. Most people with leg injuries

Figure 2.4. *Crutches and braces line the walls at Chimayo, testimony to the miraculous cures and healings. Photo by the author.*

can walk without a crutch—it's just easier and less painful to do so *with* a crutch. The truly immobile are confined to wheelchairs. There are no truly unexplained reports, such as people regrowing missing limbs. There are no artificial limbs among the crutches.

Just because patients give up a crutch or assistive device in the heat and passion of a healing does not mean that they are cured, or that they may not need those crutches or braces again very soon thereafter. James Randi, in *The Faith Healers*, examined many reports of faith healings, including those that occurred at Chimayo. "There I found supportive devices hung about the walls, and in the souvenir shop I was able to buy various photos of these adornments. But no two photos were the same. That is, the display of crutches and braces changed from time to time. The reason for this was well known to an orthopedic surgeon there. He knows the Santuario because he visits there about every six months. Why? To reclaim the orthopedic devices left there by his own patients, often poor people who cannot afford to replace the expensive mechanisms that they discarded. The priest at the Santuario knows this physician and permits him to remove what he recognizes as the property of his patients. By this time, however, they may already have been photographed" (Randi 1989, 271).

TODAY'S MIRACLE

What Deseree and Armando have in common is that they are both laypersons who suffered from a disease or injury and healed faster than they expected—but not necessarily faster than their doctors expected them to. They are not interested in statistics and average recovery rates. They couldn't care less whether the medical authorities think they were healed by God or by modern medicine. They *know that what happened was a miracle*; they have faith.

Armando and Antonia know that miracles continue in the present day. A half century ago, Armando believes, his faith and Chimayo's dirt healed him. He's hoping it will happen again. This is not a historical minimystery whose outcome was rendered ambiguous by lost records and fuzzy memories. As we finished our red chile–bathed enchiladas and concluded our interview, Armando leaned in close and told me that the miracles aren't done; there's more to come. You see, he has liver cancer.

About three weeks ago, Armando said, "I went to Chimayo for the dirt." He rubbed his belly and side. "I did go in and put dirt all over here, not just on the front but the sides. And I have a strong faith that

God will help me," he said. "I go in next month for x-rays to see about my cirrhosis. . . . If it's gone, that's a miracle." I told him I hoped so, and that I wanted to be there to scientifically document his healing—we could add a second chapter to his story.

I continued my research and moved on to other projects, but I called Armando nine months later to see how he was faring. His recorded, faintly feisty, Spanish-accented voice greeted me, so I left a message letting him know that I was looking forward to hearing from him. The next day his wife called me. In a soft voice she told me that Armando had died about three months earlier; the cancer had returned without pity or prayer and gotten the best of him. My heart sank. We'd only spent a few hours together but we'd shared stories, some laughter, and delicious enchiladas. I told Toni that I was sorry to hear of his passing; she replied that God had other plans for Armando. There would be no chapter two to his story.

Before we ended our short, somber talk she said, "I want you to know, he really enjoyed meeting you. He talked about that for a while; he loved telling you his story." I was surprised and touched, and I promised to tell Armando's story as best I could.

ACKNOWLEDGMENTS

I gratefully acknowledge Armando and Antonia Cordoba, Jennifer Lawrason, Dr. Angie Feazel Mattke, and Indre Viskontas for their help with this investigation.

REFERENCES

American Cancer Society. 2010. "Non-Hodgkin Lymphoma Overview." November 3. http://www.cancer.org/Cancer/Non-HodgkinLymphoma/OverviewGuide/non-hodgkin-lymphoma-overview-survival-rates.

Associated Press. 2010. "Medical 'Miracle' Intended to Propel Pope John Paul II to Sainthood in Doubt amid Abuse Scandal." *New York Daily News*, March 29. http://www.nydailynews.com/news/world/medical-miracle-intended-propel-pope-john-paul-ii-sainthood-doubt-abuse-scandal-article-1.162823.

Bullock, Alice. 1972. *Living Legends of the Santa Fe Country*. Santa Fe: Sunstone Press.

Cordoba, Armando. 2010. Interview by Benjamin Radford, March 20.

Dominguez-Lund, Debra. 2007. "March of the Pilgrims." *Albuquerque Journal*, April 4, A1.

Eckholm, Erik. 2008. "A Pastor Begs to Differ with Flock on Miracles." *New York Times*, February 20.

Edlich, Richard. 2010. "Thermal Burns." Medscape. http://emedicine.medscape.com/article/1278244-overview#a30.

Fraga, Andrea, Gustavo Fraga, John Noordenbos, Mayer Tenenhaus, Shannon Catle, Dhaval Bhavasr, Jeanne Lee, Raul Coimbra, and Bruce Potenza. 2010. "Beach and Campfire Burns: A Site of Pleasure and Tragedy." *Journal of Burn Care Research* 31: 184–89.

Gonzales, Julio. 2009. *El Santuario de Chimayo: The Shrine of Our Lord of Esquipulas*. Chimayo, NM: El Santuario de Chimayo.

Hróbjartsson, Asbjørn, and Peter Gøtzsche. 2010. "Placebo Interventions for All Clinical Conditions." Cochrane Library, Database of Systematic Reviews, January 20 (1): CD003974.

Kutz, Jack. 1988. *Mysteries and Miracles of New Mexico: Guide Book to the Genuinely Bizarre in the Land of Enchantment*. Corrales, NM: Rhombus Publishing.

Novella, Steven. 2010. "The Poor, Misunderstood Placebo." *Skeptical Inquirer* 34, no. 6 (November–December): 28–29.

Radford, Benjamin. 2010. *Scientific Paranormal Investigation: How to Solve Unexplained Mysteries*. Corrales, NM: Rhombus Publishing.

———. 2011. "Dowsing: Dubious, Discredited, and Dangerous." *Skeptical Inquirer* 35, no. 5 (September–October): 36–37.

———. 2013. "The Lore and Lure of Ley Lines." LiveScience, November 19. http://www.livescience.com/41349-ley-lines.html.

Randi, James. 1989. *The Faith Healers*. Buffalo: Prometheus Books.

Roberts, Kathaleen. 2011. "Spiritual Pilgrimage." *Albuquerque Journal*, April 22, D1.

Shepherd, Joseph E., and Frank A. Perez. 2008. "Kerosene Lamps and Cookstoves: The Hazards of Gasoline Contamination." *Fire Safety Journal* 43, no. 3: 171–79.

Sullivan, Randall. 2011. "Holy Dirt of Chimayo." *Miracle Detectives*, airdate January 12. Pilgrim Films and Television.

Uyttebrouck, Olivier. 2010. "Little Jerusalem." *Albuquerque Journal*, April 4, B1.

Viskontas, Indre. 2011. Interview by Benjamin Radford, November 23.

Photo by the author.

CHAPTER 3

THE MYSTERIOUS CRYSTAL SKULLS

Crystal skulls are among the strangest and most mysterious artifacts in the world. They are displayed in the world's finest museums; they have inspired Indiana Jones films; and, according to legend, they have even been used to see into the future—and to kill with terrible supernatural power.

Real skulls are, of course, made of minerals; bone is mostly calcium phosphate and calcium carbonate. Skulls are at once both mundane and macabre, symbolic reminders of both healing medicine and death.

But what of human-like skulls that are not human or even animal? What of skulls made of gems or special rocks that are said to resonate with mysterious mystical frequencies? What do we make of these objects, whose origins are shrouded in the mists of mystery?

One of the strangest—and, many claim, *enchanted*—objects in the world has a fascinating link to the Land of Enchantment.

CRYSTAL MAGIC

Of all the materials that a skull might be made of, crystal is perhaps the most intriguing. As Katrina Raphaell, author of *Crystal Enlightenment: The Transformative Properties of Crystals and Healing Stones*, notes, "Down through the ages, civilizations have used the power of crystals and stones for many purposes. The oldest legends and lore of crystal magic lead us back to the ancient continent of Atlantis [where crystals were used] to channel and harvest the cosmic force. This legendary civilization of advanced sciences would use crystals as beacons of light that would serve as a telepathic communicator to their universal forefathers.

They also used crystal power for many physical and practical purposes" (Raphaell 1985, 8).

Raphaell also tells us that ancient tribes in North and South America prized crystals for their special properties. "Mayan and American Indians have used crystals for diagnosis as well as for the treatment of disease. Large clear quartz crystals were used in special ceremonies by the elders of the American Indian villages as 'seeing crystals' in which images of the future or distant events could be seen" (Raphaell 1985, 10).

The supernatural powers and abilities attributed to crystals are numerous, from healing to scrying, divination to assassination. New Agers have constructed an intricate belief system around crystals involving auras, reincarnation, chakras, healing, vibrations, and so on. Indeed, Raphaell notes, "The power and potential of crystals cannot be overstated. It is one of the main contributors to the New Age." New Age and metaphysical stores across America and around the world are well stocked with crystals; one shop I visited in Sedona, Arizona, offered three different types of crystal skulls, each with its own powers (figure 3.1).

Figure 3.1. *A collection of carved crystal skulls in three varieties of quartz (clear, rutilated, and smoky) for sale at the Center for the New Age, a shop in Sedona, Arizona. Photo by the author.*

As for how, exactly, the crystal works to effect its mystical powers, Raphaell offers the following description: "Quartz crystals vibrate the [human] aura at such a high rate that the darker tones of karmic seeds can be dissolved and released. Quartz crystals then return that energy to its source to create higher vibrations and brighter colors to be recirculated into the aura" (Raphaell 1985, 52).

This "explanation," however, has no basis whatsoever in medical science, since such vibrations and frequencies have never been proven to exist (see, for example, Hall 2010). As Derek and Julia Parker (1990) note in *Atlas of the Supernatural*, even among crystal users and believers "there seems to be no general agreement about the relative healing powers of various crystals. . . . Crystal healers argue about the precise way in which the crystals should be used: some suggest that they should be placed in a specific pattern on the patient's body; others that the relevant stone should be placed on the relevant chakra. Yet others place crystals around the body, but not touching it" (34). All agree, however, that quartz is the most important healing crystal.

THE SAN LUIS VALLEY CRYSTAL SKULL

Clearly, a skull made from crystal is special and incredibly rare. Thus it is no wonder that people in New Mexico's San Luis Valley still talk of a mysterious crystal skull found near there decades ago. According to Christopher O'Brien, author of *The Mysterious Valley*, it all started on a hot summer afternoon in 1995, when rancher Donna Koch ("Dana") discovered a bizarre sight.

> Dana had been enjoying the uncustomarily warm February day while riding her ATV along the fence-line of her new ranch. She and her husband, Billy, a hard-working, salt-of-the-earth rancher-couple had just closed on their spread and Dana was making the half-hour trip around the perimeter of the ranch on an all-terrain vehicle. She was accompanied by the former caretaker, a teenager who had lived at the rundown ranch for several months. Sixty yards from the highway, the young man noticed a glint of sunlight from the ground and stopped to investigate. He called for Dana to come see. She braked her ATV and turned back. He was grinning, holding a glittering object in his hand, the sunlight refracting beams of light around him. (O'Brien 1996)

Figure 3.2. *A mysterious "crystal skull" identical to one discovered in the desert in 1995, said to have mysterious powers and bestow curses. From the author's collection. Photo by the author.*

Koch later contacted O'Brien with the magnificent discovery, which she presented to him wrapped in silk. "She studied my face closely as she uncovered the artifact," O'Brien later recalled.

> There in her hands was a most unusual glass skull! At first glance, it didn't look remotely human. The San Luis Valley Skull, as I've dubbed it, is six inches high and three-and-a-half inches wide, and appears to have been created from a single piece of molten glass. It does not appear to be carved. Its unique form doesn't suggest a typical human skull, rather, it is highly stylized. The three-pound skull is asymmetrical and

> was obviously not made to sit on a mantel, or altar. This asymmetric nature could be significant and unique. The smooth, graceful lines flow effortlessly through the form, suggesting to one viewer a prenatal, feminine quality. One verified unique feature is the elongated jaw which twists down and to the left with what appears to be a tongue protruding from between the upper and lower teeth. The nose hole in the front actually extends over an inch into the interior of the skull, and it features an earring hole on the right side. (O'Brien 1996)

Koch and O'Brien took the macabre object to the ranch and did some research on crystal skulls. What in the world—if indeed it *was* of this world—did she have? Was it unique, or were there others like it? What she found amazed her; one of the first skulls she read about was also the most famous, and the most deadly: the Crystal Skull of Doom.

THE SKULL OF DOOM

Arthur C. Clarke called it "the weirdest gem in the world . . . one of a handful of strange man-made objects that have challenged the ingenuity of the world's scientists" (Welfare and Fairley 1980, 51). It is a human-like skull in two pieces (including a detachable jaw), made from clear crystal quartz. It is just over five inches high, nearly five inches wide, and nearly eight inches long. It weighs eleven pounds, seven ounces.

As bizarre as the object is, the story behind its discovery is even stranger. "One day in 1927, teenager Anna Mitchell-Hedges was assisting her adoptive father, a British explorer called F. A. 'Mike' Mitchell-Hedges, in his excavations at the ruined Mayan city of Lubantuun in British Honduras (now Belize), when she made a momentous discovery" (Shuker 2009, 183). It was her seventeenth birthday, and Anna was feeling frivolous and a bit mischievous. She and some local Mayan children decided to scale one of the steep pyramid-like structures so they could get above the trees to watch a glorious sunrise. Yet something almost as impressive as the sun caught her eye: a blinding light coming from deep below her, in a hidden and ruined chamber (figure 3.3).

"It was something bright, a reflection," she later recalled. "Hitting me in the face, but I didn't know what it was" (Hunter 2005). Drawn to the beguiling, almost entrancing glow, Anna wanted to investigate but was soon chastened by her father, who sternly invoked his parental authority and demanded that she come down off the ruins before she hurt herself. Anna did as she was told but informed her father about the brilliant light she'd seen hidden deep inside the ruins below. Surely it was important, or at least worth looking for, she insisted. Eventually, her stubborn persistence convinced him to investigate the curiosity.

Anna was less enthusiastic on realizing that she herself would be the one to recover the object, being the smallest and lightest of the group. "They lowered me by two ropes. They put towels under the ropes so they wouldn't hurt me," she later recalled. Inch by careful inch, they lowered the brave girl into the musty darkness of the ruins. "I was so terrified—there were scorpions and other awful things down there," she said.

Peering around as her eyes adjusted to near darkness, she saw a human skull, which frightened her terribly. Her father, concerned for her safety, was about to pull up his daughter, but she steeled her jumpy nerves and looked more closely at the skull. It didn't seem quite right. *It was not human.* It was cold and smooth, and she realized that it was a piece of mineral. "I saw the skull, picked it up, stuffed it in my shirt and they pulled me up," Anna recalled (Hunter 2005). When the plucky girl got it back up to the top and the others saw it, they were awestruck. As if in some Hollywood movie, some of the local Mayan Indians even fell to their knees in reverence when she held the crystal above her head in the full sunlight. It was clearly a sacred, revered object of great power.

Figure 3.3. *Anna Mitchell-Hedges with her famous and powerful crystal skull, photographed in 2005 at her home in Kitchener, Ontario. Copyright 2005,* Waterloo Region Record, *Ontario.*

From then, the skull had a long and colorful history. F. A. Mitchell-Hedges wrote about the famous skull in his 1954 autobiography, *Danger My Ally*, stating that the object was "at least 3,600 years old and according to legend was used by the high priest of the Maya when performing esoteric rites. It is said that when he willed death with the help of the skull, death invariably followed. It has been described as the embodiment of all evil" (quoted in Loxton 2008).

According to Sandra Bowen, F. R. Nocerino, and Joshua Shapiro, "The Maya told them that the crystal skull was used by the high priests to will death or to heal. . . . For example if a medicine man or witch doctor was getting too old to perform the religious ceremonies, a young man was chosen to take his place. Then, at the appropriate time, both of them would lie in front of the altar with the crystal skull on top of it, and the high priest would perform a ceremony [in which] the old man's knowledge would transfer into the young boy and the medicine man would peacefully pass on, while the boy would immediately become very knowledgeable" (Bowen, Nocerino, and Shapiro 1988, 254).

Many people believed that the skull's powers were not merely legend but fact. Although the days in which the skull killed people at the command of Mayan shamans were apparently long over, some people did report strange experiences in the presence of the skull. According to researcher Karl Shuker, crystal expert Frank Dorland, who studied the skull for six years, concluded that it had mysterious powers: "It sometimes changed color or filled with a cottony haze; . . . it produced 'elusive perfume' and strange tinkling sounds; . . . images of mountains, temples, and other objects appeared within it; and . . . an aura once surrounded it for several minutes" (Shuker 2009, 184).

Stories circulated about a variety of strange things that happened in the skull's presence. For example, "The first time they kept the skull overnight in their home [researchers] Frank and Mabel were awakened by unusual noises in the house, including a jungle cat, silver bells tinkling softly, and chimes. The next morning possessions were scattered all over their living room, yet all the windows and doors were locked" (Bowen, Nocerino, and Shapiro 1988).

It's unclear what kind of sound the couple would interpret as a "jungle cat" noise, but "other times they heard what sounded like music or human voices singing strange chants. The skull also gave off what Frank calls an elusive perfume or odor, and they would see many pictures and images appearing within the skull [including] other crystal skulls, high mountains, temples, and faces" (Bowen, Nocerino, and Shapiro 1988, 261).

Others claimed that the skull mysteriously maintained a constant temperature and other bizarre qualities. In 1970 Frank Dorland took the skull to Hewlett-Packard's laboratories for analysis. "Another highly puzzling detail was that no matter what temperature the researchers subjected the Mitchell-Hedges skull to, it always remained seventy degrees Fahrenheit. All of these findings were so astounding that one of the crystalographers at Hewlett-Packard was quoted as saying, 'The damn thing simply shouldn't even be,'" Dorland reported (Bowen, Nocerino, and Shapiro 1988, xviii).

The scientists stated that the workmanship was "exquisite" and that if it was made using sand and water it could have required "an estimated 300 man-years of effort" to construct. A skull that took three centuries—nearly a third of a millennium—to create must certainly be unique.* Even the great pyramids in Egypt took only about one-tenth that amount of time to raise!

MYSTICAL VISIONS

Skull enthusiasts and psychics spent countless hours in the presence of the Mitchell-Hedges skull, meditating and trying to glean its power. Many believed that it held ancient wisdom and that it would "provide important information to scientists and healers of our world. If it should ever fall into the wrong hands, the skull would destroy itself. However over thousands of years there have been many seen and unseen forces guarding it" (Bowen, Nocerino, and Shapiro 1988, 257).

The crystal skulls—there were a few others apart from the Mitchell-Hedges skull that were found at other locations, all said to have strange powers and lacking apparent tool marks or other signs of human crafting—quickly transformed from curious artifacts into the focus of a lucrative New Age business. Writers produced books with photos of the skulls and the messages and wisdom they imparted; craftspeople manufactured miniature replicas. One Mayan priest who owned a crystal skull offered to let those interested "work with the

* It's important to remember that this conclusion was a rough estimate based upon the assumption that the skull had been found "in an abandoned Mayan temple in 1927" (Bowen, Nocerino, and Shapiro 1988). If it had been carved using modern tools or machinery, it could have been created in weeks or months instead of centuries.

skull for $500 per week, or $50 per day for each researcher" (Bowen, Nocerino, and Shapiro 1988, 10). While many crystal skull authors and researchers were sincere, they were not shy about cashing in on the New Age interest.

One researcher, Nick Nocerino, said that he had received visions from the skull showing

> pictures of several highly civilized societies, one that lives underwater, a second which lives within the Earth, and a third one which comes from some place other than our earth. The world seems to have changed its geography four times . . . each time there was a change, there appeared to be spaceships (more commonly called UFOs) which removed people. The spaceships returned at a later date when the land was stable, and people came out of them. . . . The Mitchell-Hedges skull seems to take me to civilizations that could not exist on our planet. For me, the skull is like a compact computer with a video monitor and often with accompanying audio sounds. (Bowen, Nocerino, and Shapiro 1988, 9)

Sandra Bowen, a psychic, spent nearly a month communicating with the Mitchell-Hedges skull. With the help of two extraterrestrial alien friends named Akbar and Josephat, Bowen learned from the skull that its favorite color was purple and that it had other "skull brothers and sisters" whom it had not seen in a long time, and whom it missed. According to Bowen, the crystal skull was not in fact a carved creation at all but instead "the crystallization of Sha-tree-tra's skull, a high priestess of Atlantis. . . . When she died there were seven priests who had to form a special pattern (similar to a star pattern) around her skull. With the help of the Space Beings, using the power of their minds and laser beams emanating from their eyes, they were able to crystallize her skull." In fact, Bowen said, the rest of princess Sha-tree-tra's body was "also crystallized and placed near the site of the skull. There will be a time when those parts will be discovered by people who will be guided to go there and find them" (Bowen, Nocerino, and Shapiro 1988, 211).

Frank Dorland suggested on the TV show *That's Incredible* that "the last civilization that had the skull decided that God should talk and accomplished this by cutting loose the jawbone of the skull. The priests decided that by doing this, they could control what God said. To move the jaw for purposes of barking out their religious orders, the priests would place the skull over an altar and mount it on two pivoting axes, so that the skull could nod and move from side to side. They probably used two crystal push rods from below the skull to achieve the up and down motion of the jaw and give the appearance of speaking" (Bowen, Nocerino, and Shapiro 1988, 262). He offered no evidence for this theory, however; it was apparently merely a guess.

Extraterrestrial space brothers? Galactic telephones to the past? Princesses from the lost continent of Atlantis? What should we make of all this? Some believe that these pieces of information are important mystical knowledge, while others see merely wild speculations from sincere but creative daydreamers.

THE SKULLS' ENCHANTMENT SPREADS

Anna Mitchell-Hedges, her adventurer father, Donna Koch, and various psychics were not the only ones enchanted by crystal skulls. Mitchell-Hedges occasionally took her crystal skull on tour, bringing it to New Mexico in the mid-1990s. Anthony Conforti, a crystal skull researcher living in Albuquerque, recalled that when Mitchell-Hedges arrived with her mystical crystal, "she carried it in a bowling ball bag" (Nathanson 2008). Indeed, crystal skulls became a subject of global interest. Screenwriter George Lucas said in interviews that he had been interested in crystal skulls for many years. He wrote a script about them, which finally became the 2008 film *Indiana Jones and the Kingdom of the Crystal Skull.* A Canadian company, Crystal Head Vodka (cofounded by actor and paranormal buff Dan Aykroyd), was launched in 2008, bottling its crystal-filtered libation in novelty glass skulls. Aykroyd states:

> I have always been an avid researcher of the subject of the legendary thirteen crystal heads which have been unearthed at numerous locations and at various times on our planet. The story goes that thirteen crystal heads have been found in places varying from the Yucatan peninsula in Central America to the American Southwest in New Mexico and also in Tibet. There are now seven heads known to be in mankind's custody . . . and one currently owned by a woman in the Southwest who claims that she had to finally put it in a closet after he (or she) began speaking to her [Donna Koch and the San Luis Valley skull]. Scientists estimate that it took between 300 and 500 years to carve one of these heads from a single piece of quartz. However in tests conducted on the Mitchell-Hedges head by

> Hewlett-Packard labs in the 1960s [*sic*], they could find no discernable tool marks on the head to show how it was carved. Equally fascinating is that according to both physicists and jewelers these head should not exist, but should have shattered in the course of making them. . . . The Navajo believe that they were bestowed on their people as a gift from higher beings not of this Earth as a means of cataloguing sacred cultural knowledge from the past, assessing the present, and foretelling the future. Contrary to the common perception of a skull as representing death, the people from these cultures—the Aztec, Mayan, and North American First Nations, for whom these artifacts possess sacred and mystical properties—associate the crystal heads with a life-affirming symbology. In ancient tellings, the heads are living and sentient, sources of knowledge, insight, and power.* (Aykroyd 2008)

There many skulls around the world carved out of quartz crystal, of varying sizes and designs. I've seen them in many places, especially in South and Central America, where they are sold as tourist trinkets. Those that sell for a few dollars are rather plain, but the big ones (roughly life-size) are steeped in myth and romance. There are only a handful of these larger, life-size skulls in existence, and they have inspired awe for generations. They are said to be hundreds of years old, some of them possibly of Mayan or Aztec origin. Sarah Everts, writing in *Chemical and Engineering News*, notes that "since the 1860s, dozens of skull sculptures have appeared on the art market purporting to be pre-Columbian artifacts from Mesoamerica, that is, created by the indigenous peoples of Mexico and Central America prior to Spanish exploration and conquest in the 16th century. Three such skulls have graced the collections of major museums on both sides of the Atlantic: the Smithsonian Institution in Washington, D.C., the British Museum in London, and the Quai Branly Museum in Paris" (Everts 2013, 48). The skulls are indeed a sight to behold; I examined a glowing crystal skull in the British Museum (figures 3.4, 3.5).

* Perhaps Aykroyd had been sampling some of his own product, because very little of what he says is accurate. Tool marks have indeed been found on several of the crystal skulls (see Sax et al. 2008), and Aykroyd seems unaware that some of the crystal skulls he highlights are in fact not crystal at all but instead made of blown glass—and therefore should not have "shattered in the course of making them," as he claims.

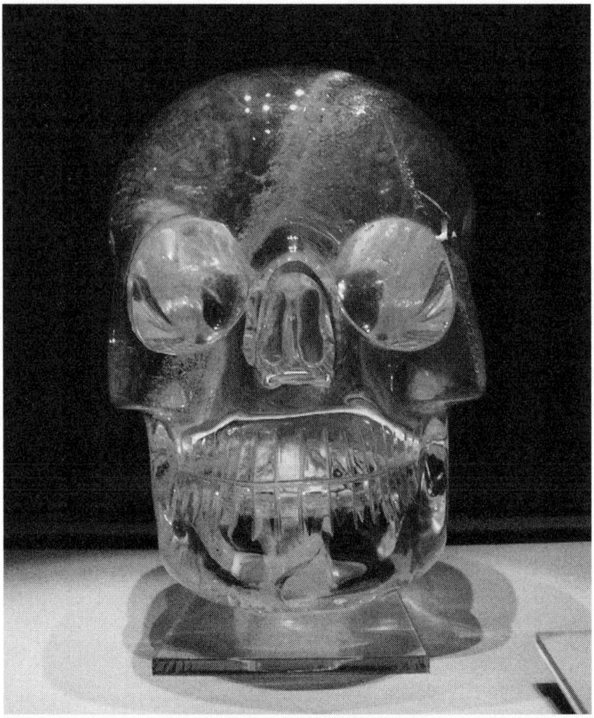

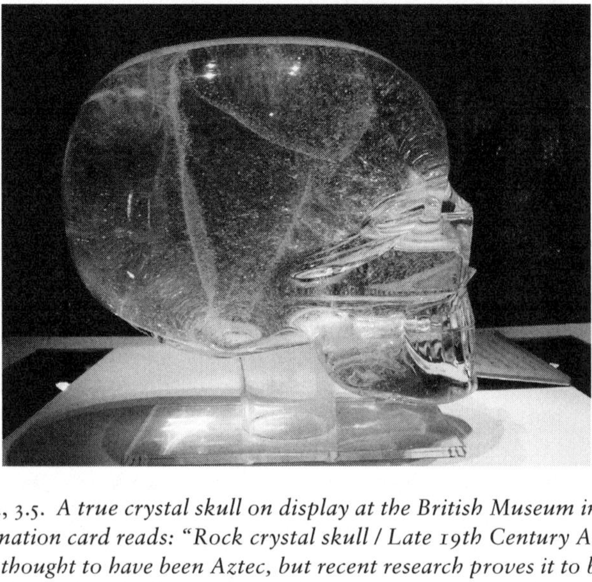

Figures 3.4, 3.5. *A true crystal skull on display at the British Museum in London. The information card reads: "Rock crystal skull / Late 19th Century AD / It was originally thought to have been Aztec, but recent research proves it to be European. Purchased from Tiffany and Co., New York, through Mr. G. F. Kunz. Ethno 1891–1." Photo by the author.*

RETURN TO THE SAN LUIS VALLEY

When Donna Koch found a mysterious crystal skull in the desert and began researching the history and lore of such artifacts, this is the sort of information she discovered: hers was apparently one of only a few in the world, possibly priceless and holding the key to unknown and even paranormal powers—both good and evil. After reading such heady stories and facts, things began happening that made Koch wonder if her own crystal skull was likewise supernatural.

It certainly *seemed* to have unexplainable powers. Koch said that the skull mysteriously repelled dirt, as if a pulsing aura or energy kept contaminants at bay. "It was all clean and shiny when I found it, but I've since discovered it doesn't get dirty," Koch said. "It just always looks the same" (Dumas 1996).

News of the curious find spread quickly among New Agers, and eager believers descended on the San Luis Valley to see the instant relic for themselves. Christopher O'Brien, the local paranormal writer, was asked to examine the skull, but when he tried to videotape the object, he claimed, his camera malfunctioned. "A psychic told me not to sleep near the skull, and to keep it wrapped in cloth in a cedar box," Koch told a *Rocky Mountain News* reporter who visited her at the time. The *Rocky Mountain News* story continues,

> Koch now keeps the skull hidden, but she agrees to bring it to a small rock and crystal store near her home so we can photograph it. As she walks through the door, a crystal stand shatters, and the rock resting on it clatters to the floor. No one's surprised. "I don't think it's evil, but so many things have happened I believe it's connected to power," says Koch. "It's like it's saying, 'Take heed! I'm here!'" Koch brought the skull to Denver a couple years ago to have it looked at by art collectors and by the Denver Museum of Natural History. But no one would hazard a guess on its age and origins. Although she was offered $20,000 for it by a collector of the paranormal from Washington, she doesn't think she'll sell. "I just have the feeling that if it was sold, nothing good would come of it," says Koch. "I get the feeling it came to me to protect it. It's very strange. Everyone who looks at it feels something different. Some people tell me it's healed their souls. Other people hate it and won't touch it." (Dumas 1996)

Koch confided to friends that she believed the mysterious crystal skull was cursed. "Some people are plumb scared of it when they first see it," she said. "A friend came to see it and now she won't step foot on our property" (O'Brien 1996). Her son, who had volunteered to remove the skull from the ranch and take it into town to have it examined by an expert, was hit in the head with a hammer. "It damn near laid me out," he reported after recovering from the blow. Not long after, her husband was hit on the head by a truck boom. Although both were accidents (and neither Koch's son nor her husband was seriously injured), the Koch family wondered if dark forces might be at work.

Not all of the skull's effects were overtly dangerous. Many of the phenomena echoed what Koch had read about other people's experiences with other skulls. Some were subtle and mysterious—hard to define or objectively prove—such as strange feelings and smells. Koch's husband said that when he "opened up the cabinet where the skull was kept, he smelled 'a ladies perfume that about knocked me over. It smelled just like a busted bottle of perfume. We couldn't locate the source of the smell and we've never smelled it since'" (quoted in O'Brien 1996).

Other odd, random things seemed to happen around the same time to other people who came into contact with the skull. According to O'Brien, one woman "took the skull outside to look at it in the sunlight. As she approached her pickup, parked in the driveway, a spare tire laying in the back of the truck exploded." (It's not clear what O'Brien meant by "exploded," although tires may burst if overinflated and heated by the sun, or go flat if punctured.)

Of course, as with the Mitchell-Hedges Skull of Doom, psychics and sensitives were especially drawn to the skull. As one writer noted, "More than one hundred people arrived to gather around the skull beneath a full moon at Colorado's White Eagle Village Inn, Retreat, and Conference Center, coming from as far away as St. Paul, Minnesota, and Sedona, Arizona, to meditate around the skull for hours and record their impressions" (Smith 2008a). One psychic told Koch, "It is very old. It's not man-made and not of this Earth. You must be very careful with it. It can be very detrimental. . . . You must be balanced, or you will be hurt." He also told her that someone would soon contact her and help guide her in trying to decide what should be done with the skull. When O'Brien showed up, Koch concluded that he must be the chosen one the psychic had referred to.

SCIENTIFIC ANALYSIS AND THE SKULL SOLUTION

Koch's skull was eventually taken to the Denver Museum of Natural History, where curators determined that it was actually crafted from glass, not crystal. This revelation somewhat diminished the gleaming skull's mystique, since of course if it was not made from crystal quartz, then there would be no reason to believe it had any of the mystical healing or scrying properties attributed to that particular rock. After all, it was quartz specifically (not glass, granite, or any other mineral) that New Age experts claimed possessed special powers and vibrations.

But questions remained: if it was glass, then who would have made it, and how, and why? Skeptics noted that ordinary glass skulls were not uncommon in folk art, and in fact they could be found for sale in art and curio shops around Colorado, New Mexico, and elsewhere. But if it was a piece of art, why would it be lying abandoned on the ground out in the desert? And why wouldn't the artist have signed the piece, or left his or her mark on the magnificent work? None of it seemed to make sense; it was a true mystery.

As bizarre as the tale was, soon the story took a stranger twist when the Denver Museum of Natural History located the source of the San Luis Valley skull. It had not come from the severed head of an Atlantean princess, or from aliens, or from ancient civilizations, but from a young man named Brad Chadez.

Chadez, a Denver glassblower, owned a piece of vacant property in Colorado, and sometimes he and his wife would go over the property, planning where they might build their dream house one day. "We left one of my skull paperweights as kind of a cornerstone where we were going to build the house," Chadez told me. "I had been making these for years. When me and my wife got together, we used to go to Day of the Dead fairs in New Mexico and elsewhere and sell them. This was about half size. It was really awful, for one of my paperweights . . . the mouth went wrong, and so it was technically one of my seconds. The neighbor, Donna Koch, had been looking to buy that property for years, and she was out walking the property and found that paperweight. And that's pretty much where it all started."

Wanting to get to the bottom of the mystery that had drawn New Age pilgrims, psychics, and curiosity seekers from across the country, officials had "called glass studios in the area that may have produced such a thing," and they found Kit Karbler, owner of the Blake Street Glass Studio in Denver. Based on the description, Karbler was pretty sure it was one of Chadez's pieces.

"I didn't know all this was going on at first," Chadez told me. "My wife and I were in New Mexico, and when I got home, I got a pile of voicemails about my paperweight being in the newspaper. It was just awkward, because there was no credit or anything. I sold the skulls around town, so I'm pretty well known around Denver, especially the Denver glass scene, for my skulls. Everyone recognized it right away and called me up. That was when Christopher O'Brien's book [*The Mysterious Valley*] first came out."

Chadez was shocked and puzzled when he learned of all the commotion and speculation over the flawed glass paperweight he'd placed on his property to mark the location of his future home. "I couldn't believe it," Chadez later said. "I guess they had some sort of sessions with it, and a kind of healing thing, and there was even a series of accidents they attributed to it" (Smith 2008b).

Donna Koch's mysterious, magical crystal skull was neither mysterious nor magical (nor crystal). Chadez had a bemused laugh over the whole affair and thought nothing more about it. The strange little mystery had been solved. "I don't know whether it just perpetuated itself, or what," he said. "The answer just wasn't that far away for it to be so crazy. I think it just got into the New Age circles, and then it took on a life of its own."

But months later, Chadez heard that Koch was still displaying and promoting his paperweight as a mysterious, supernatural crystal skull. In fact, if anything, the skull was gaining international publicity as more and more New Agers and others came to see it. Perhaps Koch did not want to believe that the skull was not what she had thought it was; perhaps the lure of fame was too tempting not to exploit. Perhaps Koch was making good money off it. Whatever the reason, according to Chadez, "She knew [the truth] but failed to disclose it for another eight months" (Smith 2008a). Chadez told me that Koch "still tried to keep it going. It was something she didn't want dropped, she was pretty famous in the area at the time. . . . She thought she had a gold mine on her hands until the time the story broke." When Chadez first identified the skull as one of his own, he says that Koch "was not surprised. She knew who I was because of property, she knew me by name. So it should have been dropped right there. But what happened was, I think the book was already in the works, and she did not come clean on it. She kept the myth going."

Finally, after an article on the San Luis Valley skull appeared in the *Rocky Mountain News* in November 1996, Chadez, along with his parents and others who were concerned that the deception had gone too far, confronted Koch and demanded that she stop claiming that the skull was mysterious or had special powers. Finally, Chadez himself set the record straight in a piece published in the *Crestone Eagle* newspaper, which explained the whole situation and told people not to be fooled. When the truth finally came out, "the psychic channeling of the skull's ancient spirits rattled to an abrupt and sheepish halt" (Smith 2008b). It must have been deeply embarrassing for Koch and others who had spent considerable time and effort on the skull—not to mention the psychics who claimed to receive mystical messages and spiritual visions from a defective glass paperweight.

Why wasn't it immediately recognized? Since it was not intended for sale, Chadez had not put his mark on it. Although the glass skull did not have any seams, because it had been cast hot ("hot wound"), there were many signs that it was a manmade object. Chadez finds it hard to believe that anyone would not immediately recognize it as a glass sculpture: "There were gather marks—you can see the striations in the glass. There's also what are called 'stones' in the glass, which is where part of the brick crystallizes and creates little pebbles that fall into the glass, and there were even obvious glass inclusions in it."

But what about all the mysterious phenomena? All the visions and accidents and strange smells? Even if it was glass instead of crystal, made a year earlier instead of millennia ago, and made by a guy named Brad instead of by aliens or an Atlantean princess, surely *something* unexplained was going on, right? Many of the mysteries vanish once we look at them more closely. Take, for example, Koch's claim that the skull was clean and shiny when she found it, and that it doesn't get dirty. Any round, smooth glass object will naturally repel dirt, so that's not very mysterious (more on this shortly).

Some of the mysterious events were likely just coincidences. There's little evidence, other than Koch's story, that some of the events even occurred (for example, the spare tire "exploding"; perhaps it did, perhaps it didn't, but the tire was never examined or analyzed). There's no reason to doubt that Koch's son and husband were both injured, but also no reason to think that the incidents are related to the paperweight. More likely, Koch, O'Brien, and others were simply making a common psychological mistake in assuming that the odd occurrences must have been caused by the skull they found. This is another excellent example of the logical fallacy called *post hoc ergo propter hoc*, literally, "after this, therefore because of it." People sometimes make connections that don't exist and assume that two unrelated events might be somehow linked by cause and effect. Each day, tens of thousands of people get into accidents or have flat tires; if such an event were to occur just after the person found some strange object that he believed for some reason might be cursed, he may well assume that there must be some connection. In the case of the skull, the visions and messages originated from the psychics' imaginations and the power of psychological suggestion; there's no evidence of anything else.

A FINAL TWIST

There's yet another strange twist to the story. According to Chadez, when he placed the skull out as a property marker, he did not leave it out in the open; instead, it was left inside a very distinctive—and decidedly earthly—vessel, namely a purple velvet Crown Royal whiskey bag. "I put it inside a Crown Royal bag," Chadez said. "Someone had given me a bunch of them for that exact reason, to carry around paperweights in them."

That explains why the skull "was all clean and shiny" when Koch first saw it. Surely even a round glass object would have at least a little dirt or dust if left out in the open—unless it was found inside a bag. Remember, according to one version of the story, Koch did not personally find the skull; it was found some distance away by her teenage ranch hand, who noticed it, went over to it, and brought it back to her.

If her assistant simply pulled it out of the bag and left the bag on the ground without mentioning that detail to Koch, the skull's dirt-free appearance would be all the more mysterious to her.

So was it all a hoax, a deliberately planned publicity stunt? Or merely a series of mistaken assumptions and misunderstandings? We may never know the full truth.

RETURN TO THE SKULL OF DOOM

The San Luis Valley skull turned out to be less than meets the eye, a product of wishful thinking, mistaken assumptions, and self-deception. But what of the information that Koch and so many others had learned about Anna Mitchell-Hedges, her swashbuckling father, and the Skull of Doom? After all, Koch and others in many ways have used the Skull of Doom as a template for understanding their own crystal skulls. The stories of the Mitchell-Hedges skull told them what to expect with their own experiences. The Skull of Doom involved plenty of mysterious phenomena—some of it even proven by scientists at a lab.

The Skull of Doom, too, turned out to have some metaphorical cracks in its story that only appeared after careful investigation. Although dramatic, the Skull of Doom story is largely myth, falling apart under close analysis. F. A. Mitchell-Hedges was not the brave archaeologist adventurer he claimed to be; in fact, Joe Nickell (2006) refers to Mitchell-Hedges as "a habitual liar and faker" who was revealed to be a con man who had been caught in a string of lies and scandals ranging from financial fraud to adultery.

Adding to the suspicion, Mitchell-Hedges was evasive about how he came to acquire the skull in the first place: "How it came into my possession I have reasons for not revealing," he wrote. In fact, Mitchell-Hedges's story changed significantly, and as researcher Daniel Loxton (2008) noted, the story he told was that Mike Mitchell-Hedges *himself*—*not* his daughter Anna—had discovered the famous Skull of Doom. Nickell notes that Mitchell-Hedges "made no reference to the skull at the time of his return from Lubantuun or in the years immediately following" (2006, 15) and in fact only made the first published reference to the skull in a 1936 issue of an anthropological journal. This silence about such a remarkable discovery is odd indeed; why would he have kept such an amazing thing a secret for so long?

Loxton notes that F. A. Mitchell-Hedges is not the only person to have fabricated (or greatly embellished) information about the skull. Anna Mitchell-Hedges changed her story about how she got the skull at least twice; she first stated that she and her father found the skull together beneath an altar in a ruined temple in 1926, but in a 1983 account she claimed that she was with a worker who was felling trees in the jungle, saw something shiny beneath the stones, and dug it up on the spot. Her most recent version of the story, in which she recovered the skull in 1924 after being lowered into the temple with ropes, was related earlier, and—in a bit of circular irony—seems directly inspired by an Indiana Jones film. It gets worse: there's no evidence that Anna even visited the ruins at Lubantuun, where she claims to have found the skull. For an excellent, detailed analysis of the Mitchell-Hedges clan and their Skull of Doom, see Daniel Loxton's 2008 article in *Junior Skeptic*.

The truth is that neither Anna nor her father found the skull, whether amid the Lubantuun ruins, on eBay, or anywhere else. F. A. Mitchell-Hedges bought the skull from a collector named Sydney Burney in 1933, and he then sold it to pay a debt. It was later purchased by his daughter Anna, who made up a romantic and adventurous story about finding it on her seventeenth birthday in the jungle ruins of a lost city. All the fanciful, adventurous stories about discovering the crystal skull amid ruins in the Central American jungle (and the dramatic Mayan reports of its amazing powers) were just myths created to craft a colorful backstory to the strange skull. "I discovered it in a long-lost, ruined jungle temple" is more fun than "my father bought it from a guy at an auction."

No less a person than Dr. Jaime Awe, director of the Institute of Archaeology of Belize, fell for the hoax. In 2012 Awe sued the makers of the film *Indiana Jones and the Kingdom of the Crystal Skull*, claiming that the story is based on a national treasure looted nearly a century earlier from his small Central American country. According to the *Hollywood Reporter*, "one of the most entertaining lawsuits of the year was filed in Illinois federal court. It comes from Dr. Jaime Awe, director of the Institute of Archaeology of Belize. This real-life Indiana Jones is suing on behalf of the nation of Belize over the Crystal Skull artifact, popularized in the 2008 Steven Spielberg film *Indiana Jones and the Kingdom of the Crystal Skull*. Awe is demanding the return of the Crystal Skull from a treasure-hunting family that allegedly stole it 88 years ago from Belize."

Awe sued Lucasfilm, the Walt Disney Company, and Paramount Pictures. Awe states that the crystal skull described in the film was stolen by F. A. Mitchell-Hedges during a visit to the Maya ruins of Lubantuun in the early 1920s. In his complaint, Awe cited a 1928 antiquities ordinance that prohibited the removal of artifacts from what was then British Honduras without express government permission. Since the crystal skull had been illegally removed from the ruins and used as a basis for the most recent Indiana Jones film, Awe and Belize wanted a cut of the profits and the return of the stolen skull, which they saw as part of their cultural heritage. "Lucasfilm never sought, nor was given permission to utilize the Mitchell-Hedges Skull or its likeness in the Film," says the complaint. "To date, Belize has not participated in any of the profits derived from the sale of the Film or the rights thereto." Soon after I wrote an article for Discovery News (Radford 2012) revealing the true story of the crystal skull, Awe quietly dropped the lawsuit.

What of the supposed scientists who declared that the Mitchell-Hedges skull was "impossible"? A discussion of the skull's analysis in the Hewlett-Packard publication *Measure* tells a somewhat different story from the one Frank Dorland related. According to scientists who studied it over the course of two days in December 1970: "For the Mitchell-Hedges skull the lab performed two significant tests. . . . The lab people first determined that it was almost certainly a single quartz of crystal, rather than a composite of three crystals as Dorland had suspected. Next, they probed the lower-jaw question. Was it originally an integral part of the crystal? The orientation of its X-Y axis and the 'veils' revealed by the polarized light showed that it had indeed come from the same crystal" (Hewlett-Packard 1971). That's it: the only tests they conducted on the skull were to see if it was crystal (it was), and if it was carved from one piece (it was). No tests that might "verify" any mysterious qualities of the skull (for example, that it was capable of maintaining a specific temperature) were done; such qualities were mostly exaggerated.

Doubts about the various skulls' authenticity and origins have circulated for decades. One of the most famous crystal skulls in the world is on display at London's British Museum (figures 3.4, 3.5). It was purchased from Tiffany, an auction house, in 1897 and "has attracted worldwide attention from those who credit it with special powers and believe it to be a source of ancient knowledge with the ability to heal. While it has always been the subject of interest and curiosity scientists have long doubted its authenticity." According to the British Museum display, "Although the crystal skull is highly polished, traces of tool marks remain from its carving. Moulds have been made of these indentations using special silicon dental wax and these have been examined at high magnification in a scanning electron microscope. The detailed investigation revealed clear evidence that some features were carved using rotary cutting wheels. This kind of equipment was not available until after the Spanish conquest in 1521, so the skull cannot be of Aztec manufacture. Instead, it seems likely that it was in fact made by Europeans in Germany or Brazil during the late nineteenth century."

In 2005 an anthropologist at the Smithsonian Institution examined several skulls and found that the cuts in the crystal unmistakably showed evidence of modern, not ancient, carving techniques. Not only had the cuts been done with modern lapidary wheels, but the skulls themselves had been polished with modern machinery. Researcher Margaret Sax noted "the reality that no quartz skulls have to date been retrieved from well-documented official archaeological excavations" (Sax et al. 2008, 38). Jane Walsh, an archaeologist at the Smithsonian's National Museum of Natural History, has traced the origin of most of the famous crystal skulls. "It was a French dealer named Eugène Boban who capitalized on this fascination with the macabre, as well as Europe's growing interest in and ignorance of Mesoamerican artifacts, to slip some of the first sham skulls into museums. . . . [It was Boban] who sold them to art dealers who then sold them to the museums more than 100 years ago" (Everts 2013, 49). It seems likely that, for the most part, they are well-crafted European sculptures (often later passed off as much older relics with more exotic origins), nothing more.

Yet the mystery of the crystal skulls remains. The truth about the Skull of Doom has been revealed, as has the truth about the San Luis Valley skull. When myths are stripped away—and fact is sorted from fiction—the crystal skulls reveal more about human nature than the mysteries of the universe.

ACKNOWLEDGMENTS

I gratefully acknowledge Dorion Cable, Brad Chadez, and Daniel Loxton for their help with this chapter.

REFERENCES

Aykroyd, Dan. 2008. "Dan Aykroyd's Crystal Head Vodka." YouTube video, 8:02. Posted November 12. http://www.youtube.com/watch?v=SKqjIv91Zx8.

Bowen, Sandra, F. R. Nocerino, and Joshua Shapiro. 1988. *Mysteries of the Crystal Skulls Revealed*. Pacifica, CA: J & S Aquarian.

Bower, Bruce. 2008. "Skullduggery Worthy of a Film." *Science News*, June 21, 12.

Dumas, Alan. 1996. "Valley of Lights: San Luis Hamlet of Crestone, a Strange Range Where the Deer and Maybe Even Aliens Play." *Rocky Mountain News*, November 10, 14D.

Everts, Sarah. 2013. "Crystal Skulls Deemed Fake." *Chemical and Engineering News* 91, no. 9 (March 4): 48–49.

Hall, Harriet. 2010. "Power Balance Technology." *Skeptical Inquirer* 34, no. 3 (May–June): 47–49.

Hewlett-Packard. 1971. "History or Hokum?" *Measure*, February, 8–10.

Hunter, Colin. 2005. "Caretaker to a Mystery." *Waterloo Region Record* (Kitchener, Ontario), August 20.

Loxton, Daniel. 2008. "Crystal Skulls." *Junior Skeptic* (*Skeptic* magazine) 14, no. 2: 89–96.

Nathanson, Rick. 2008. "Trail of the Skull." *Albuquerque Journal*, June 6, E1.

Nickell, Joe. 2006. "Riddle of the Crystal Skulls." *Skeptical Inquirer* 30, no. 4 (July–August): 15–16.

O' Brien, Christopher. 1996. *The Mysterious Valley*. New York: St. Martin's Press.

Parker, Derek, and Julia Parker. 1990. *Atlas of the Supernatural*. New York: Prentice Hall.

Radford, Benjamin. 2012. "'Indiana Jones' Makers Sued over Crystal Skull." Discovery News, December 8. http://news.discovery.com/human/archaeologist-sues-indiana-jones-makers-over-crystal-skull-121208.htm.

Raphaell, Katrina. 1985. *Crystal Enlightenment: The Transformative Properties of Crystals and Healing Stones*. New York: Aurora Press.

Sax, Margaret, Jane Walsh, Ian Freestone, Andrew Rankin, and Nigel Meeks. 2008. "The Origin of Two Purportedly Pre-Columbian Mexican Crystal Skulls." *Journal of Archaeological Science* 35, no. 10 (October): 2751–60.

Shuker, Karl P. N. 2009. *The Unexplained: An Illustrated Guide to the World's Paranormal Mysteries*. New York: Metro Books.

Smith, Mike. 2008a. "Crystal Skulls (Real or Imagined) All the Rage." *Local IQ*, May 29–June 11.

———. 2008b. "The San Luis Valley Crystal Skull." *Skeptical Briefs*, December, 3–5.

Welfare, Simon, and John Fairley. 1980. *Arthur C. Clarke's Mysterious World*. New York: A & W Publishers.

CHAPTER 4

THE GREAT AZTEC UFO CRASH

The most important case involving the recovery of an alien craft took place outside the little town of Aztec, New Mexico, in 1948.

UFO researcher Timothy Good,
Above Top Secret: The Worldwide UFO Cover-Up

The UFO crash outside the tiny town of Aztec, New Mexico, is overshadowed by its much more famous cousin in Roswell, on the other side of the state. But many believe that what is said to have happened in Aztec in 1948 could be the single most important event in human history. The Aztec incident is the first time that the U.S. government was alleged to have recovered—and then hidden—an intact extraterrestrial spacecraft and its occupants. Whether one is a skeptic or a believer, it's no exaggeration to say that the events surrounding the Aztec UFO crash are among the most bizarre in the Southwest's colorful history.

About fifteen minutes outside of Aztec, following a highway, then dirt roads, then finally a meandering hiking and mountain-biking trail, there lies a small area many believe once held materials forged in another galaxy. These days there's little unusual about the setting: it's scenic, hilly, and dusty. You'll find scrub brush, cacti, and snakes (along with many small oil-pumping stations and machinery) amid the plentiful evergreen pines (figure 4.1).

What exactly happened there—if anything—is a question that has been discussed for half a century. The events of the original and best-known version could have come from a Steven Spielberg film or an episode of the 1960s sci-fi television series *The Outer Limits*:

Figure 4.1. *The author near Aztec, New Mexico, near where a UFO is said to have crashed. Photo by the author.*

> It was 1948 and three radar sites tracked a UFO as it streaked across the New Mexican sky. Something apparently happened to it and it struck the ground. Using the information from the three radar sites to triangulate the position of the crash, soldiers, scientists, and police officers began a systematic search that led them to the downed craft. They spent two days observing the disc-shaped UFO before they ventured close to it. Through portholes in the craft they could see the bodies of sixteen alien beings. Probing through a broken porthole with a long rod, they accidentally hit a knob or button that opened the hatch. (Randle 1989, 41)

Unlike the Roswell flying saucer, which was supposedly largely destroyed, "the ship was whole and practically unmarred, having made a gentle pancake landing. . . . The material of the ship puzzled them. [It was] very light—two or three men together could lift one side of the saucer which measured 99.99 feet in diameter—[and] it looked like aluminum but wasn't. In the laboratory it would prove to resist 150 tests and 10,000 degrees of heat in scientific efforts to determine its composition. Dismantling the ship proved to be a problem. There were no rivets, bolts, or screws" (Cahn 1952).

Top scientists from across the country were summoned to investigate this flying saucer, prominent among them a man known as "Dr. Gee," a "mysterious and anonymous electronic wizard who had masterminded submarine locating devices for the government" during World War II (Cahn 1952, 107). This elite team, reminiscent of 1950s pulp hero Doc Savage and his group of superhero scientists who were popular at the time, bravely "entered the craft then carefully removed the bodies, laying them out on the ground. They were between three and three and a half feet tall, human looking except for the size, and wearing old-fashioned clothes made of cloth that was nearly indestructible. The skin was dark brown. . . . From studying the bodies outside the craft, Dr. Gee was able to draw a series of conclusions about them. Because they were tiny, he believed they came from Venus. Studying their features, he determined they were between thirty-five and forty, and he noticed that every one of them had perfect teeth" (Randle 1989, 41).

From the measurement of the saucer—99.99 feet exactly—the eminent Dr. Gee concluded that "Venusians used a mathematical method, not unlike ours, known as the 'system of 9's'" (Cahn 1952, 102). (Why Dr. Gee assumed that Venusians use the North American anthropometric measurement of the foot—as opposed to the meter, cubit, or some unknown, alien unit of length—was not explained.) The researchers searched the ship, and the mystifying metallic objects they found, along with other technology and materials recovered from the saucer, were unlike anything anyone had ever seen.

The saucer was soon carted off to an air force base, and the incident was covered up. Eyewitnesses were warned against speaking out, and all traces of the event were destroyed (with the exception of the UFO, its technology, and its alien occupants, of course).

On the face of it, the whole story seems like a tall tale. Who would believe that this actually occurred, much less near the Four Corners area of New Mexico? These days, aliens and UFOs are staples of science fiction films and TV shows, but in 1948 flying saucers were just coming into the public consciousness—in part because of Kenneth Arnold's seminal and widely reported 1947 sighting of a UFO mistakenly reported by a careless journalist as a "flying saucer."*

Yet two men who had learned about this amazing Aztec incident weren't afraid to speak their minds. To this day, no one would have heard about it if not for Silas Newton and Frank Scully.

* For more on Kenneth Arnold's sighting, see Philip J. Klass, *UFOs Explained* (New York: Random House, 1974).

Silas M. Newton was many things, but to many he was mainly an oil man. Newton knew something about the Aztec crash, and he also knew he needed someone else to help him tell his story. He contacted a friend, Hollywood reporter Frank Scully, and convinced him to write about the Aztec crash. Scully trusted Newton completely; he'd known him for years. If Scully had any doubts about the story, they were quickly quashed when Newton explained that he had proof. He couldn't produce the saucer or the aliens, of course—they were likely hidden at some top-secret air force base where only military personnel with the highest level of security clearance could even hope to hear a rumor of their existence—but he had the next best thing: a firsthand eyewitness. And not just any eyewitness—not the town drunk or some shady con man—but a respected scientist who had personally examined the saucer and its contents: Dr. Gee.

Dr. Gee had to remain anonymous to the public: he was risking his professional career—and possibly even his life, Newton hinted darkly—to break the code of silence. But Newton could absolutely vouch for Dr. Gee, and Scully would be given his real name and the ability to check his bona fides and interview him at length. Scully would be given access to top-secret documents that would verify Dr. Gee's information about what had crashed in Aztec.

Scully soon met with Dr. Gee, who, as promised, revealed his real name: Leo GeBauer. GeBauer was a stocky, middle-aged man with pale, deep-set eyes and the gift of gab. He also had a colorful past, degrees from prestigious universities, and a seeming command of technical and scientific matters far beyond the Hollywood entertainment reporter's expertise. Scully was mightily impressed, later referring to GeBauer as having "more degrees than a thermometer." GeBauer talked at length about his involvement in the Aztec flying saucer crash; he even showed Scully one of his prized possessions: a small, round piece of metal from the alien ship that had defied analysis by the world's top scientists.

Realizing that he had a worldwide (if not universal) exclusive on the news story of the century (if not the millennium), Scully committed to writing about it. He agreed to keep GeBauer's identity a secret; after all, his eyewitness was brave enough to break a conspiracy of silence and denial. It was the least he could do to protect this patriot, who felt that the world deserved to know the truth.

In October and November 1949 Scully published columns in *Variety*, telling the story of the Aztec UFO incident as related to him by Newton and GeBauer. The following year he expanded the magazine columns into a best-selling book: *Behind the Flying Saucers* was both hugely successful and very influential in the public's perception of UFOs. It sold some sixty thousand copies, was widely discussed in magazines and newspapers, and "affected, in some degree one way or another, the thinking of millions of people" about UFOs and aliens (Cahn 1952, 103).

OIL, SILAS NEWTON, AND DR. GEE

While Scully was busy working on his book, Newton and GeBauer were also busy. They were actually somewhat less interested in the Aztec UFO than Scully. While the reporter and his readers reeled with the realization that extraterrestrial life had been found here on Earth, Newton and GeBauer seemed largely indifferent to the implications of human-alien contact; their interest lay not above the earth but inside it. Newton, the oil entrepreneur, explained to Scully that he wanted to find deposits of oil and had hired GeBauer to help him. The eminent scientist had come through with flying colors, developing a device whose success at finding the black gold was out of this world. At least the technology was: GeBauer had used his vast knowledge of advanced electromagnetism and combined it with information gleaned from his in-depth study of the alien technology recovered from the Aztec saucer to create the device.

Any profits from the sale of Scully's book were small potatoes compared to the untold riches that such a machine could yield—in the right hands. The publicity Newton and GeBauer received from Scully's *Variety* articles and subsequent book boosted both their profile and their credibility. Like any entrepreneurs, Newton and GeBauer couldn't go it alone, even with the benefit of alien technology. They needed capital, and so they actively courted hundreds of potential investors.

For example, GeBauer showed his device (referred to as a "doodlebug") to an investor named Herman Flader, who was floored by the amazing machine.

> GeBauer had his machine with him: a metal box about eighteen inches square with antennae protruding from either end. The antennae were tipped with small metal balls about the size of marbles. These, GeBauer confided, were plutonium and worth $3,800 apiece. One side of the box was covered with dials, knobs, and small lights. . . . Flader had recently dug five water wells on one of his ranches. Just by twirling the machine's dials until the lights lit, GeBauer located each well and read

> its exact depth. A couple of times a red light on the machine flared and GeBauer announced they were over oil, reeling off the precise depth of the deposit. . . . "Old Betsy," GeBauer's pet name for his machine, was apparently infallible. . . . In the course of the tests, GeBauer revealed—confidentially, of course—that "Old Betsy" operated on the same magnetic principles as the flying saucers. As a matter of fact, he added casually, when the first saucer had landed on earth, he had been called into consultation by the government because of his outstanding work in the field of magnetics.* (Cahn 1952, 69)

But there was more—much more. Not only could Old Betsy magnetically detect oil, water, and natural gas, but it could diagnose any medical problems the user might have: "By taking a firm grip on her plutonium-tipped antennae, GeBauer could give you a reading on the state of your health" (Cahn 1952, 70). It seemed that the only thing this little piece of alien technology could not detect was fraud.

Those who wanted to examine the machine were refused; in fact, they were told that doing so could be deadly. Old Betsy's "circuits were so secret the government had insisted GeBauer put demolition charges in each machine. . . . If Flader so much as tried to peek inside the machine, he would be blown to bits" (Cahn 1952, 70). With the death penalty a consequence of curiosity, Flader promised not to look. Instead, he ended up giving Newton and GeBauer over a quarter of a million dollars.

CAHN'S GAME

Newton and GeBauer's oil exploration and investment gathering went on for months, finally drawing the attention of an intrepid journalist, *San Francisco Chronicle* reporter J. P. Cahn. As he later described in a pair of articles for *True* magazine, Cahn doggedly investigated the strange case. He first interviewed Frank Scully to learn more about the information in his book *Behind the Flying Saucers*. Scully seemed completely and sincerely convinced of the story that Newton and the anonymous Dr. Gee had told him. Cahn wrote that in asking Scully about his book, he "gave me the impression that he had only the vaguest idea of what he was talking about, but he believed every word he was saying" (Cahn 1952, 103).

* This is, of course, completely unscientific; plutonium is highly radioactive, and neither water nor oil are magnetic.

Scully was pleasant but not especially cooperative, refusing to reveal the identity of his primary source, Dr. Gee. Cahn then turned to the other public figure in the book, Silas Newton. Newton agreed to meet with Cahn. Silas Newton was a short, compact man in his sixties who looked younger than his age, with "the sort of face you'd expect to find on a middle-aged elf—tanned, deep-seamed, high-browed, and crackling with good humor" (Cahn 1982, 104). He had charisma, made friends easily, and could talk a million miles a minute. He always seemed eager to share a secret with a new friend. He used scientific words and technical phrases—although not always accurately, Cahn noted.

ANALYZING THE ALIEN METALS

During one meeting, Newton showed Cahn a few pieces of metal that he claimed had been recovered from the Aztec saucer and given to him by Dr. Gee. This mysterious metal, as described above, had stumped the world's best scientific minds. Using a basic magician's palming move, Cahn boldly and secretly swapped the small piece of alien metal for another he'd prepared. Immediately after the interview, Cahn took the metal to the Stanford Research Institute in Menlo Park, California, for analysis. Cahn was eager to find out what the metal was. Could he really be holding something created by an alien race on Venus or elsewhere in the universe?

Cahn reported that the Stanford scientists "gave the disk the full treatment. They clipped off a tiny piece and checked its melting point. They did a simple gravimetric analysis. They mounted it in plastic, polished a portion of it to a mirror finish and examined its structure microscopically. They sent another piece of the disk over to Stanford University for a spectrochemical analysis."

It was the first—and most comprehensive—scientific analysis of an alleged extraterrestrial artifact ever recorded, and its results would more or less definitively prove or disprove the whole story. "Newton's precious unknown metal that Dr. Gee had supposedly taken from a crashed flying saucer, the same that had refused to melt in Dr. Gee's laboratory at 10,000 degrees, melted quite nicely at Stanford Research Institute at just 657 degrees Fahrenheit. It was plain old aluminum, 99.5 percent pure, a quality commercially described as grade 2S and used in the manufacture of nothing more cosmic than pots and pans" (Cahn 1952, 110).

Cahn, doing the kind of investigative journalism that has all but vanished in these sorts of inquiries, dug into the facts, and what he discovered made the whole story seem less and less plausible with each new revelation. He learned, for instance, that Silas Newton was not the famous and well-respected oilman Scully had described. In fact, nobody Cahn contacted in the oil business had ever heard of him.

Cahn contacted Scully with his concerns about Newton's credibility, but he was summarily dismissed. Through detective work, Cahn soon identified the mysterious Dr. Gee as Leo GeBauer. Once GeBauer was unmasked by this skeptical inquirer, his web of lies collapsed. "Instead of holding degrees from Armour Institute, Creighton University, and the University of Berlin, as Scully wrote, GeBauer only claimed a degree in electrical engineering from the Louis Institute of Technology in Chicago around 1931 or 1932, he couldn't remember which." During the time he claimed to have been employed in top-secret government magnetic research defense programs, he had actually been employed at a company called AiResearch—not as a scientist but as a maintenance man (Cahn 1952, 111).

Even Herman Flader, whom GeBauer had so impressed with his oil-locating device, eventually broke his promise to not look inside the contraption. When Flader finally opened Old Betsy, he found some wires and "a little 20-cent battery" that lit up the red light indicating when oil was found. There was no alien technology: "The machinery turned out to be the tuning units of U.S. Army radio transmitters. They still had the Signal Corps identification plates on them" (Cahn 1952, 70). An electronics expert later testified in court that the unit "couldn't indicate the presence of anything"—much less water, oil, gas, gold, or cancers. It was all a lie—a huge, bold, complete, and utter con job.

They were caught. Investigations revealed that Newton and GeBauer (according to Cahn, "as slippery a pair of swindlers as ever came down the pike") had "individually, or as a team, . . . been hawking phony stock and fake machines in a dozen states for the last 25 years" (Cahn 1952, 69). Cahn and police investigators uncovered dozens of victims. Some declined to prosecute because they were embarrassed at having been conned by fraud artists who had somehow convinced them to invest in technology they had been told was developed on Venus. Many others could not prosecute because the statute of limitations had expired. But not Mr. Flader; he was hopping mad and happy to put the UFO hoaxing criminals behind bars. According to writer Nick Redfern, GeBauer was also revealed in FBI files to have been a Nazi sympathizer, quoted as saying: "What this country needs is a man like Hitler. . . . It would be God's blessing if we had two men in the United

States to run this country like Hitler. . . . We should tend to our own damn business and let Germany give England what they had coming" (Redfern 2004).

On October 14, 1952, FBI agents arrested GeBauer in Phoenix and Newton in Hollywood. On November 10, 1965, the pair went on trial. When in front of a jury, GeBauer insisted that Old Betsy could do what he claimed, although he changed his story and said that the device was not based on alien technology recovered in Aztec but instead on his study of the aurora borealis, or northern lights. Working scientists with legitimate academic degrees testified at the trial, explaining that there was not a shred of science, truth, or credibility to anything that came out of GeBauer's mouth—quite a turnaround from his original claims of being so esteemed a scientist that the U.S. government had asked him to personally inspect the world's first recovered UFO.

The jury saw right through Newton and GeBauer's mountain of lies; the pair were found guilty on two charges each of fraud and conspiracy. They both faced the maximum of thirty years in prison.

Veteran investigator Robert Sheaffer, in his book *UFO Sightings*, interviewed Cahn, who explained that "the purpose of the UFO fable was to expand their 'sucker list.' When credulous letters sent to Scully and forwarded to Newton and GeBauer suggested that the sender had money, the latter would contact the sender to regale him with stories of saucer crashes—and of fantastic new devices for discovering oil" (Sheaffer 2012).*

Newton and GeBauer left a long line of conned victims, but one is often overlooked: Frank Scully. Most people believe that Frank Scully was himself an innocent rube and that "despite solemn prefaces by both the author and publisher, [his] book was a complete hoax" (Cahn 1952, 36).

* Robert Sheaffer told me about his encounter with Cahn: "J. P. Cahn, who called himself 'Jape,' was a colorful figure who often had a mischievous side. He was a great storyteller who enjoyed retelling the events of his 'crashed saucer' investigation, or almost anything else. One day his hackles were raised by a writer calling him a 'journalist.' 'I'm not a journalist, I'm nothing but a good, old-fashioned newspaperman, and that's all I've ever been.' But he also wrote a lot of freelance articles, sold cars, and organized trade shows. By the time I met Cahn in 1982, he was living alone in a house in a prestigious neighborhood up on San Francisco's Mount Davidson. He said that, prior to the discussions he and I had about his investigations of the Scully book, he had not spoken about that subject with anyone in a very long time. However, by the mid-1980s, interest in the subject was increasing, and he was contacted by several researchers. Cahn's health declined during the 1990s (he was in his seventies). He sold his house in 1997 and moved into an assisted-living home. He died in 2004" (Sheaffer 2012).

He had been suckered into endorsing a fictional UFO crash and been an unwitting accomplice in helping Newton and GeBauer rob and scam people of their life savings. Scully's reputation never recovered, and his career and credibility were badly damaged; he died in June 1964. Decades after his death, however, Chris Carter, the creator of *The X-Files* television series, paid tribute to Scully by naming one of the program's lead characters after him.

AZTEC ALIEN TECHNOLOGY REVISITED

So the eyewitnesses are not reliable; but what about any hard evidence that anything mysterious crashed in Aztec? As we have seen, the most notorious piece of technology developed from the crashed saucer was Old Betsy—the fantastic, although completely fictional and fraudulent, "doodlebug" that GeBauer and Newton claimed could find water, oil, natural gas, and cancer. While even the most diehard UFO believers admit that the device was completely phony, some people still believe that a flying saucer crashed in Aztec and that not only were alien bodies recovered but alien technology was indeed adopted by the U.S. government and is currently being used in military applications. UFO writer Timothy Good claims: "The most important case involving the recovery of an alien craft took place outside the little town of Aztec, New Mexico, in 1948. . . . A great deal of technical and other intelligence resulted from this recovery, intelligence which gave the Americans a giant leap forward in technology and weaponry unparalleled in human history" (quoted in Dennett 2011, 232).

This is hardly the first time that a UFO conspiracy buff has claimed that high-tech weapons were reverse-engineered from alien technology. Basically, scientists take an unknown object, break it down into smaller components, see how they work, and reassemble it. There is nothing unusual or arcane about the process; it is standard practice around the world when foreign powers are able to capture or shoot down their enemies' high-tech surveillance devices.

However, the claim that American scientists have access to far-advanced technology flies in the face of logic and evidence. For example, it's curious that despite allegedly having access to faster-than-light spacecraft technology for over half a century, America's top scientists still haven't been able to develop a flying saucer. Nor can they prevent their (real) top-secret aircraft from occasionally crashing and being recovered by foreign powers, as happened in Pakistan in May 2011 when a stealth H-60 Black Hawk helicopter crashed during the raid that killed Osama bin Laden, and the following year when a top-secret U.S. spy drone was captured by Iranians when it landed in their country (Hennigan, Cloud, and Dilanian 2011; Quinn 2011). If what Good and other alien technology reverse-engineering conspiracy theorists claim is true, it's odd that the military chooses not to use any of the ultra-high technology available to it—or, if they are using it, it appears to be just as fallible as the homegrown advanced technology the military already uses.

THE FBI INVESTIGATES

The Aztec UFO claims have not gone away; indeed, they resurfaced as recently as 2011. UFO researchers have long sought "smoking gun" evidence that would prove that the U.S. government knows more than it admits about crashed flying saucers. In 2011 the news media and the UFO community were abuzz with a recently discovered "top secret" FBI file proving that flying saucers and alien bodies had been recovered in New Mexico. The (UK) *Sun* ran a story headlined "Aliens Exist, Say Real-Life X-Files," quoting UFO expert Nick Pope as saying, "These are the real life *X-Files*. This document could be the smoking gun that proves UFOs are real." Bill Birnes, the publisher of *UFO Magazine* and a star of the television show *UFO Hunters*, endorsed the document as hard evidence of the Roswell UFO crash on an episode of the show *Unsealed: Alien Files* broadcast in 2013.

This "smoking gun" was a March 22, 1950, memo from Washington bureau agent Guy Hottel to the director of the FBI (figure 4.2). It has the subject line "Flying Saucers, Information Concerning," and states:

> An investigator for the Air Forces stated that three so-called flying saucers had been recovered in New Mexico. They were described as being circular in shape with raised centers, approximately 50 feet in diameter. Each one was occupied by three bodies of human shape but only 3 feet tall, dressed in metallic cloth of a very fine texture. Each body was bandaged in a manner similar to the blackout suits used by speed flyers and test pilots. According to Mr. [blacked out] informant, the saucers were found in New Mexico due to the fact that the Government has a very high-powered radar set-up in that area and it is believed the radar interferes with the controlling mechanism of the saucers. No further evaluation was attempted . . . concerning the above.

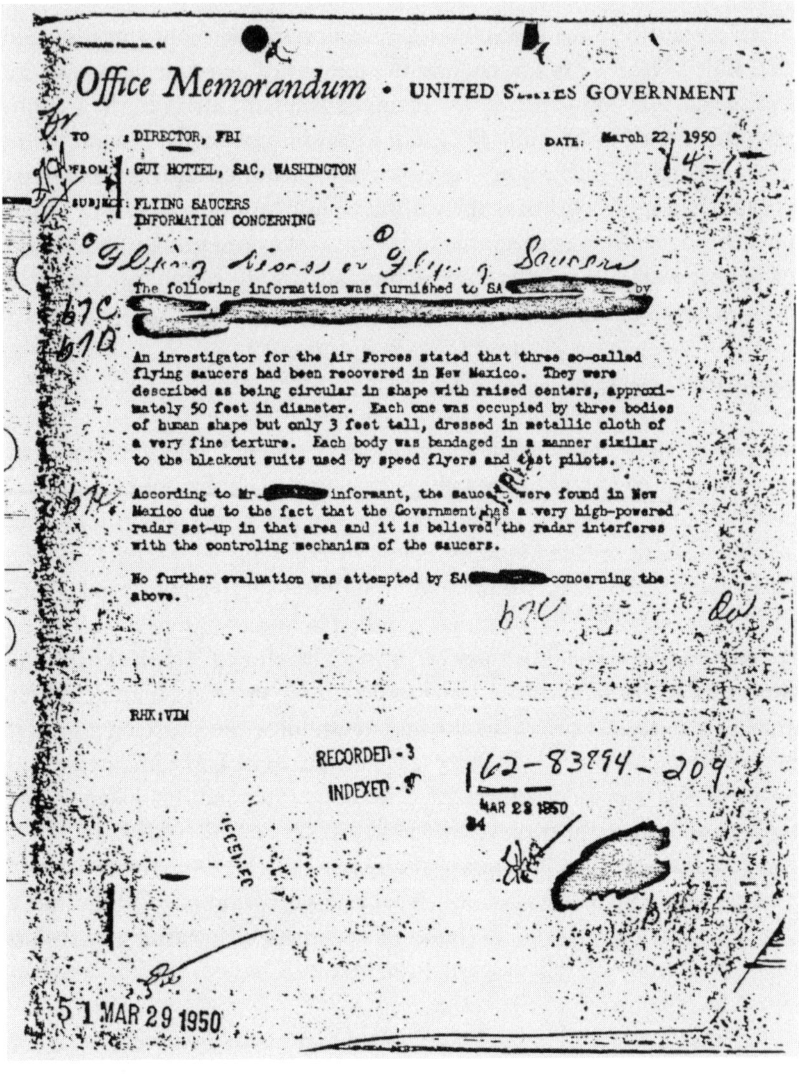

Office Memorandum • UNITED STATES GOVERNMENT

TO : DIRECTOR, FBI DATE: March 22, 1950

FROM : GUY HOTTEL, SAC, WASHINGTON

SUBJECT: FLYING SAUCERS
INFORMATION CONCERNING

The following information was furnished to SA [redacted] by [redacted]

An investigator for the Air Forces stated that three so-called flying saucers had been recovered in New Mexico. They were described as being circular in shape with raised centers, approximately 50 feet in diameter. Each one was occupied by three bodies of human shape but only 3 feet tall, dressed in metallic cloth of a very fine texture. Each body was bandaged in a manner similar to the blackout suits used by speed flyers and test pilots.

According to Mr. [redacted] informant, the saucers were found in New Mexico due to the fact that the Government has a very high-powered radar set-up in that area and it is believed the radar interferes with the controling mechanism of the saucers.

No further evaluation was attempted by SA [redacted] concerning the above.

RHK:VIM

RECORDED - 3
INDEXED - 8

62-83894-209

MAR 28 1950

51 MAR 29 1950

Figure 4.2. *A 1950 FBI memo discussing the recovery of a UFO and alien bodies in Aztec, New Mexico.*

I was asked by Discovery News to examine the document, and I concluded that it was indeed a smoking gun. But instead of proving that the military had covered up a UFO crash, it proved that the public, reporters, and UFO "experts" like Nick Pope hadn't analyzed the document very closely.

To start with, most people assumed that the memo was referring to New Mexico's most famous UFO crash, but a close reading reveals that Roswell is not mentioned anywhere in the memo. It merely says that the saucers were "recovered in New Mexico." Since the alleged saucer crash in Roswell is the most famous such incident in the world, one might assume that any reference to UFOs in New Mexico is a reference to Roswell. However, none of the Roswell eyewitnesses had described "flying saucers . . . circular in shape with raised centers, approximately 50 feet in diameter" or three-foot-tall aliens wearing metallic space suits. Instead, the informant's words match a description given by Silas Newton about the Aztec UFO crash.

It's also suspicious that this "smoking gun" document is just an ordinary office memo. Contrary to the sensational headlines and blog posts circulating at the time, it's not classified as Top Secret, or even Secret; in fact it's not classified at all. This supposed proof of crashed saucers is in the form of an ordinary memo, carrying no more secrecy or concern than a request for more office staplers. Given the supposedly explosive nature of the memo's contents, one might think that the FBI would do a better job of ensuring that ordinary office employees wouldn't have access to a document admitting that they were hiding three crashed saucers and nine alien bodies.

Not only was the FBI memo about Aztec, not Roswell, it wasn't "newly discovered." The memo had been discussed in UFO circles since the mid-1980s, and a close reading reveals that Agent Hottel is not verifying, validating, or endorsing any of the information presented in the memo; he's merely telling the FBI director what an air force investigator had said that an informant (Silas Newton, his name blacked out) had *told him* about the crashed saucers. He's not saying that any of the information is accurate; he's just reporting what he was told. Again, we see third- and fourth-hand information being presented as truth.

The FBI memo doesn't prove anything other than that what Silas Newton had told an air force investigator about a UFO crash in Aztec was passed along to Agent Hottel, who then told the FBI director. It's little wonder that the FBI took no further notice of or action on such an implausible story ("no further evaluation was attempted")—at least not until the agency began its criminal investigation of Newton and GeBauer.

David E. Thomas, a physicist and UFO researcher in New Mexico, explains how the Hottel memo story took off:

> Guy Hottel described an investigator's report of a flying saucer recovery in New Mexico, with mention of three saucers, three-foot-tall bodies, metallic cloth, and bandaged alien bodies. The crash was supposedly due to interference from high-powered radar. But all of these elements (saucers, aliens, cloth and tape, radar site) have been firmly traced to the yarns spun by our two swindlers! William Moore even traced how the story got from Silas Newton to J. Edgar Hoover: Newton told George Koehler (employed at radio station KMYR in Denver), who told Morley Davies, who told Ford dealers Murphy and van Horn, who told auto dealer Fick, who told the editor of the Kansas City *Wyandotte Echo*. By that time, Koehler had become "Coulter," just like a game of "Gossip"! This article was picked up in the news, where it caught the interest of the OSI. The OSI agent passed the story on to Guy Hottel of the FBI, and he gave the eighth-hand story to Hoover. (Thomas 1998)

THE AZTEC UFO ENDURES

With the two con men convicted and all the evidence related to the Aztec UFO discredited, the episode faded away. As John Michael Greer (2009) noted in *The UFO Phenomenon*, "The story dropped out of the UFO debate immediately thereafter, and nobody but debunkers mentioned it for some two decades after that. In the late 1970s, however, Leonard Stringfield resurrected the Aztec hoax as one of a litany of supposedly crashed UFOs in the Air Force's possession, and the story has been repeated by a great many [UFO researchers] since then" (119). Like the phoenix, the long-discredited Aztec story continues to rise from the ashes of disrepute, fueled by sloppy scholarship and the desire to tell an outlandish UFO story, facts be damned. Variations on the story have cropped up, especially given that Newton and GeBauer changed their story depending on who they were talking to. Sometimes a dozen alien bodies had been recovered; other times fourteen or sixteen. Sometimes the description of the alien saucer stuck with Scully's report; other times there were three (or more) smaller saucers.

Folklore is a living, mutable form; it constantly changes and adapts, and sure enough the fictional Aztec 99.99-foot UFO and its unfortunate, perfect-toothed aliens soon popped up four hundred miles away, in Roswell. "Many of the details cited by Scully in his book about the Aztec crash reappeared, sometimes verbatim, in accounts of the Roswell incident published in the 1980s. In his study of the Roswell story as a modern myth, Charles Ziegler has argued that this shows the way folktales normally grow, by picking up themes and details from other sources" (Greer 2009, 119).

The Aztec UFO case, although conclusively shown to be a complete hoax, won't go away. Indeed, what may be one of the grandest hoaxes of all time has garnered the attention of other hoaxers who sense the chance to revive the tale for money, publicity, or just fun. When the stories reappeared, this time there were several new crashes—one of them directly involving the president of the United States!

> In 1974 the Scully stories of crashed saucers and the tales of little bodies were back. This time it was Robert Carr and he had new information about the crash that Scully had claimed happened near Aztec, New Mexico. Carr was very secretive about his sources, refusing to reveal them. He did say, however, that there had been more than one crash and that President Eisenhower had been taken to Muroc Air Force Base to view the craft and the aliens. Later all the material was transferred to Wright Field for safekeeping and further study. . . . Researchers then went to work trying to learn if Carr was right or if he was merely telling the same tales. Was it Frank Scully again? One man went to Aztec, talked to local residents, read the newspaper files, and spent days trying to locate the crash site. He concluded that Carr's information about Aztec was wrong. (Randle 1989, 43)

Indeed, in *The UFO Casebook*, Kevin Randle insists that "there might be something to their rumors of the crashed discs" after all. "Now it seems that there was some truth to the Scully stories" he says, although he admits that "Newton and GeBauer might have added details to dress up their story." Yes, Randle believes that the factual details of a real crashed flying saucer and its sixteen dead alien bodies wouldn't be sensational enough to interest the public—these two con men needed to embellish the truth with fanciful details and exaggerations. Those who buy Randle's bizarre the-hoax-hides-the-truth claim likely would have been happy to purchase beachfront New Mexican property from Newton and GeBauer in the 1950s (Randle 1989, 45).

Preston Dennett, relying largely on William Steinman and Wendelle Stevens's discredited 1987 book *UFO Crash at Aztec*, claims that new witnesses have since emerged confirming the Aztec UFO story.*

* Interestingly, Wendelle Stevens's daughter, CeCe, claims to be a psychic and crystal skull expert (see chapter 3). She offers a variety of New Age healing services from her home in Sedona, Arizona.

Dennett writes that Steinman "has raised a convincing case that the whole affair was an attempt to discredit Scully and the entire Aztec UFO crash by providing real information mixed with disinformation, coming from a less than credible source" (Dennett 2011, 233). Dennett thus paints J. P. Cahn's whole investigation as part of a grand UFO conspiracy bigger than anyone imagined; he was not an enterprising investigative reporter but instead a government puppet.

The suggestion that there are real eyewitnesses to UFO crashes seems tantalizing and intriguing until one actually reads their stories and realizes that they are not actual witnesses but (assuming they are sincere and not telling tales for profit, fun, or attention) are merely repeating what other people have told them.

For example, "One new witness has recently been discovered. In 1952, Bill Devlin . . . says that he befriended a soldier and got to talking about UFOs. The soldier revealed that he had personally been involved in a UFO crash incident in Aztec. The soldier told Devlin that he was one of three drivers who delivered the remains of the saucer from Aztec to Fort Riley" (Dennett 2011, 233). Dennett refers to Devlin as a "witness," although it's clear that he didn't "witness" anything. An unknown person named Devlin, who may or may not be credible, is simply passing on what he says an anonymous soldier (who may or may not be credible) *told him* about the Aztec crash. If this sounds familiar, it should: it's an example of the elusive friend-of-a-friend (FOAF) tales so common in rumors, folklore, and urban legends. This sort of "somebody told me that someone said . . . " statement holds no credibility in a court of law (it's called "hearsay"), but it's unfortunately all too common in UFO research. The same sort of reliance on unreliable sources destroyed Frank Scully's credibility and career. Dennett's complaint that "less than credible sources" have been used to support the UFO case is especially ironic.

Scott Ramsey is yet another UFO researcher who insists that, despite all evidence to the contrary, the Aztec crash really happened. Ramsey claims that at least a dozen people, mostly oil workers and police officers, saw the saucer firsthand. Yet, as is typical of these cases, these are nothing more than stories. Not a shred of hard evidence nor a single photograph of the saucer has ever emerged—which is not surprising, since it was the product of two con men's imaginations.

When interviewed on a Paranormal Paracast podcast in 2010 about evidence for the crash, Ramsey claimed that he had "thousands" of documents about it: "Well, we've got eyewitness testimony of people through the years. . . . We have FBI reports, CIA reports, army/CID reports, air force/OSI reports." As support for his theory, Ramsey related a story he'd heard about a newspaper reporter allegedly caught in a sting operation by government authorities trying to buy photos of the Aztec saucer. He tried to follow up on that story, yet could find no evidence at all: "I spent months with the archivist and the reporters at the *Baltimore Sun-Times* [*sic*], they never had a reporter by that name ever work for them." Ramsey also tried to verify his story at the army's Criminal Investigation Command archives in Quantico, Virginia, and once again came up empty-handed.

So what does all this mean? Even Ramsey admits that he has no idea what to make of his information. The Paranormal Paracast cohost asked Ramsey, "So we have a nonexistent reporter for the *Baltimore Sun* seeking an allegedly nonexistent photograph. I'm confused." Ramsey admitted, "So are we. . . . You said you're confused, I am too."

Normally when an investigative reporter realizes that statements he's been given don't check out and aren't supported, that reporter assumes he's been misinformed. However, as is typical of conspiracy thinking, Ramsey assumed that the reason he couldn't find documentation was that it had been hidden as part of a government cover-up—not that the story about the *Baltimore Sun* reporter trying to buy photos of the Aztec saucer that Newton and GeBauer had dreamed up years earlier is one of the many hoaxes and tall tales that have cropped up in the wake of the fiasco.

When asked for hard proof of the crash, Ramsey offered just two pieces of evidence: a few tree limbs that had allegedly been broken by the saucer, and a "one-meter square concrete slab that measures about nine or ten inches thick" containing rebar that he deems suspicious. To Ramsey, the best explanation for its existence is that it was used by the military to handle "an incredible amount of weight" (presumably the Aztec saucer, although Ramsey conveniently ignores the fact that eyewitnesses said it was very light and could be lifted by only a few men). "We cannot come up with an intelligent reason why it's there," he said.

This is an example of a logical fallacy called *arguing from ignorance*: trying to use a lack of information or knowledge to support a claim. Just because he can't think of a good reason for something doesn't mean it's mysterious. Ramsey promised to reveal all his evidence in a soon-to-be-published book on the Aztec UFO, which he did self-publish in 2012.

Several of the Aztec "witnesses" claim that they read about the crash in the local newspaper: "As possible further confirmation, a newspaper article about the crash appeared in the *Farmington Daily Times* following the incident. Several witnesses claim to have seen this article" (Dennett 2011, 233). It seems that the Aztec UFO cover-up was not nearly as thorough as claimed, if soldiers and others involved in the crash retrieval talked freely about it in the local newspaper! Predictably, it's not true; the witnesses are either wrong, misremembering, or lying. There is no record of any article in the *Farmington Daily Times* at that time about the Aztec UFO crash.

In 1985 one of the main proponents of the Roswell crash, William L. Moore, gave a "brilliantly researched and argued paper" to a UFO symposium sponsored by the Mutual UFO Network (MUFON). In it, he discussed how the Aztec UFO hoax had spread, and how it had continued to fool UFO researchers: "The key thing for crashed saucer researchers here is that Newton told his story, with variations to suit the particular ear he was bending, to large numbers of people all over the West. And many of these people freely repeated it to others, either without naming the original source, or in painting Newton (and of course GeBauer) with labels of unquestionable respectability. The story, now third-hand and embellished accordingly, went heaven knows where from that point" (quoted in Brookesmith 1996, 159). Five decades later, the Aztec story continues to fool people.

Peter Brookesmith, in *UFO: The Government Files*, notes: "There is, then, good reason to believe that in the minds of 'witnesses' quoted many years later, the legends and the reality did coincide over time—and that, no doubt with perfect sincerity, they recounted memories that conflated history, mental associations with more recent stories, and ancient rumors into 'fact.' Repeated retellings to the flock of interested researchers will, of course, have solidified and smoothed these memories. And some 'witnesses' were probably not sincere" (Brookesmith 1996, 160).

CONCLUSION

In the end, the entire Aztec UFO crash story rests completely on two proven liars and convicted con men who found a sympathetic ear in Frank Scully, whose subsequent book Cahn describes as "now proved to be, in effect, one of the greatest scientific hoaxes to hit the country since the old Cardiff Giant was rooted out of the soil of the Onandaga Valley in 1869" (Cahn 1952, 12). Once again, well-meaning UFO buffs were suckered by hoaxers, con men, and liars. Anyone who thinks that modern UFO researchers have wised up needs a refresher course in human gullibility—and especially UFO believers' worldviews. There's an old proverb that says, "Fool me once, shame on you; fool me twice, shame on me," but some UFO writers continue to fool themselves (and their readers) over and over again.

This not only casts serious doubt on their credibility (if they'll believe and repeat a story completely lacking in evidence and concocted by a pair of convicted con men, what *won't* they believe?) but also undercuts other, more sober UFO investigators, because it makes the whole field look silly. Observers come to believe that there's no UFO story so outlandish and thoroughly discredited that some prominent authors and "experts" won't endorse it.

Indeed, the story lives on. The town of Aztec, seeing the publicity and tourist dollars that Roswell has attracted, held their own annual Aztec UFO symposium. It was successful for a few years but finally ended in 2011. Organizer Katie McClure was quoted in the *Farmington Daily Times* as saying that declining interest and attendance were to blame, along with the difficulty of finding local volunteers to organize the event. The fact that the Aztec UFO crash was made up as part of an elaborate con game was not mentioned.

REFERENCES

Brookesmith, Peter. 1996. *UFO: The Government Files*. New York: Barnes and Noble.

Cahn, J. P. 1952. "The Flying Saucers and the Mysterious Little Men." *True* magazine, September.

———. 1956. "Flying Saucer Swindlers." *True* magazine, August.

Dennett, Preston. 2011. *UFOs over New Mexico*. Atglen, PA: Schiffer Publishing.

Greer, John Michael. 2009. *The UFO Phenomenon: Fact, Fantasy, and Disinformation*. Woodbury, MN: Llewellyn.

Hennigan, W. J., David Cloud, and Ken Dilanian. 2011. "Drone That Crashed in Iran May Give Away U.S. Secrets." *Los Angeles Times*, December 6. http://articles.latimes.com/2011/dec/06/business/la-fi-1206-drone-iran-20111206.

Quinn, Ben. 2011. "Pakistan 'Gave China Access' to Downed U.S. Helicopter." *Guardian*, August 14. http://www.guardian.co.uk/world/2011/aug/15/pakistan-china-access-us-helicopter.

Ramsey, Scott. 2010. The UFO Chronicles, Paracast, March 3. http://www.theufochronicles.com/2010/03/researcher-scott-ramsey-reveals-new.html.

Randle, Kevin. 1989. *The UFO Casebook*. New York: Warner Books.

Redfern, Nick. 2004. "Incident at Aztec." *Fortean Times*, April.

Sheaffer, Robert. 2012. Interview by Benjamin Radford, February 4.

Steinman, William, and Wendelle Stevens. 1987. *UFO Crash at Aztec*. Sedona, AZ: UFO Photo Archives.

Thomas, Dave. 1998. "The Aztec UFO Symposium." *New Mexicans for Science and Reason Reports* 4, no. 6 (June). http://www.nmsr.org/aztec.htm.

CHAPTER 5

THE SANTA FE COURTHOUSE GHOST

New Mexican ghosts are notoriously camera shy.

Oh, sure, they will show up now and then. They like to appear briefly, often out of the corner of your eye, sometimes when you least expect it. Like chaste flirts, they tease with hints of their true charms, but they always hold back, just out of reach, leaving frustratingly little evidence of their visit. Without some sort of proof, it's just another story, another *cuento* to tell around the campfire as smoke and embers twist their way into the inky night sky.

Very few New Mexican ghosts have been photographed, and none as clearly as the mysterious, glowing white blob that was captured on video in the state's capital in 2007. Early on the otherwise mundane Friday morning of June 15, 2007—at 7:27 and eleven seconds, to be exact—Santa Fe deputy policeman Alfred Arana saw a ghost.

He had been reviewing surveillance video from the previous evening at the First Judicial District Courthouse on Catron Street (figure 5.1) when he saw a mysterious, glowing white spot of light. The entity seemed to come out the courthouse's back door at the top right-hand corner of the frame, cross in front of a parked police car, and then move diagonally off screen, covering the distance in about ten seconds.

Arana walked to the side door to see if the bizarre object might still be there. Instead of a glowing ghost, he saw only an empty dirt area and a few bleary-eyed commuters heading to work or the nearest coffee shop.

A shorter version of this chapter appeared as chapter 9 of my book *Scientific Paranormal Investigation: How to Solve Unexplained Mysteries* (Corrales, NM: Rhombus Publishing, 2010).

Figure 5.1. *A ghostly figure was recorded on a surveillance camera at the Steve Herrera Judicial Complex in Santa Fe. Photo by the author.*

He waited until Sergeant Vanessa Pacheco arrived. "I've got something you should see," he told her. "I can't explain it, I don't know what it is." The pair stood in front of the video screens, rewound the video, and watched the footage together. As more court personnel showed up, the theories multiplied as each new person marveled at the ghostly white figure.

It was soon dubbed the Courthouse Ghost, and what started out as a minor local curiosity soon took on a life of its own as a full-blown mystery when state, national, and finally international press reports carried the story. The "ghost video" (figure 5.2) was eventually seen in various versions nearly one hundred thousand times on YouTube.*

THE THEORIES

Theories about the strange entity circulated outside the courtrooms, in downtown cafés, and on the *Santa Fe New Mexican*'s website. Some

* Available at http://www.youtube.com/watch?v=ZBR6wD6rzPg.

skeptical Santa Feans suggested earthbound explanations, such as a video glitch, a hoax, an insect, cottonwood tree fluff, or a reflection from a passing car. However, Santa Fe being, well, Santa Fe, the ghost theory stuck. "Generally, most people who have seen the video believe it is some type of spirit or ghost," Sergeant Pacheco told the *Santa Fe New Mexican*. "I don't believe in ghosts, so I don't think that's what it is," she added skeptically.

Several people noted that the object seemed to be trailed by a shadow as it moved across the video screen. Others saw odd faces in the blurry images; one woman, Marylou Parna, saw a male's face in the image of the police car: two eyes, a nose, and lips. One anonymous woman who posted to the *New Mexican*'s website claimed to be a spiritual reader and said that the video was definitely of a ghost. In fact, she saw not just one but five separate spirits in the video—including a man near the tree, a child, and a woman with a hat.

Santa Fe New Mexican journalist Jason Auslander noted other reactions among the courthouse staff; for instance, lawyer Steve Aarons said, "To me, it looks like a person walking, but I don't know why they have

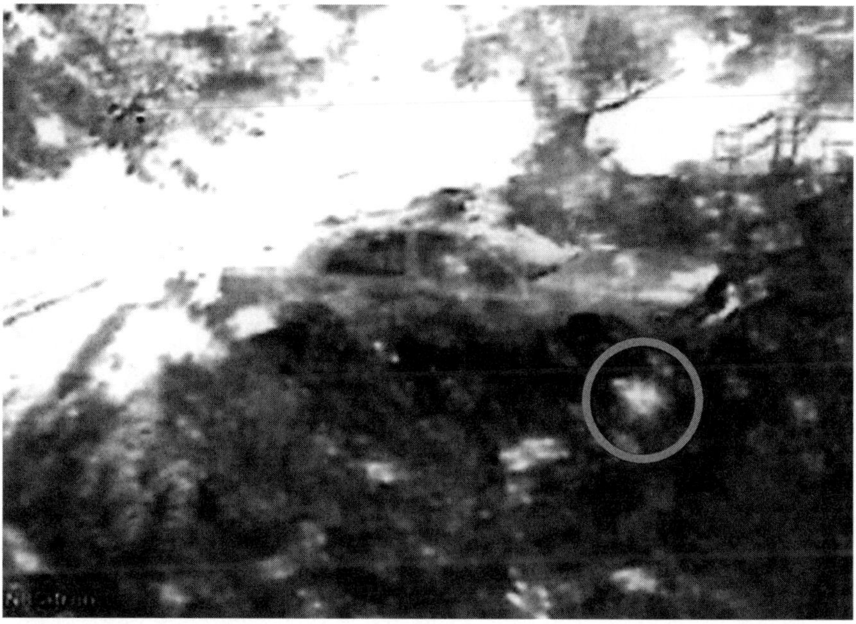

Figure 5.2. *A white, ghostly entity (circled) was captured on camera and made national news.*

this neon light on their head." The light looked slightly crab-shaped and seemed to crawl like a bug, although Pacheco and others who regularly look at footage from that surveillance camera said that they've seen bugs on the lens before, and they don't look like the image captured that Friday.

Perhaps the most bizarre aspect of the image is that it appears to cast shadows that look a bit like the movements of the invisible monster in the 1987 John McTiernan/Arnold Schwarzenegger film *Predator.* Many who watched the video said that the shadows looked like legs. Mary Marlowe, another lawyer, said that she saw hands in the image. Courthouse employees debated whether it might have been a reflection. However, the angle of the sun at that time of day wouldn't have created such a reflection, and a large tree outside the door shaded most of the area from above.

"It looks like a reflection of something but the angle of the sun is all wrong," said Juanita Sena-Shannon, a court clerk. District judge Michael Vigil said that he, too, thought it was a reflection at first, perhaps from a passing car. But when he looked closer, he realized that a reflection would have moved in a straight line, which the light did not. "It doesn't make sense," the judge said. "It is bizarre." Arana said that the footage was clearer when he first watched it than when it was replayed over and over on Friday. During that first viewing, he said, it looked as if the light had stars arrayed in a diamond pattern, which were each spinning clockwise. Arana said that he had no idea what the cameras might have captured.

One deputy suggested that the ghost was the spirit of a convict who had been killed at that very courthouse, not far from where the ghost was seen, in 1985. (This specific spectral speculation was scuttled within days after the widow of the murdered convict allegedly threatened to sue any courthouse personnel who publicly repeated the story.) One woman said that she sensed the ghost was the spirit of a little girl who had gotten lost on her way home and met an untimely end; another woman noted that a vacant lot nearby was being excavated for a new building and suggested that perhaps an Indian burial ground had been accidentally disturbed, releasing a restless Native American spirit (despite this popular idea, archaeologists found no evidence at all of any early American Indians at the site; see Hay 2012). Yet another asked if any local psychics had been asked to contact the ghost and help put it to rest.

Jude Torres, employed as a courthouse janitor for four years at the time of the sighting, said that sometimes he encountered spooky sounds at night: phantom footsteps or doors closing apparently on their own accord. Despite his spooky experiences, he thought that the ghost was in fact just a spider. Public defender Earl Rhoads was similarly skeptical of the video, suggesting that a floating piece of cottonwood fluff carried in the wind was the culprit.

Hundreds of people posted their comments to the YouTube video page, swapping ideas and discrediting each other's theories. A sampling:

- "It's a piece of plant matter, like a dandelion seed."
- "It's a bug, a spider or something."
- "The problem with the bug supposition is that it doesn't account for the translucent shape that moves along underneath it. If it was a bug crawling across the lens it would be far blurrier and it also wouldn't appear to give off light. As the light ball passes in front of the cruiser, you can see right through it."
- "People who view the surveillance footage regularly know what bugs look like when they crawl across, and that it does not look like a bug of any sort. They would have known if it was any kind of bug or spider."
- "It's obviously a ghost. Of a spider. That is haunting that parking lot. Where it met its untimely death the day before, when it got run over."
- "It's a hoax! None of the pixels in the image change in the slightest except the moving light. It's a still image with the light photoshopped into each frame."
- "It's Bigfoot!"
- "A mirror reflecting sunlight or a flashlight."

And so on. Dozens and hundreds of theories and guesses, but no answers. Yet.

THE INVESTIGATION

I was asked by Auslander from the *Santa Fe New Mexican* to investigate this latest, and highest-profile, New Mexico ghost case. It was certainly mysterious, and I was intrigued. He asked me what kind of gear I would use. I explained that when I see television programs featuring self-styled ghost hunters, I often cringe at their lack of science. They parade around dark, spooky mansions with high-tech gear such as electromagnetic field detectors—never mind that there's not one shred of evidence that ghosts emit (or are associated with) electromagnetic fields.* It's a popular theory based on nothing but supposition and speculation.

* For more on this, see chapter 4 of my book *Scientific Paranormal Investigation* (Radford 2010).

Figure 5.3. *The author conducting an experiment to determine the origin of the Santa Fe courthouse ghost. Photo by the author.*

I told Auslander I'd seen dozens of videos and images very similar to this courthouse ghost. Often they're simply misperceptions, camera artifacts, or common objects like dust or insects. The quality of the image is often inversely proportional to the belief that the object is a ghost: the fuzzier and more ambiguous the form, the more likely it is to be interpreted as a ghost. I didn't approach the investigation trying to prove or disprove the ghost but merely to find out what was going on. The video seemed like good evidence: could I possibly prove it *was* a ghost?

I began by listing all the possible explanations and quickly found that many of the "rational" explanations simply did not fit the facts. If it was a prank, why would a hoaxer choose to create such an odd, easy-to-miss phenomenon—not to mention doing so on a courthouse surveillance camera, where police might be watching? If it was a reflection from a passing car, why wasn't the vehicle seen on the tape, and how could one explain the wrong positioning of the sun to create such a reflection? If it was an insect on the camera lens, why didn't it look like a bug (for example, it should have been much larger), and why was it glowing? If it was a piece of fluff from cottonwood trees, why did the object glow and seem to move with intent across the scene? If it was a video glitch or artifact instead of a physical object, why did it seem to cast a shadow, and what sort of weird malfunction could cause such a pattern? And, of course, if it was a ghost, why would it appear there, in that form?

Nothing seemed plausible; the case was mysterious indeed.

VIDEO ANALYSIS

I contacted the local TV station to get the highest-quality original image that I could; the YouTube version was of such low resolution as to be nearly worthless, like trying to admire a postage-stamp Picasso. I spent hours examining the video, watching it over and over again with each hypothesis in mind, seeking any sign, any clue, that might favor one explanation over another.

The first question was about the shadow: was it real or an optical illusion? There did seem to be a slightly darker patch following underneath the object as it moved, but a closer inspection revealed that the "shadow" closely followed the movements of the object on the video screen—not the texture of the terrain beneath it, as a shadow would do. Shadows from passing clouds, for example, will change shape and size as they move over objects below (such as buildings or ditches). But the ghost's shadow stayed the same shape and size: I deduced that the shadow was on the lens itself, not on the ground. Very strange.

A second clue came from the angle of the sun; at one point, the shadow appeared to be directly beneath the object, yet the video was shot at 7:27 in the morning, not midday when the sun is high overhead. The sunlight explanation just didn't add up. Furthermore, if the object was giving off its own light—as it seemed to be doing—it would not cast its own shadow (light bulbs do not cast their own shadows). I realized that the object was *reflecting*, not emitting, light. It was something the sun was hitting—not a video artifact, not itself a reflection, and not a glowing ghost.

The next question was of size. Since nothing in the video is in focus (you'd think a bottle of Windex would be within the court's budget), it's hard to tell how far away the object was from the camera. Was it a tiny object near the lens and therefore out of focus, or a large, amorphous object farther away? Logic suggested that people living in the apartments across the street (and walking and driving nearby) would have noticed a large glowing orb near the courthouse. So it was instead small, and probably close to the camera. But what?

GHOSTLY SCIENTIFIC EXPERIMENTS

After analyzing the video, I concluded that the two most likely explanations that fit the facts were a piece of floating tree debris or an insect of some sort. I needed to eliminate these remaining possibilities before entertaining the ghost hypothesis. As Sherlock Holmes noted in Arthur Conan Doyle's *The Sign of Four*, "when you have eliminated the impossible, whatever remains, however improbable, must be the truth." Could an insect or debris from a tree have created the ghost image? Possibly, but without further investigation I couldn't make any assumptions about how either would appear on camera.

I headed up Interstate 25 to Santa Fe and began an investigation at the courthouse, starting by taking measurements of the area. The camera was mounted twelve feet above the ground, thirty-five feet from the street, and about forty-eight feet from the police car seen in the video image (figure 5.3).

A few courthouse employees watched me curiously as they (and I) went into work. "Are you looking for our ghost?" one woman asked me as she passed by on the sidewalk. I nodded and told her I'd show her when I found it—preferably in a small box. Within a few hours, a local television station got wind of my investigation and dispatched a reporter and camera crew to do a short segment on the ghost, which by then was getting national attention.

Normally I don't like having news media around when I'm doing an investigation; they tend to get in the way and expect quick, easy, TV-friendly sound-bite answers to what can sometimes be difficult and complex mysteries. Investigations can rarely be solved on cue and within a few minutes (or hours; some of my investigations have lasted many months or even years). Definitive answers aren't always possible, and investigations are often solved by tedious trial and error. If television producers edit footage of an investigation selectively or illogically, the investigator can come out looking like a fool. But the reporter, an attractive brunette with a pretty smile, seemed genuinely interested, so I gamely explained what I was trying to do.

My first experiment tested the floating cotton hypothesis. I wanted to float a ball of cotton past the surveillance camera to see if it later resembled the ghost. This was easier said than done, as the camera was far too high to reach without a long extension ladder. I searched the area and on the street corner found a few fallen tree branches bundled for the garbage collector. I grabbed the longest one, sheared some extraneous twigs with a knife from my investigation kit, and attached a long plastic tube to it with some bits of wire. I then gently poked some cotton fluff into the top of the tube, hoisted it up near the camera, took a deep breath, and puffed. Two bits of cotton popped out and rather unconvincingly wafted back to the ground.

I probably looked a bit silly, a serious investigator blowing cotton fluff through a makeshift periscope tube, but the reporter remained interested. After all, while plenty of water-cooler investigators and armchair theorists in New Mexico and on the Internet were idly guessing about what the ghost was, I was the only person on the scene investigating the mystery.

After a few attempts, the reporter and I went inside the courthouse to review the resulting video with the court's deputies. The results were not impressive: the cotton did appear as a fluffy ball, but it didn't glow, nor did it move across the screen as the ghostly image had. A piece of windblown cotton seemed less likely than I had first expected. The reporter asked me if I was disappointed, and I replied that I was not disappointed at all; the experiment hadn't failed but in fact had been a success. It had demonstrated that the ghost was probably not a piece of floating cotton fluff; any experiment that helps narrow down the possibilities is a good one.

The reporter left with a tentative explanation, and the TV segment that would air later that night showed my far-from-definitive experiments. Out of ideas and needing a green chile refuel, I headed over to a local Burrito Company restaurant for lunch and ghost-hunting analysis. It was pretty clear to me that the entity was something floating or moving close to the camera, but proving this to my satisfaction was turning out to be a difficult task. I felt tantalizingly close to solving the case but despaired of finding a conclusive answer to the mystery that thousands of people were discussing and watching on YouTube at that very moment.

Cotton, fluffy and white as it is, was unlikely, which left insects as a possible solution before I would move on to the ghost hypothesis. But I had no idea how to arrange an appropriate experiment. I couldn't just buy a box of spiders, aphids, or trained fleas at the local supermarket or Trader Joe's; even if I could, how would I get them onto the camera and to cross the lens in exactly the same way, in the same light? I drove home, mulling the case over.

That evening, I reviewed the video footage once again. The object looked more like an insect than ever, steeling my resolve to test it. The only insects I could think of that I could buy in quantity and on short notice were ladybug beetles (genus *Coccinella*). I rushed to a nearby greenhouse just before it closed and purchased a bag of 1,750 ladybugs, with a few smaller incidental insects included as well. (It's a business expense, although I expected that itemizing "ladybugs for ghost investigation" would trigger an audit.)

SAY HELLO TO MY LITTLE FRIENDS

The next morning, an hour before sunrise, I grumpily returned to Santa Fe for a final attempt. It was important that the experiment's conditions be as close to the original as possible. I arrived just before seven, cut out the top of a plastic liter bottle, and attached it to a collapsible aluminum pole designed for cleaning pools. As a few amused office workers stood by, I dumped a few hundred sleepy (or chilly) ladybugs into the makeshift cup and then onto the top of the camera. I noted the time, took photos of the bugs, and waited for them to crawl around. Many tumbled off the camera immediately. Some flew away, but a few lingered. I could only hope that they were feeling cooperative and would dutifully crawl across the lens.

As I watched, I realized with wry irony that, after all my preparation, video analysis, and research, the definitive success or failure of my ghost investigation might come down to which direction, if any, some bugs decided to walk. So much for the glamour of ghost hunting; I'm a long way off from *The X-Files*.

I repeated the process two more times, in ten-minute intervals. By seven thirty, I had run out of time, ladybugs, and steam. This was it: either I had found my ghost or I hadn't. I couldn't invest any more time on the case. A deputy policeman came out to watch me, and we went inside to check the courthouse's camera monitors.

LET'S GO TO THE TAPE

The deputies gathered around to rewind the video, replaying the past fifteen minutes. I saw myself on the small screen, unpacking my gear, setting up, and sipping coffee. I'd forgotten that I was going to be seen and felt relieved that I hadn't absently picked my nose. For a few boring minutes, three police officers and I stared blankly at the video screen watching nothing unusual (except me). It was getting slightly embarrassing for me, but finally a ladybug crawled across the screen . . . and my heart sank. It did not match our ghost at all. It looked exactly like a ladybug, was dark instead of light, and was far too large. A few minutes later, a second insect also crossed the screen; it too was not a match for the Santa Fe courthouse ghost. I sighed and began thinking of ways to put the best face on the case (and where to begin looking for ghosts) when, at 7:26 a.m., the ghost appeared.

"There it is!" I nearly shouted, pointing at the video monitor in vindication. "That's it!" Sure enough, the courthouse ghost moved across the video monitor, exactly as it had less than a week earlier. Everyone agreed that the image was exactly the same as the original ghost in every respect, including size, shape, color, and movement. "You got it," Deputy John Lucero said. "I'm convinced it was a bug."

I was in a celebratory mood: I'd just solved a mystery that had stumped people across the country. But there was a nagging question—yet one more puzzle: since it was a bug, why didn't it look like one? Why, for example, was it glowing, and why was it so small? I noted, as others had, that if the bug was directly on the camera lens, it should have appeared huge. Other bugs in the same experiment had been dark and enormous; why did this bug look like the ghost while the others didn't? I went out and looked closely again at the camera, and I noticed an important detail that everyone (including myself) had missed: the surveillance camera was encased inside a housing to protect it from the environment. The ghost bug was not on the camera lens itself but instead on the outer glass. Thus it appeared smaller and fuzzier and seemed to glow because sunlight was hitting it. The bugs inside the casing appeared larger (because they were directly on the lens) and darker (because they were shielded from the sunlight by the housing).

The mystery was solved: the Santa Fe courthouse ghost was a bug. While I can't identify the exact species, there is no doubt that it was the unwitting YouTube star. It would be a remarkable coincidence if the ghost just happened to reappear at exactly the same time that my test insects crawled across the lens. The insect or spider explanation fit all the facts. The object was purposely moving, not floating; the object was blurry because it was close to the security camera's lens; it was glowing because direct morning sunlight hit the lens from a low angle; and the shadow it cast was on the glass of the camera casing. Plus, it appeared at almost exactly the same time of day, under the same conditions.

That the Santa Fe courthouse ghost turned out to be an insect doesn't take away from its role as a ghost; in fact, the one thing that most ghost investigators agree on is that many, many things can be mistaken for a ghost. Since no one knows for certain what a ghost is, it helps to have cases like these that have been conclusively solved, for it tells us which nonghost phenomena have been interpreted as ghosts. Still, it's a bit sad that the best ghost video in New Mexico's history did not lead to a supernatural explanation. Once again, the ghosts tease us and taunt us, throwing us some red herrings (or red enchiladas). Maybe tomorrow, next month, or next year . . .

REFERENCES

Auslander, Jason. 2007a. "What Was It at the Courthouse?" *Santa Fe New Mexican*, June 15. The video can be seen at http://www.youtube.com/watch?v=jPhCuMA-aaE; accessed February 27, 2014.

———. 2007b. "Ruling on Courthouse Ghost: Not Likely." *Santa Fe New Mexican*, June 21. The story is archived at http://archive.is/DLL3s; accessed February 27, 2014.

Hay, Kiera. 2012. "Past Meets Future." *Albuquerque Journal*, December 16, B1.

Radford, Benjamin. 2007a. "Capturing the Santa Fe 'Courthouse Ghost.'" *Fortean Times*, November.

———. 2007b. "Santa Fe 'Courthouse Ghost' Mystery Solved." *Skeptical Inquirer* 31, no. 5 (September–October).

———. 2007c. "Catching the Courthouse Spirit." *Weekly Alibi* (Albuquerque) 16, no. 43 (October 25–31).

———. 2010. *Scientific Paranormal Investigation: How to Solve Unexplained Mysteries*. Corrales, NM: Rhombus Publishing.

CHAPTER 6

THE LORETTO CHAPEL'S MIRACULOUS STAIRCASE

Santa Fe's Our Lady of Light Chapel, better known as the Loretto Chapel, harbors a mystery known around the world (figure 6.1). Inside the ornate yet unassuming exterior lies what many consider a miracle; it is "one miracle of old Santa Fe that can still be seen and experienced to this day: we can stand beside it, touch it and marvel, even though this particular miracle occurred more than a hundred years ago" (Kutz 1988, 61). This wondrous attraction is Saint Joseph's Stairs, or simply the Miracle Staircase; what makes it so special is that the spiral staircase makes two complete turns from the floor to the choir loft—without a single nail or even a center pole for support (figure 6.2).

As amazing as the staircase is, how it came to exist in the first place is itself quite a story. It all began when, at the end of the famous Santa Fe Trail, the Sisters of Loretto established a religious school in 1853 with about three hundred students. Construction of the chapel began in 1873, and it was completed about five years later. The chapel was to be twenty-five feet by seventy-five feet in area, and eighty-five feet high; it was almost finished when a dreadful mistake was discovered.

According to one version,

> The large circular staircase that was needed in the construction of a new church was simply impossible to build in the space provided. It should have been built first, and the church erected around it. According to the story, a traveling carpenter arrived one day and offered to solve the problem [of creating a spiral staircase connecting the upper and

> lower floors]. The rest of the workers scoffed, but told him that if he wanted to waste his time, go right ahead. The strange man was seen taking some measurements as the rest of the work crew went home for the night. But when the work crews returned the next morning, the carpenter was gone, and in his place was a beautiful staircase elegantly built into the impossible space. As the workers examined it in awe, a sudden realization was made; each riser of the staircase was supported by the one *above* it! The strange man would have had to build the staircase from the top down! And except for that support, no other means of bracing was used. It was an architectural miracle. Cases like this one have been too well documented to simply dismiss as urban myth. Could it be divine intervention in our midst, the work of guardian angels, or perhaps the craftsmanship of the master carpenter himself, St. Joseph? (MacRorie 1997, 21)

Columnist Phyllis Schlafly compared the significance of the miracle to nothing less than the Shroud of Turin—the reputed burial cloth of Jesus.

Figure 6.1. *The entrance to Santa Fe's Loretto Chapel offers a wood carving of Saint Joseph, said to have created the miraculous staircase within. Photo by the author.*

"Many believe that another visible, tangible miracle exists in an old convent in Santa Fe, N.M. It is called St. Joseph's Stairs. . . . Experts say the stairs should have crumbled the first time weight was put on them. No one can explain how they have withstood a century of use" (Schlafly 1979).

Figure 6.2. *Visitors marvel at the world-famous miracle staircase in Santa Fe. Photo by the author.*

A miracle would indeed seem to be the only explanation. A staircase built overnight, from the top down, and with no visible means of support surely defies not only rational explanation but physics itself: a genuine miracle in the Land of Enchantment.

The "official" version of the events from the Sisters of Loretto goes like this: "The chapel work progressed with some financial worries and a maximum of faith on the part of the Sisters. It was not until it was nearly finished that they realized a dreadful mistake had been made. The chapel itself was wonderful and the choir loft was wonderful, too, but there was no connecting link between the two. . . . Mother Magdalen called in many carpenters to try to build the stairway; but each, in his turn, measured and thought and then shook his head sadly saying, 'It can't be done, Mother.'"

The Sisters of Loretto then prayed for nine days to Saint Joseph; finally, "on the last day of the novena, a gray-haired man came up to the convent with a donkey and a tool chest. Approaching Mother Magdalen he asked if he might try to help the Sisters by building a stairway! Mother gave her consent gladly and he set to work. . . . The only tools he had were a hammer, a saw, and a T square. It took him six to eight months to complete the work. When Mother Magdalen went to pay him, he had vanished. She went to the local lumber yard to pay for the wood, at least. They knew nothing of it there. To this day there is no record stating that the job was ever paid for" (Florian 1960).

The stairway seemed of little note until the early 1900s, when it gradually grew more famous; it even appeared in *Ripley's Believe It or Not!* twice—first in 1939 as "the Miraculous Stairway built without support and without nails." *Ripley's* ran it again in 1956; according to Mary Jean Cook, "with this added publicity the staircase became famous as more and more tourists began to include the Chapel of Our Lady of Light as part of their historic Santa Fe tour" (Cook 2002, 59). By 1960, visitors "came from all over the world to see the wonderful stairway" (Florian 1960)—among them were claimed to be architects and engineers who said they could not understand how the staircase could possibly have been created, or even how it remained standing. It's been famous ever since and was even the subject of a 1998 CBS television movie called *The Staircase*, starring Barbara Hershey and William Peterson. The national, then international, attention helped the chapel financially as well. As religious pilgrims have always done, the visiting faithful donated money to the Sisters.

THE SECRET OF THE MIRACLE STAIRCASE

As they say, all that glitters is not gold, and it's clear that at least some parts of the story are not true on the face of it. For example, the staircase is not made entirely of wood; instead, a significant part of the stairs (under the treads and between the stringers, or supporting sides) is painted to look like wood but is in fact reinforced plaster, made from hydrated lime, sand, water, and horsehair (Florian 1960). Casual visitors would not notice this, of course, and might assume that the entire staircase is wood. While it's true that the staircase is made without nails, it is held together with glue and hundreds of hardwood square wooden pegs, which can be almost as strong as nails—or, stranger, even better than nails, as we will see. And although it was originally constructed without any brace or support, the staircase is no longer free-standing, as a large supporting and stabilizing metal brace was added years ago (figure 6.3).

Figure 6.3. *Although the Loretto staircase was originally constructed without any support, a large stabilizing metal brace was added years later. Photo by the author.*

As unique and remarkable as the story is to the public, it actually follows a pattern very familiar to folklorists. Indeed, the Loretto story is only one of many similar legends that have been told around the world through the ages: "Over the centuries, stories have surfaced of the wandering carpenter or stone mason, who mysteriously appears in a town, completes a task, usually for a grieving family or for a group that desperately needs help, and vanishes as soon as the work is completed" (MacRorie 1997, 20).

This suggests that perhaps the legend is more myth than truth. Mysteries are to be explored, if not explained, so let's dig a little deeper into this famous New Mexico mystery, beginning with who built it.

WHO WAS THE MYSTERIOUS CARPENTER?

If the mysterious carpenter was not Saint Joseph, who could it be? Over the years a handful of people have contacted the Sisters of Loretto, believing that their relative may have built the staircase. Such claims were (usually) politely entertained but dismissed when no historical evidence was forthcoming. The various claimants—surely all sincere—came and went without being able to offer anything more substantial than family lore. As the decades passed by, it seemed to grow more apparent that, if the mysterious carpenter was indeed a mortal man and not a saint, his true identity would never be known.

All that changed around the turn of the last century when Mary Jean Cook, a Santa Fe historian, researched her book on the Sisters of Loretto and their famous chapel.

"After many years of mystery, an elusive Frenchman named François-Jean Rochas has been documented as the carpenter of the legendary spiral staircase in the Chapel of Our Lady of Light. While other carpenters may have assisted him during the construction, Rochas was called its builder by his friend Quintus Monier, contractor of the St. Francis Cathedral in Santa Fe, who also worked on the chapel." Cook discovered a nondescript obituary in the *Santa Fe New Mexican* that revealed a shocking secret. The January 5, 1895, piece, written by Monier, stated that "Frank Rochas . . . a Frenchman, was favorably known in Santa Fe as an expert worker in wood. He built the handsome staircase in the Loretto Chapel" (Cook 2002, 60).

The information is clear and unmistakable. There is only one staircase in the Loretto Chapel, and Monier would be in a position to know firsthand that Rochas had built it. Monier had no reason to lie or be mistaken about it, and it seems unlikely that he would have falsely credited Rochas with building the staircase in a public newspaper—especially so soon after its construction.

Who was "Frenchy" (as he was often called) Rochas? Although records from the time are understandably incomplete, we do know something about Rochas. He was born on September 22, 1843, near the Isère River south of Grenoble, France. He was the eldest of four children and probably moved to New Mexico in the 1870s. He was something of a recluse and hermit, possibly due to his training as a *compagnon* (a member of a celibate French artisan brotherhood) (Cook 2002, 61).

Further research uncovered another tantalizing clue in the Sisters' logbook from March 1881: "Paid for wood by Mr. Rochas, $150.00." This proves that Rochas had been employed by the Sisters of Loretto as a carpenter, on the staircase and/or on the new Loretto Academy building, which was completed in 1881. Cook acknowledges that "documentation of any earlier payment to the carpenter Rochas for construction of the spiral staircase could not be found in the sisters' books" (Cook 2002, 62). Obviously, a receipt or entry explicitly stating that Rochas built the staircase (or a photograph of him doing so) would be definitive proof, although as we will see nearly all of the other evidence points to the same conclusion. In her book *Loretto: The Sisters and Their Santa Fe Chapel*, Cook documents other intriguing evidence, including Rochas's name on the manifest of a cargo vessel from France; could he have purchased precut staircase wood and brought it with him to Santa Fe? Cook also spoke with a compagnon—a French carpenter of the same woodworking guild as Rochas—who recognized the miracle staircase's design and craftsmanship.

The legend says the mysterious carpenter vanished after his work was done, and in a way that's what Frenchy Rochas did. Like many itinerant carpenters hired to do a job, he finished up and moved on. A few things are known about the reclusive carpenter after he finished his work at the Loretto Chapel. He went south to Dog Canyon, where he settled a small homestead. Frenchy raised cattle, did occasional carpentry work for neighbors, sometimes traded supplies with Apaches, and kept to himself, as he always had.

Frenchy tried to stay out of trouble—but, as often happened in the Old West, trouble found him. Pete Eidenbach (1998) states that

> Frank appeared in 1886 in county legal records and local news, when he swore out a warrant against a former employee named Morrison

> for horse theft. Morrison was arrested, but released, and on July 1 he ambushed Rochas at his Dog Canyon homestead where Frank was constructing the stone walls that kept his cows out of the narrow, treacherous canyon and its permanent stream. The *Rio Grande Republican* reported the incident two days later in some detail. Although he was wounded twice, Frenchy reached his cabin, barred the door, and out-waited his assailant: "About 10 o'clock that night, Morrison broke open the door to finish his bloody work when Rochas fired, wounding him. . . . He escaped. . . . When last heard from, he had not been caught. Rochas will recover."(3)

Rochas would not survive a second attack on his homestead less than a decade later; he was found dead in his stone cabin on Christmas Eve, 1894, by a man named Dan Fitchet. He'd been shot, probably by thieves or Apaches (although possibly by his own hand in a suspected suicide).

SCIENCE MEETS THE UNEXPLAINED

Thus it seems that the true carpenter was not Saint Joseph but rather a reclusive Frenchman. That part of the mystery is solved, but a greater mystery remains: How did Frenchy create a spectacular staircase that has been called miraculous and, allegedly, defies rational explanation? How could he create something so incredible that a saint had been credited for his work? Surely not even a celibate master carpenter could construct a staircase supported by only prayer and thin air.

Indeed, part of the staircase's legend is that its structure is scientifically unexplainable. Various sources suggest, for example, that "the stairway confounds architects, engineers, and master craftsmen" (Brokaw 2002, 1), and "experts say the stairs should have crumbled the first time weight was put on them" (Schlafly 1979). The stairway has even been referred to as a "supernatural feat of engineering" (Harold 1996).*

The staircase not only supported its own weight but—as seen in a photo taken around 1959—even a choir of over a dozen women at once.

* This is a common claim for supposedly miraculous or unexplainable buildings and structures around the world. For example, the mysterious Coral Castle, a Florida tourist attraction consisting of large blocks of rock, is widely claimed to have baffled top scientists for decades. Yet investigations have determined that no scientists have ever been stumped by Coral Castle; no legitimate research has concluded that the castle's construction is in any way baffling (Stollznow 2010; Radford 2006).

From these authoritative declarations one might assume that dozens—perhaps hundreds—of scientists have examined the staircase over the years and found that it defies physics or natural laws. If such studies were ever carried out, however, there seems to be no record of them, save for two reports.

The first, done by engineer Carl Albach (1965), was published in the journal *Consulting Engineer*; Albach offered no opinion on whether the staircase was a miracle ("we will not attempt to answer that question," he writes) but merely noted a slight springy movement as he climbed the stairs (something others had previously described). The article actually contains no analysis of the staircase, likely because Albach was an electrical, not a structural, engineer. The second report was a 1996 analysis by Forrest Easley that identified the type of wood used as spruce.

Thus there has been only one professional analysis done (on the wood, not on the staircase structure itself). The stories of countless stymied scientists, architects, and engineers is apparently a part of the myth. This situation seems likely to remain the case; the organization that owns the chapel as a private museum has refused scientific testing or analysis of the staircase (Cook 2010).

THE SCIENCE BEHIND THE MIRACLE

The staircase is supported by two stringers, with seven pieces of thick wood on the inside stringer and nine pieces on the outside. There are several theories that could explain how the staircase functions without a center pole of support. Most scientific analyses suggest what's called the "'shear theory' . . . that each major segment of the staircase, treads, risers, and stringers were put together with extraordinary craftsmanship using square pegs and therefore well-fitted pegs would have to shear off in order to collapse. The square pegs, well fitted, might create a virtual solid entity" (Brokaw 2002, 15).

A spiral staircase that is essentially a solid structure could explain it (figure 6.4). But I wanted to go beyond speculation to get real answers. Is that plausible? Could physics and engineering really explain how the staircase could support a dozen people at once, without a center support pole? It seemed that there was one profession whose expertise was conspicuously absent in all the speculation and publications to date. Who better to analyze the wooden staircase than a carpenter?

I interviewed Mick Harper, a carpenter in Corrales, New Mexico, with thirty-five years of woodworking experience. He had previously examined the staircase personally, although a closer inspection of the staircase was now off limits. Still, we pored over photographs, diagrams, and sketches of the staircase, and he helped shed some light on this centuries-old mystery.*

I began by asking how the staircase could have been constructed without a center support, and how it had moreover supported the weight of nuns going up and down it twice a day for decades. "You have to appreciate two or three things about the properties of wood as a building material to understand how this was constructed," he began. "The reason that wood is so good as a building material is that it's very good at compression. That's why post and beam and stud framing works—[the wood] doesn't distort along the grain. You can soak, or soak and steam, the wood, and cause some of those fibers to compress."

I noted that, according to the Sisters of Loretto, the carpenter who had built the staircase used tubs of water along with strong wood glue—likely made of horsehide or horse hoofs, a compound widely used at the time. The sixteen long pieces of strong, flexible wood, when expertly joined, glued, fitted, and finished, would create an incredibly strong structure that is actually stronger than the sum of its parts. "The glue migrates into [the wood's] moisture cells, so when you put glue on the edge of the adjoining boards, the resins in the glue migrate into the former moisture cells and the vehicle, the solvent for the glue—which is water, mostly—evaporates and it leaves behind the resins that are now inside the former moisture cells. It's cemented—so that bond is now stronger than the bond between adjacent cells."

"So that would essentially create a solid piece of wood?" I asked.

"Actually it's superior to a solid piece of wood because you have all these glue lines that keep one plane of wood fibers from slipping on the next plane of wood fibers. That's why you have seven laminations on the inside, and nine on the outside," he explained. Each long wooden splice overlaps the others in different places, creating a solid, continual load-bearing column. Two, in fact, and since there are two stringers, the weight is more or less evenly distributed between the two. The inside stringer would be the strongest because of the center of gravity (and because it makes smaller loops). That would also be where most of the weight from people on the risers would be carried. Remember that the

* At least one craftsman duplicated the technique in the late 1970s and created a model of the spiral staircase. Oscar Hadwiger, who at one point mistakenly claimed that his grandfather Yohon had built the staircase, spent several months on his reconstruction (Longto 1970).

original staircase had no banister, and thus people ascending or descending the staircase would naturally step close to the center—the strongest stringer—to avoid getting too close to the sides and risking a dangerous fall.

Figure 6.4. *A model of the Loretto staircase by Robert Lamping, on display at the Loretto Chapel. Photo by the author.*

WOODEN PEGS

The engineering and architecture explanation made sense. But why use wooden pegs? I asked. "The part about no nails, that's easy to buy," Harper said. He explained that the carpenter's choice of using wooden pegs instead of metal nails is one of the keys to understanding both the stairway's strength and its longevity. Although many people assume that the pegs were used mainly for aesthetic reasons, nails and screws likely would have caused the spiral miracle to collapse decades ago.

Harper explained why: "Wood is hydrophilic—it absorbs and loses moisture from the atmosphere. If you have wood pegs and wood dowels in a wooden construction, they expand and contract together. What happens to wood around a metal fastener is that eventually the fibers in the wood right around the metal fastener go through shrinking and swelling, and eventually those fibers get crushed—it's called compression set. But since it's wood, it's all shrinking and swelling together, and staying together." The joints don't pull loose. That of course doesn't happen with metal nails and screws, which is probably why Rochas chose to use hundreds of hardwood pegs and dowels to assemble the staircase. In a curious twist to an already strange story about a spiral staircase, the longer-lasting nails would have created a shorter life for the staircase. Those who wonder how a staircase could have stood for so long without using metal nails have the logic exactly backward: it could *only* have stood for so long by having used *wooden* pegs.

But there's one last mystery: how was the exquisite craftsmanship done with only Frenchy's basic tools? As Sister Florian wrote, "One of the most baffling things about the stairway is the perfection of the curves of the stringers. . . . How this was done in the 1870s by a single man in an out-of-the-way place with only the most primitive tools [according to the legend, only a T-square, a hammer, and a saw] has never been explained" (Florian 1960).

This mystery evaporates when we realize that Frenchy had far more than "the most primitive tools." In fact, upon his death his possessions "pointed clearly to a master carpenter and cabinetmaker: five saws, a saw clamp and set, nine planes, nineteen moulding planes, two squares, five gauges, six chisels, two gouges, a draw knife, a brace, three augers, ten auger bits, a reamer, two clamps, and a pair of trammel points (for drawing large circles)" (Eidenbach 1998, 9).

All the pieces fit—both literally and figuratively. The fact that Harper had a pretty good idea of how the staircase was built did not diminish the accomplishment; if anything, he appreciated its craftsmanship more than a casual observer would be able to, because, as a carpenter himself, he recognized how much work and care went into it. "The execution is just incredible," he said. "The theory of how to do it, to bend it around in a two-turn spiral, that's some difficult arithmetic there."

If the staircase was built by Frenchy Rochas (most likely with the help of other carpenters) and his achievements are impressive yet explainable, what of the other mysteries surrounding the staircase?

THE MIRACLE WOOD

What of the reports of the strange wood that was not purchased locally and that couldn't be identified? That, too, is at least partly a myth. As noted earlier, while the wood remained unknown for many years, it was identified in 1996 as spruce (Easley 1996). But it's not a local species of spruce, which is why it took so long to identify it. So where did it come from?

If the local wood materials were not of high enough quality (or hardness) to build the staircase, it's logical that the carpenter would have sent for the wood he needed to do the job. Cook suspects that the wood for the staircase was designed and precut in France, shipped to Santa Fe, and assembled in the chapel. Indeed, Cook points out, "It also would explain why the Sisters of Loretto have no record of having paid for the staircase; it may have been paid for when it was purchased—perhaps by Archbishop Jean Baptiste Lamy—in France" (Fauntleroy 2002).

Could Frenchy have shipped the wood from France to build the staircase? At first it seems unlikely: the staircase seems far too big. But it must be remembered that the staircase seen and photographed today is only partly the staircase Frenchy originally built. The banister, which makes the staircase look more substantial than it really is, was added years later, and when we consider the amount of wood actually needed to build the staircase, we find that it's not that much—all the wood together probably took up no more space than a large desk. Shipments of that size and even larger were routinely sent across the Atlantic by boat and across North America by train and wagon. Furthermore, we know that other large pieces of the Loretto Chapel were shipped from Europe—the hand-carved wooden altar, for example, was not made locally but was brought in from Italy (Brokaw 2002, 1). If the staircase came from France—either in precut pieces or partly assembled—it would be only one of several imported components of the chapel.

THE FRENCH CONNECTIONS

There's yet more evidence that Frenchy Rochas created the staircase. The chapel's design was specifically French; indeed, the original architect, Antoine Mouly, "had been involved in the renovation of Sainte Chapelle, in Paris, France, in the early 1800s. Mouly was encouraged to fashion the Loretto Chapel after the Sainte Chapelle" (Brokaw 2002, 4). According to Sister Florian, "Because Bishop Lamy was from France, he wished the Sisters to have a chapel that was similar to his beloved Sainte Chapelle in Paris." Not only was the chapel ordered to be designed by a French architect and built by a Frenchman, but many of the craftsmen were also French (Florian 1960). It is quite plausible that one of those French carpenters, Rochas, built the staircase.

Much has been made in the legends that a single person (typically Saint Joseph) succeeded in building the staircase where others had failed (or had not even attempted the job, assuming that it was impossible). Although there were undoubtedly dozens of skilled carpenters in New Mexico in the 1870s from a variety of cultures (Mexican, Italian, and so on), it makes perfect sense that a master French builder and carpenter intimately familiar with French architecture would be the best person (if not the *only* person in the Southwest) who could do the job. The choice of lumber, mentioned earlier, also answers another mystery that traces back to the original legend: why couldn't local carpenters have created the staircase? The answer might be that they simply did not have the skill, and also that the local lumber they were familiar with (and had used all their lives) was too soft, or not flexible enough. Frenchy likely realized that he could succeed where others might fail by using his connections back in Europe—and his knowledge of more suitable varieties of wood that were available there.

THE MYSTERIOUS CARPENTER

Another mystery is why the carpenter is not better known. His staircase is, after all, a magnificent piece of work. Of course, it is usually a building's architects and funders—not the laborers and woodworkers—who get credit, recognition, and plaques for such achievements. Still, it seems odd that Frenchy Rochas's name and fame have been so obscured.

There are several reasons. First, Frenchy was a reclusive hermit; he lived alone and often worked alone. Although a skilled craftsman, he was by no means a high-profile individual and was essentially an itinerant laborer. Second, his employers, the Sisters of Loretto, would not likely have gotten to know him well, for "during these times it was considered immodest for the Sisters and the girls to carry on a conversation with a male laborer" (Brokaw 2002, 12). Even had one of the Sisters (or others) tried to speak to him about matters other than his work, they wouldn't have gotten far, as Frenchy spoke little English (Eidenbach 1998). It was certainly good enough to communicate his basic work-related needs (a few others there spoke French as well), but it's unlikely that this bachelor hermit spent much time socializing.

Cook believes that it was common knowledge in the late 1800s that Rochas had built the miracle staircase. At the time, when news of the staircase was first beginning to spread, it was not regarded as a miracle but "merely" a handsome staircase. Then, as fantastic stories about the staircase's construction began to capture public imagination, "there were those who knew [Rochas's] name but who did not wish to betray the legend. The staircase builder's identity was of little interest to the public until his accomplishment reached legendary proportions some time during the early decades of the twentieth century. By then, those who had known or worked with Rochas were dead" (Cook 2002, 60).

Another reason for the silence, Cook believes, is that it was the Sisters of Loretto themselves who were pivotal in creating and perpetuating the legend, and people who knew very well that Frenchy had built the staircase understandably didn't want to tarnish or undermine the beloved Sisters' story. There's little benefit to being a curmudgeon who pours cold water on a quaint idea, by pointing out for instance that it had been an ordinary French hermit instead of Jesus's father who had built a magnificent staircase. There's no need to invoke a *Da Vinci Code*–type conspiracy to see why those who knew the truth weren't eager to ruin a good story by giving Frenchy his due—he had died by then, after all. Furthermore, Frenchy didn't leave behind any family who might wish to claim credit for their relative's achievement. In fact, Rochas's family back in France rarely heard from him and apparently knew nothing of his work on the staircase (Cook 2010).

A booklet available for purchase at the Loretto Chapel is dismissive of Cook's conclusion that Frenchy built the staircase. It acknowledges that Rochas received payment for working on the building in 1881 (that is a matter of public record and beyond dispute) but states that "Mother Magdalen is said to have written that she did not know the name of the mysterious carpenter. She would have indeed known the carpenter's name as he also worked for them after the staircase was finished and his payment was recorded" (Brokaw 2002, 19).

The argument presented by the chapel's booklet is flawed, for it relies on thirdhand stories, not hard evidence. Reporting that Magdalen "is said to have written" that she didn't know the carpenter is merely saying that *someone said that they think she wrote* that she didn't know who had built the staircase. Did Mother Magdalen write that she didn't know the carpenter, or didn't she? Either such a statement from her appears in the records, or it does not.

The Sisters have not offered any evidence of this. In fact, Cook told me, "There is nothing in the letters of Magdalen, she was the Mother Superior, where she speaks of the staircase. Not once" (Cook 2010).

The fact that the Mother Superior of the Loretto Chapel never mentioned the famous miracle staircase that drew countless visitors to its doors is curious indeed. Clearly she knew about the pious legend that was growing around the staircase; Cook believes that Magdalen likely was embarrassed by it. If she knew that Frenchy Rochas had really built the staircase attributed to Saint Joseph (a story from which her Sisters and the public drew faith, inspiration, and strength), she could hardly be blamed for ignoring the truth. Frenchy was long dead and, by not commenting on the staircase (or its origins) one way or the other, she could avoid explicitly endorsing or discrediting the myth that Saint Joseph had built the stairs.

"I think she just felt that society could not accept [the truth]," Cook says. "Because she had done a great deal of research. You don't want to ruin the legend, and the legend was still alive and well. I understand why the Sisters did it. They had to put food on the table. They did it for a reason. . . . I don't think it was malicious at all. They just veered from the truth a little bit, and they could rationalize that. They desperately needed the money." That money came in from tourists and pilgrims, as it still does today—although the chapel and its miracle staircase is now under private ownership.

There remains one final mystery in this complex case: Why are there apparently no other existing identical staircases? Surely Frenchy—or one of his compagnons—would have built another, similar staircase somewhere else. Cook believes that they were common in 1800s France—so common, in fact, that they were not considered special or unusual enough to be preserved. As old buildings were torn down to make room for newer, stronger, and larger buildings, perhaps the spiral staircases—beautiful and fragile as they were—were simply impractical to keep intact.

Perhaps a better question is, why *would* there be another staircase just like it? It was a unique job, done under specific circumstances and constraints that likely were not to be found at other locations in New Mexico. After all, the staircase was originally built to address an architectural oversight in the Loretto Chapel specifically. Unless other incompetent architects elsewhere *also* made exactly the same mistake in a building of precisely those measurements and requirements (and forgot to connect the chapel floor with the loft), there would be no need to build an identical spiral staircase. Saint Joseph's staircase was a beautiful, jury-rigged patch-up, and Frenchy himself would probably be shocked to discover that it's still standing.

The staircase's basic design (a spiral without a center support) is inherently unstable; the fact that the staircase has been stabilized by a metal brace for years and can no longer be climbed is proof of that. But just because the design is unstable does not mean that the staircase cannot continue to stand or that it will come crashing down if one steps on it. Nor does it mean that world-class craftsmanship and design cannot overcome its limitations.

In fact, there is at least one report of an identical miracle staircase. It can be found in the February 15, 1944, edition of the *Santa Fe New Mexican*. According to the report, Bonnie Foster, "a government official dealing with labor problems" who had examined the Loretto staircase, found a close match during her travels: "Over in Danzig, seaport, town and first-class fortress of much-hated Prussia, Mrs. Foster found an extraordinary wooden staircase similar to St. Joseph's. It is tall, spiral, and without steel nails, but the wood is different. It is in the town hall, of the 14th to 16th century. . . . She declared it is strikingly like St. Joseph's in design" (*Santa Fe New Mexican* 1944, 5). If this eyewitness is right—and there seems little reason to doubt her veracity—then Foster provides an important clue documenting a European-crafted miracle staircase that had been built at least a century before the one in Loretto Chapel. Danzig, now the city of Gdańsk in Poland, likely incorporated at least some French influence in its buildings, given that French culture and artistry were broadly disseminated across the continent. Perhaps another architect did make a similar mistake.

A similar staircase can also be found in the south of France; and in the United States another one (albeit with fewer turns) can be found at the Washoe Club, a historic three-story brick building in Virginia City, Nevada. A sign there reads, "Spiral Staircase: The spiral staircase was featured in *Ripley's Believe It or Not!* as being the longest of its kind without a supporting pole. It was custom designed and built for the millionaire's club of the Washoe during the 1870's." According to the caption of an old photograph on the Washoe Club's website, "This historic old winding staircase . . . was once used by such famous men as Mark Twain, Sandy Bowers, and a host of others."

The Washoe and Loretto spiral staircases were both built in the 1870s; Cook told me that Frenchy Rochas never visited Nevada, so he could not have created the Washoe Club's staircase. But clearly, more than one person knew how to build such staircases at the time.

MYSTERY SOLVED

What began as a supernatural religious miracle, a mystery on par with the Shroud of Turin, turns out to be extraordinary but explainable through careful research and analysis. Piece by piece, the ornate legend falls away. Many parts of the story are completely false, such as the claims that the stairway was built overnight, from the top down, by a carpenter whom no one knew; other parts of the story are partly true, such as that a mysterious man was the only one who could create the staircase after others failed; and yet other parts are completely true, such as the curious fact that none of the wood was local, and that the carpenter used tubs of water in the construction.

Truth, in this case, is almost as strange as fiction, and the fact that the staircase was almost certainly made by a reclusive French woodworker instead of Saint Joseph does not detract from the magnificence of the work. Archbishop Michael Sheehan was philosophical about the matter, saying, "It will always be referred to as a miraculous staircase. It was an extraordinary piece to have been done in its time" (Steiber 2000).

As for Frenchy, he's again getting credit for his work. His grave can be found in the Nuestra Sonora de la Luz Cemetery near Alamogordo. His tombstone reads, "'Frenchy' François Jean Rochas / Sept. 22, 1834–Dec. 26, 1894 / Gunned down at his rock cabin in Dog Canyon." The man whose brilliant work had been credited to none other than Saint Joseph himself died a lonely and mysterious death—another unsolved mystery in the Land of Enchantment.

REFERENCES

Albach, Carl. 1965. "Miracle or Wonder of Construction?" *Consulting Engineer*, December.

Brokaw, Bill. 2002. *Loretto Chapel: The Miraculous Staircase.* Lawrenceburg, IN: Creative Company.

Cook, Mary J. Straw. 2002. *Loretto: The Sisters and Their Santa Fe Chapel.* Santa Fe: Museum of New Mexico Press.

———. 2010. Interview by Benjamin Radford, August 12.

Easley, Forrest. 1996. *Loretto Chapel Museum Staircase Wood Analysis.* Privately printed, December.

Eidenbach, Pete. 1998. "The Stockman and the Carpenter." In *Things Remembered Otero County, New Mexico, 1899–1999*, edited by Linnie L. Townsend, 1–18 Alamogordo, NM: Alamogordo/Otero County Centennial Celebration.

Fauntleroy, Gussie. 2002. "The Continuing Mystery of Rochas, the Staircase Carpenter." *Santa Fe New Mexican*, July 14, E3.

Florian, Sister M. 1960. *The Inexplicable Stairs: Answer to a Prayer to St. Joseph.* Reprinted from *St. Joseph Magazine*, April.

Gumbell, Andrew. 2002. "In Foreign Parts: The Mystery of Santa Fe's Miracle Staircase." *Independent* (London), September 21.

Harold, Wanda. 1996. "The Secret of the Spiral Staircase." *Fate*, July, 78–79.

Harper, Mick. 2011. Interview by Benjamin Radford, August 23.

Kutz, Jack. 1988. *Mysteries and Miracles of New Mexico: Guide Book to the Genuinely Bizarre in the Land of Enchantment.* Corrales, NM: Rhombus Publishing.

Longto, Ron. 1970. "'Miracle Staircase' Carpenter Identity Revealed!" *New Mexican*, February 26, 1.

MacRorie, K. T. 1997. *Hoosier Hauntings.* San Diego: Thunder Bay Press.

Nickell, Joe. 2007. *Adventures in Paranormal Investigation.* Lexington: University Press of Kentucky.

Radford, Benjamin. 2006. "Mysteries of the Coral Castle." *Skeptical Inquirer* 30, no. 3 (May–June).

Santa Fe New Mexican. 1944. February 15, 5.

Schlafly, Phyllis. 1979. "Modern Miracles for Doubters." *Daily Intelligencer* (Doylestown, PA), April 13, 6.

Steiber, Tamar. 2000. "Loretto Staircase Mystery Unravels." *New Mexico* magazine, January, 62–66.

Stollznow, Karen. 2010. "Coral Castle: Fact and Folklore." *Skeptical Inquirer* 34, no. 1 (January–February).

CHAPTER 7

THUNDERBIRDS

MYSTERIOUS GIANTS IN THE SKY

One hundred million years ago, dinosaurs roamed the vast plains of New Mexico; to this day their bleached bones can be found by the intrepid explorer, baking under the sweltering sun. Scientific evidence suggests that they finally died out about sixty-five million years ago. Yet according to some eyewitnesses, a few dinosaurs—namely the flying ones—may have somehow survived, remaining hidden from the modern world in the lonely vastness of the desert.

There are reports of giant, winged creatures flying high in the New Mexican skies. Indeed, as we will see, there are scattered reports of such beasts from all over North America. To some they are mere legend; to others they are very real. Scott Francis, in his book *Monster Spotter's Guide to North America*, seems certain that they exist, stating that "*the fact is* that a large mystery creature haunts the skies of the United States and may offer scientists a chance to discover a believed extinct species and monster enthusiasts the opportunity to witness a living myth" (Francis 2007, 139; emphasis added).

MONSTER BIRDS OF THE ORGAN MOUNTAINS

One of the most famous modern sightings of giant birds in the Land of Enchantment happened just before the turn of the last century when Las Cruces resident Dave Zander saw something he couldn't explain. Zander has lived near the Doña Ana Mountains for more than thirty years, hiking, camping, and hunting in the area. I interviewed Zander in 2007 and again later in preparation for a televised segment on KRQE Channel 13. He told me that his sighting had occurred nearly a decade earlier, in June or July of 1998 or 1999: "It was on the north side of the mountains looking south," he said. "Way atop the rocks up there. At first I thought it was people, like two people who had climbed up there—though that would be a pretty rough hike."

He estimated that the figures were about a mile away. Zander had a pair of binoculars, and even through them the details were hard to make out. But their bodies seemed to be solid black, with bald or pink heads and necks. As he and his friend watched, one of the figures leapt (or fell) off the rock! Thinking that these were perhaps hikers, Zander became horrified at the thought that he might be witnessing a suicide—or worse yet, a murder.

But within a second or two after leaving the precipice, he said, two huge wings spread out from the falling figure, and he saw "at least a twenty- or twenty-five-foot wingspan," he told me, "the size of a small plane." The animal beat its massive wings and soared off, with the second creature quickly following in the same manner. Zander and his friend stood there in shock, hardly able to believe their eyes. Whatever it was, it was the biggest flying animal they'd ever seen. It was "not a normal bird," he said. "Definitely of a giant variety. It made you feel like it could come over and carry you off if it wanted." When he got home, Zander tried to find out more about it. "I called the Audubon Society, but they weren't helpful," he told me. "Nobody seemed to care."

One researcher, Ken Gerhard from Texas, interviewed Zander in 2007. "I found him to be both knowledgeable and very credible," Gerhard told me. "As an avid hiker, Zander had encountered a variety of wildlife and his testimony has remained consistent throughout the duration of our correspondence."

Gerhard and others have suggested that Zander may have seen a living dinosaur called a teratorn. "Enormous, raptor-type birds known as teratorns inhabited the Americas a mere ten thousand years ago," Gerhard said. "Some possessed wingspans over twenty feet across. Accounts of living pterosaurs are much harder to explain of course, since there is a gap in the fossil history that spans sixty-four million years. Yet I have interviewed many sincere eyewitnesses who are adamant that they have seen these flying reptiles."

Indeed, the biggest problem with the teratorn theory is that all the scientific evidence shows that the animals died out a long time ago—a *really* long time ago. If we're going reach that far back for an explanation, we might as well accept that *Jurassic Park*–like pterosaurs are still flying around.

In his self-published book *Live Pterosaurs in America: Sightings of Apparent Pterosaurs in the United States*, Jonathan David Whitcomb (2009) relates a story told to him by another New Mexican man in the wake of the publicity of Zander's sighting that followed Gerhard's interview with Zander in 2007:

> I live in central New Mexico. Fourteen years ago [in 1993] in Socorro, me and a close friend, who now has a masters in biology, were hiking during the midday sun at [a] box canyon and something blocked the sun for a moment. We both looked up to see what did that and saw a large flying animal. It had a twenty to thirty foot wingspan and was about the same length long. It had a long tail with a seeming spike at the end. Its head was very pterodactyl shaped with a fluted back pointy head. It glided at about 700 feet in a westward direction. It was black and we watched it glide . . . and land somewhere in the southern expanse of the Magdalena Mountains. (51)

Whitcomb's anonymous correspondent could offer no proof of his encounter but said that it had occurred around March or April 1993—and that he and his friend "joked for years that we saw a dragon" (Whitcomb 2009, 51). Perhaps even more amazingly, the man claimed that he saw it again a month later, although there were apparently no other eyewitnesses, and he didn't have a camera handy. In the end there is no record or evidence of either sighting. But other reports of such aerial monsters in the southwestern skies can be found—in nearby Arizona.

THE WINGED MONSTER OF HUACHUCA

According to one rumor, "in 1886, a group of ranchers in Tombstone, Arizona, claimed that they had actually shot and killed a thunderbird. After pinning the dead creature to the side of a barn, they measured its wingspan at about thirty-five feet" (Blackman 1998, 98). This story, although widely circulated and repeated, has been shown to be mere myth. There is nothing in the historical record of anything like that happening, nor has any photograph of the massive bird ever been found. Blackman coyly notes that "the wing tip has been lost for decades," misleadingly suggesting that evidence of the rest of the story is intact and valid, and that if only the wing tip could be found the story would come together.

Figure 7.1. *Legends say that a band of Arizona cowboys shot and killed a bird the size of a barn in the 1800s; searches for an elusive photograph of the event (represented here) have been fruitless. Illustration by the author.*

But there is another story that seems to offer more than ranch rumor. According to a newspaper report in the April 26, 1890, *Tombstone Epitaph*, a monstrous flying creature was found in the Arizona desert. The article, headlined "Found in the Desert: A Strange Winged Monster Discovered and Killed in the Huachuca Desert," read:

> A winged monster, resembling a huge alligator with an extremely elongated tail and an immense pair of wings, was found on the desert between the Whetsone and Huachuca mountains last Sunday by two ranchers who were returning home from the Huachucas. The creature was evidently greatly exhausted by a long flight and when discovered was able to fly but a short distance at a time. After the first shock of wild amazement had passed, the two men, who were on horseback and armed with Winchester rifles, regained sufficient courage to pursue the monster and after an exciting chase of several miles succeeded in getting near enough to open fire with their rifles and wounding it.
>
> The creature then turned on the men, but owing to its exhausted

> condition they were able to keep out of its way and after a few well directed shots the monster partly rolled over and remained motionless. The men cautiously approached, their horses snorting with terror, and found that the creature was dead. They then proceeded to make an examination and found that it measured about ninety-two feet in length and the greatest diameter was about fifty inches. The monster had only two feet, these being situated a short distance in front of where the wings were joined to the body.
>
> The head, as near as they could judge, was about eight feet long, the jaws being thickly set with strong, sharp teeth. Its eyes were as large as a dinner plate and protruded about half way from the head. They had some difficulty in measuring the wings as they were partly folded under the body, but finally got one straightened out sufficiently to get a measurement of seventy-eight feet, making the total length from tip to tip about 160 feet. The wings were composed of a thick and nearly transparent membrane and were devoid of feathers or hair, as was the entire body. The skin of the body was comparatively smooth and easily penetrated by a bullet.
>
> The men cut off a small portion of the tip of one wing and took it home with them. Late last night one of them arrived in this city for supplies and to make the necessary preparations to skin the creature, when the hide will be sent east for examination by the eminent scientists of the day. The finder returned early this morning accompanied by several prominent men who will endeavor to bring the strange creature to this city before it is mutilated.

It's quite an amazing story—and, curiously, nothing more came of it. No mention of what happened to the animal's carcass, what the scientists and local prominent men concluded about it, or anything else appeared in following issues of the *Tombstone Epitaph* or anywhere else. As the late researcher Mark Chorvinsky (2002) wrote, "To the best of my knowledge, this is the last that anyone ever heard of this creature. There is no mention of any photograph being taken. The article claims that the creature's wingspan was 160 feet."

Another question is whether the original newspaper article was accompanied by a photograph of the strange creature. Some people reported having seen it, but no one has yet found it. Chorvinsky spent years searching for the elusive thunderbird photograph. It was like chasing a ghost, or an urban legend: memories changed, friend-of-a-friend eyewitnesses reported having seen it, and so on. In the end, he found nothing.*

In 1969 J. K. Parrish repeated a story about the incident in *Old West* magazine, which "prompted a letter from Harry F. McClure [who] recalled details of it and [claimed to have] seen the two ranchers himself as a youth in Lordsburg, New Mexico, where the story was much discussed at the time. . . . According to McClure, it was never captured, let alone killed" (Hall 2004, 134). Since this New Mexican's statement contradicts the whole premise of the *Tombstone Epitaph* story, it's likely to be a tall tale with no backing record whatsoever.

If the unidentified flying object recovered in the remote desert had been a flying saucer instead of a dead giant bird, many people would assume that a government conspiracy had covered it up—how else could all records of such an amazing, unique discovery (reported in the local newspaper, no less) have simply disappeared without a trace? Did President Benjamin Harrison, upon being notified of this spectacular find through top-secret channels, immediately dispatch federal agents (such as James T. West and Artemus Gordon of the TV show *The Wild Wild West*) to secure the site, remove all evidence, and threaten or bribe witnesses into silence?

This seems less likely than a pterosaur in a bird cage, so let's examine other explanations. It's fair to point out that the *Tombstone Epitaph* is no *New York Times* when it comes to credibility. In fact, from a historical perspective, newspaper hoaxes were fairly common in the 1800s, and "true" stories of exotic monsters and fantastic creatures were particular reader favorites. The competition for readers among newspapers was fierce, and most editors were happy to bend the truth or sensationalize a story—or flat-out make one up—if it meant selling some broadsheets.**

* As remarkable as the story is, the story behind the story is equally fascinating. For years, many people denied that the *Tombstone Epitaph* article even existed; writers such as prominent thunderbird researcher Mark Hall, John Keel, and Ivan T. Sanderson claimed that the article had never been published anywhere, that it was just another wild rumor (like the earlier story of the thunderbird found by cowboys and propped up against a barn). Finally, Chorvinsky did some investigating and found that the article had in fact appeared in the newspaper. Others had somehow failed to find it despite having the exact correct date. (In fact, most never bothered to look, which doesn't speak well for their researching skills.) (See Chorvinsky 2002; Hall 2004, chapter 12.)

** In our book *The Martians Have Landed!: A History of Media-Driven Panics and Hoaxes* (2012), Robert Bartholomew and I discuss many newspaper hoaxes, including when the *New York Sun* printed a story in 1835 claiming that scientists had discovered colonies of bat-like men living on the moon!

One researcher found a similar story in the *Macleod Gazette* of Fort Macleod, Alberta. The story, published on November 3, 1892, and titled "A Winged Monstrosity," claimed that a man in Quebec had seen an immense creature in the sky that he first took to be a monstrously sized eagle. It had apparently been carrying off his sheep in the dead of night, and the man shot it out of the sky with his rifle. After a struggle, "the monster lay dead at his feet. It had two great wings measuring fifteen feet from tip to tip. The head, which was fifteen inches in circumference, resembled that of a large monkey. The body was five feet long, and the back part was covered with a fur or coarse hair. The feet or claws resembled the legs of a wolf, and under the tail feathers was a long appendage with a tuft at the end that looked like the tail of a large calf. Lying with wings extended on the ground, the monster looked as big as a horse" (Benedict 2002, 16).

As with the Tombstone story, there seems to be no record of any such thing anywhere else (including in Quebec, where the supposed incident took place). Coming just two years after the *Tombstone Epitaph* story, it seems very likely to be exactly what it appears to be: one of many wild newspaper stories that editors occasionally added to their real news to spice things up.

Although no one ever located any photo of a huge bird or pterosaur taken in 1800s Arizona, a bizarre photo did appear with nearly identical content—except it was said to have been taken during the Civil War. The photo (actually there are at least two similar photos) was posted sometime after 2000 on the Internet and appeared to show Union soldiers posing around the carcass of a giant winged beast that looks like a pterosaur. They all have rifles, and the scene suggests that the soldiers shot the creature out of the air and are now posing around their trophy.

The idea that Civil War soldiers battled giant flying reptiles and dinosaurs seems absurd, and many immediately smelled a hoax. One of the photos was indeed soon revealed as fake; veteran researcher Loren Coleman, curator of the Cryptozoology Museum in Portland, Maine, explained: "As it turns out this photograph was a promotional tool of Orlando, Florida's Haxan Production (producers of the movie *The Blair Witch Project*), to develop interest in their forthcoming sci-fi television program, *Freaky Links*. The series, first broadcast on Fox TV in 2000, involved the character 'Derek Barnes,' an investigator of the unknown. The photograph was a hoax, using Civil War reenactors and a pterodactyl created as a prop exclusively for two episodes of *Freaky Links*" (Coleman 2007). A second photo from an anonymous source was revealed as a digitally faked image—along with one showing Civil War soldiers with a dead triceratops.

If living dinosaurs seem too far-fetched, there's another explanation for the sightings: the fearsome thunderbirds of Native American lore. These birds allegedly have a wingspan far in excess of any known feathered animal; their flapping wings create a thunderous roar. But are these giants in the sky merely mythical? Some New Mexicans say no.

CLASSIC THUNDERBIRDS

When it comes to classic thunderbirds, descriptions vary. Scott Francis (2007) states: "Some describe a large condor-like bird, and in other instances they tell of a prehistoric pterodactyl-like creature" with a wingspan of between fifteen and thirty-five feet. "In most cases the creature is a large bird with huge wings that it can beat together to create thunder. Lightning shoots from the thunderbird's eyes, its shadow blocks out the sun and wherever it goes, storms tend to follow. The thunderbird of legend is so large that entire lakes may form on its shoulders, and on occasion it flies over oceans to prey on whales" (137).

In his book *The Mythic Bestiary: The Illustrated Guide to the World's Most Fantastical Creatures*, Tony Allan relates one Native American story:

> Nobody ever doubted the thunderbirds' terrible power. The Ojibwa of the Great Lakes region told of two rash youths who decided to explore a mountain peak where the birds were said to live. Without performing any of the necessary rites, the two set off on their climb. The summit was shrouded in mist, but the more foolhardy of the two pressed on. His friend heard him shout, "I see them! I see them!" as he disappeared into the cloud. Then there was a terrible crash and a blinding flash of light. As the friend staggered backward, he saw the lifeless body of his companion tumbling down the mountainside. (Allan 2008, 16)

However, the thunderbirds, as great and powerful elements of the sky, could also be beneficent. Allan continues, "For those who treated them with respect, the thunderbirds could be valuable helpers. The Makah people of the Northwest Coast had a story of a thunderbird that saved a village from famine by snatching a whale from the ocean and delivering it to the community, which fed off its flesh for many weeks" (Allan 2008, 16).

Mark Hall (2004), author of *Thunderbirds: America's Living Legends of Giant Birds*, offers the following description of thunderbirds: "The bird is distinguished by its size and lifting capabilities exceeding those of any known bird living today anywhere in the world. Wingspan estimates are necessarily all guesswork. But observers sometimes have the benefit of a measurable object for comparison or the benefit of time to observe a resting bird. The results most often provide sizes of 15 to 20 feet."

In many cultures and mythologies, birds are associated with the air, elements, and weather. Weather is of course a major force in people's lives, and it always has been—from deadly snowstorms to floods and tornados. So it's not surprising that legends, superstitions, and mythologies arose surrounding forces and animals associated with the airy realms. Some Native American groups carved totem poles in the shape of thunderbirds as a way to honor unseen spirits—and to provide protection from their wrath (figure 7.2).

Figure 7.2. *A northwest coast–styled Kwakwaka'wakw totem pole depicting a thunderbird, erected at Thunderbird Park in Victoria, British Columbia. Photo by the author.*

MODERN DINOSAURS?

Many people believe that the thunderbird—if it exists—is probably a giant version of some known bird or a dinosaur that somehow escaped extinction millions of years ago. Indeed, several of the descriptions might apply to dinosaurs, and the idea has a strong popular appeal. The best-known flying reptiles were the pterosaurs (often incorrectly called pterodactyls); pterosaurs were not technically true dinosaurs, although they existed at the same time as their close cousins and were far larger than humans (figure 7.3).

Figure 7.3. *Size comparison of a pterosaur and a human. Illustration by Daniel Loxton. Originally published in* Junior Skeptic *magazine; used by permission.*

Veteran investigator Massimo Polidoro points out in *Skeptical Inquirer* that "the original idea for dinosaurs still living in the modern era and interacting with humans dates back to 1912 when Arthur Conan Doyle, then already a celebrity thanks to the adventures of his cool private detective Sherlock Holmes, published one of his most famous novels, *The Lost World*. . . . In Doyle's book, a group of explorers sets sail for a lost land in South America . . . and discovers that dinosaurs, long believed to be extinct, still live" (Polidoro 2002).

Indeed, prior to Doyle's famous novel, few had considered the idea that dinosaurs could still exist—and certainly no one took it seriously as an explanation for odd or unexplained animals. It was only decades later that monster buffs and cryptozoologists would try to link modern monster sightings (such as the Congo's Mokele-mbembe, Scotland's Loch Ness Monster, or the thunderbirds of the American Southwest) to extant remnant populations of animals long extinct. The connection makes a certain amount of sense—of all animals known to have existed, dinosaurs come the closest in size and shape to many alleged modern monsters—as long as one ignores the incontrovertible evidence that dinosaurs died out millions of years ago.

ROCS, GRYPHONS, AND MARCO POLO

Thunderbirds aren't the only huge birds of legend around the world. There's also the roc, described in Persian stories—most famously those about Sinbad the Sailor in the *One Thousand and One Nights*. In one adventure, Sinbad spies a white dome in the distance, believing it to be a building. But, as he approaches, he realizes that it's actually an enormous bird's egg, and he soon meets its protective parent: a gigantic winged monster whose size temporarily blots out the sun. The roc chases Sinbad back to his ship, swooping down to pick up—and then drop—massive boulders onto the fleeing sailors.

The Sinbad stories are fiction, but the travelogues of real-life explorer Marco Polo also contain reports of thunderbird-like creatures. In *The Travels of Marco Polo*, the Venetian vagabond wrote that Madagascar and other islands off the East African coast, which he visited around 1290, were said to be

> inhabited by gryphon birds, which make their appearance here at certain seasons of the year. But they are by no means such as men in our country suppose, or as we portray them—half bird and half lion. According to the report of those who have seen them . . . the actual eye-witnesses report that in build they are just like eagles but of the most colossal size. They report that they are so huge and bulky that one of them can pounce on an elephant and carry it up to a great height in the air. Then it lets go, so that the elephant drops to earth and is smashed to pulp, whereupon the gryphon bird perches on the carcass and feeds at ease. They add that they have a wing-span of thirty paces [about forty-eight feet, or fifteen meters] and their wing-feathers are

> twelve paces long. . . . I should explain that the natives call them *rukhs* and know them by no other name and have no idea what a gryphon is. But I feel sure from the monstrous size they attribute to the birds that they cannot be anything but gryphons. (Polo 1958, 300)*

Polo found these stories credible, partly because he himself "had seen a roc's feather, brought back by envoys to the court of the Great Khan, whose quill measured twice the width of his hand. Scholars have speculated that this might have been a frond of the raffia palm, passed off as a roc's feather to impress the Chinese visitors" (Allan 2008, 148). To a credulous audience steeped in stories of exotic beasts in far-off lands, a dyed palm frond could easily be taken for a giant feather (especially if the recipients had never seen a raffia palm).

There may be a scientific basis for these roc/gryphon stories. The peculiar wildlife of Madagascar included a giant flightless bird, *Aepyornis maximus*, also known as the elephant bird. The animals, which vaguely resembled massive emus or ostriches, went extinct only relatively recently (a few hundred years ago); at about ten feet in height, they towered over humans. It's possible that early explorers who saw these creatures fully grown mistook them for newborn birds, as they also could be imagined to resemble baby chicks, and assumed that they would grow up to be far larger—thus spawning stories about the roc.

NATIVE LEGENDS AND MODERN MONSTERS

What's the connection, if any, between Native American stories of thunderbirds and modern sightings of giant birds? Thunderbirds are of course not the only mysterious creatures that appear in the lore of ancient cultures. In fact, the field of cryptozoology is actively engaged in the search for such creatures.

One example is the Ogopogo lake monster, said to lurk in the deep, cold waters of British Columbia's Lake Okanagan. As with many lake monsters, native Indian tales have been used to suggest a historical precedent for the creatures. Ogopogo is supposedly based on Indian legends of a fearsome water spirit called N'ha-a-itk, who would demand a toll from travelers for safe passage near its reputed home of Rattlesnake

* It should be noted that the veracity of Marco Polo's writings has long been challenged; while Polo traveled widely, several of his accounts seem to have come from other sources and may have been fictional.

Island in Lake Okanagan. Hundreds of years ago, whenever Indians would venture into the lake, they brought chickens or other small animals to drop into the water to ensure a safe journey.

N'ha-a-itk would use its mighty tail to lash the lake's waters into a fierce storm, drowning its victims. According to Mary Moon (1977, 32), author of *Ogopogo*, "The Indians . . . looked on it as a superhuman [supernatural] entity." Other writers agree, including W. Haden Blackman (1998), who points out that the Sushwap and Okanakane Indians "believed that it was an evil supernatural entity with great power and ill intent." N'ha-a-itk's paranormal connection to the elements is perhaps the strongest of any lake monster. Not only does N'ha-a-itk seem to have supernatural control over the lake's waters, it also commands aerial forces: "The Indians said no boat could possibly land [on Rattlesnake Island], for the monster would cause a strong wind to blow and baffle the attempt. . . . The monster was something more than an amphibian. It was always in some way connected with high winds" (71).

Such stories and descriptions suggest that, to First Nations peoples, N'ha-a-itk was a disincarnate force of nature, not a real creature actually living, eating, breathing, and breeding in the cold waters of Lake Okanagan. Just because a given culture has a name for (or tells stories about) a strange or mysterious beast—be it Sasquatch or Ogopogo, fairies or leprechauns—doesn't necessarily mean that those names or stories are meant to reflect reality. As folklorist Michel Meurger points out in his *Lake Monster Traditions*, claiming native evidence for unknown creatures is an "old gimmick of portraying the sighter as a kind of 'noble savage,'" a process he aptly names "the scientification of folklore" (Meurger and Gagnon 1989, 13).

Writer Noah Nez, in his analysis of the thunderbird traditions, offers a Native American perspective:

> Thunderbirds are unlike any extinct, prehistoric, or living species of birds presented by many cryptozoologists and monster enthusiasts because they are mythical creatures inspired by the animals, relative to the groups of people living at the time these stories originated, as a way to explain the natural world. The evidence of modern thunderbird sightings is an exaggeration of similarities, which are not supported by Native American stories. In fact, no person has ever seen a thunderbird, even in dreams or in the "visions" of medicine men. According to the Native American mythologies, thunderbirds have no actual physical form. . . . The majority of the "evidence" proposed for this mythic

> bird-like creature is often given as literal interpretations of Native American folklore. However, the ancestral stories are explicit in stating that these creatures represent formless "thunder beings" which cannot be seen, even in dreams or visions, thus any eyewitness sightings (and certainly those by non-Natives) by definition cannot be thunderbirds. In fact it may even be considered *disrespectful* to suggest that a person could see, or has seen, a thunderbird. Some may have looked to the thunderbird legend to help rationalize these various strange encounters that people experience, but in doing so, they bastardize these legends, misinform their readers, and do a disservice to the people or their tribal culture. If any part of the story should be taken out of the legend of Wakinyan Tanka, it should be that thunderbirds are a link between the supernatural and natural worlds which reflect their power in a contradictory fashion expressed with the "paradox of life." They do not exist, but they are very real in the hearts and minds of Native American people. (Nez 2011)

Thus it's clear that only by misunderstanding and mischaracterizing the true interpretation of the thunderbird can modern writers claim them as evidence for modern "big bird" sightings. Native Americans would laugh at (or be offended by) the idea that some large creature a white man reported seeing in the sky while driving on a highway outside of Albuquerque was a thunderbird.

Many American Indian tribes incorporate thunderbird designs in their art, and the images are even used in commercial signs and names (figure 7.4). Petroglyphs depicting Native American thunderbirds have been found in several places in New Mexico, including at the Three Rivers petroglyph site in the desert north of Tularosa. The petroglyphs, carved into basalt rock, are believed to have been carved between 600 and 1,100 years ago by the Jornada Mogollon group (figures 7.5a, 7.5b). "Originating in the Pacific Northwest, its image somehow migrated south, catching support from the tourist trade and the jewelry artists at Kewa Pueblo, formerly known as Santo Domingo. 'Supposedly the first thunderbird came off of cave paintings,' said folklorist Roddy Moore, a co-curator of a new show at the Wheelwright Museum of the American Indian. 'It exploded when the railroad started using it and when (hotel owner Fred) Harvey copyrighted it,' continued Moore, the director of the Blue Ridge Institute and Museum in Ferrum, Va. 'That same form is on American coinage—on some half-dollars. It's on Mexican coinage. It's on military insignia. It's been in a lot of different places'" (Roberts 2011).

Figure 7.4. *A sign along historic Route 66 in Gallup, New Mexico, featuring the name and image of the legendary thunderbird of Native American lore. Photo by the author.*

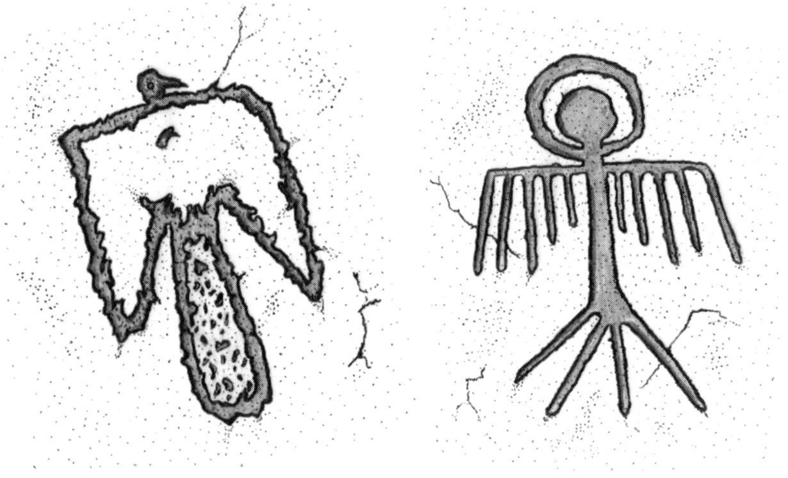

Figures 7.5a, 7.5b. *Two petroglyphs depicting Native American thunderbirds were discovered on basalt rocks in the desert north of Tularosa, New Mexico. The petroglyphs are believed to have been carved between 600 and 1,100 years ago by the Jornada Mogollon group. Illustrations by the author.*

THUNDERBIRD EYEWITNESSES

So, setting aside hoaxed newspaper accounts from the 1800s and Native American legends, all we are left with as evidence for modern-day monstrous avians is a handful of eyewitness reports, since "claims for photographic evidence in support of the birds have not been persuasive" (Hall 2004, 132).

Let's return to Dave Zander's sighting of two giant birds in the desert near Las Cruces. What could he have seen? One possibility is that Zander saw a pair of condors. Condors are the largest flying birds in the Western Hemisphere and can reach a wingspan of about nine feet. The California condor (*Gymnogyps californianus*) is a type of vulture primarily seen in California, the Grand Canyon area, and Utah's Zion National Park. Birds, of course, ignore state lines and roam wherever they wish. The condor is also a remarkably long-lived bird, with a lifespan of up to sixty years, so it's quite possible that the same particularly large condor might be sighted at locations distant from each other, and years apart.

Perhaps most telling, the condor's colors closely match Zander's description: the birds are black, with some patches of white on the underside of the wings and a mostly bald head with pink to red skin color.

Do California condors live in New Mexico? They certainly did at one point; fossil remains of these birds have been found in New Mexico dating back to the Pleistocene Epoch (from 2.5 million to about 12,000 years ago).

It is true that the range of the California condor normally doesn't extend as far east as New Mexico. However, it is certainly possible that a pair of condors could have reached the Organ Mountains near Las Cruces. In fact, nearly three dozen California condors were released in the neighboring state of Arizona in December 1996 (two years before Zander's sighting) as part of a wildlife reintegration plan (Grahame and Sisk 2002). It seems likely that Dave Zander (and others) could have seen one of these. (In fact, Zander himself acknowledged that he might have seen a pair of condors—although ones that were far larger than any others reported, by his estimation.) Indeed, as Texas cryptozoologist Ken Gerhard (2012) admits, "We can't completely rule out the possibility that the man-sized birds he spotted were wayward California condors, since there is an extant population in Arizona and these immense birds are known to have a tremendous range."

The fact that it took almost ten years for Zander's sighting to be scrutinized has made it all but impossible to fully investigate the incident and come to a final conclusion. At this point, fifteen years later, we cannot definitively determine what large birds might have been in the area at the time, although condors are a reasonable guess.

The large size of the birds described by Zander remains problematic; condors don't have a twenty- to twenty-five-foot wingspan, as Zander reported. One obvious possibility is that Zander simply overestimated the size of the creatures he saw. This is not a far-fetched explanation: How many people could accurately estimate the wingspan of a moving, unknown object from a distance of about a mile—with or without binoculars? Without some scale of reference, any estimate would be little more than guesswork, even for trained ornithologists.

In my fifteen years of investigating mysterious creature sightings and reports (including Bigfoot, the chupacabra, and lake monsters), I have discovered that eyewitnesses consistently overestimate the size of unidentified creatures they see. Part of the reason is that people are not good at estimating distances, and if one doesn't know the distance to an object, one can't accurately estimate its size unless there is an adjacent object of known size or scale for quick reference.

For example, in my investigation of Champ, the monster in Lake Champlain, I examined the most famous photo of the beast, taken by Sandra Mansi in 1977; it is considered the best photographic evidence in the world for any lake monster (Kirk 1998; Zarzynski 1988). The Mansis estimated that the creature's neck protruded about six feet out of the water and that its size was about twelve to fifteen feet long from neck to end. The family got a good long look at it, as the sighting lasted a remarkably long time—between five and seven minutes. Joe Nickell and I investigated (and re-created) the photo for a Learning Channel television show, and we discovered that all previous estimates of the creature's size had been dramatically overstated. The neck sticking out of the water was nowhere near the previous estimates of six to eight feet or more. Instead, the creature's neck extended just over three feet out of the water, and it was altogether about seven feet across. The "monster" was less than half the size the eyewitness had claimed. (For more details on the photo and my investigation, see Radford and Nickell 2006, chapter 2.)

In another investigation, of the Ogopogo lake monster, my investigation team determined that, in recording the most famous video footage of the monster, Arthur Folden overestimated the animal's size by at least a factor of two. Despite getting an extended look at the animal—

and even capturing it on film—he estimated that it was twice what we determined would be its actual size. (For more details, see Radford 2010, chapter 8.)

Thus it seems likely, based on my research and that of others, that Dave Zander overestimated the size of the flying animals he saw by a factor of two or three; instead of a twenty- to twenty-five-foot wingspan, it was probably closer to between eight and ten feet—still quite large, but within the size range of known large birds such as the condor. Of course it's possible that his size estimate was correct—or even low—but the evidence suggests otherwise.

CONCLUSION

Upon close examination, there's good reason to be skeptical that there are giant, living birds or pterosaurs flying in the skies above New Mexico. Despite a few mistaken claims to the contrary (for example, Blackman 1998*), they are rarely if ever sighted by those who spend most of their time looking at the skies: ornithologists and airplane pilots. In 2012 there were nearly 30,000 commercial airline flights crisscrossing the United States on any given day—more than 1,500 in any given hour—at a wide variety of altitudes, on a wide variety of routes, and in every direction. That's nearly eleven million flights per year, and there is no report of a single airline pilot or passenger ever having spotted one of these modern-day dinosaurs flying around. If any flying creatures

* In his mystery-mongering book *The Field Guide to North American Monsters*, Blackman suggests that a thunderbird encounter "could have been responsible for the crash of a United Airlines plane in November 1962. When the wreckage was discovered in a wooded area of Maryland, rescuers found no survivors but did stumble upon a mass of bloody feathers. Investigators also noted huge gouges and slash marks on the plane, especially near the tail assembly" (Blackman 1998, 99). In fact, nearly everything about this account is wrong: United Airlines Flight 297 indeed crashed on November 23, 1962, after colliding with birds—but the birds were a large flock of whistling swans. The swans—not a thunderbird—damaged the airplane and led to the death of seventeen people. According to aviation officials, "The Viscount was flying at 6000 feet, en route from Newark to Washington when it penetrated a flock of whistling swans. At least two of which were struck by the aircraft. One swan which was struck penetrated the leading edge of the left horizontal stabilizer and egressed from the rear surface causing damage to the elevator as it did so. This so weakened the structure that failure occurred which rendered the plane uncontrollable" (Flight Safety Foundation 2012). Bird strikes are not uncommon in aviation, and despite Blackman's claim to the contrary there was nothing unusual or mysterious about the loss of this flight. It's unfortunate that Blackman used this very real human tragedy as fictional evidence for thunderbirds.

remain undiscovered in North America, they are much more likely to be tiny avians hidden away in the dense foliage of forests—not massive birds with twenty- to sixty-foot wingspans.

There are also biological and zoological arguments against the existence of massive, unknown birds. Like other unknown creatures such as Bigfoot, the Loch Ness Monster, or the chupacabra, there cannot be only one of them. If these animals are real and have existed and evolved for millennia, there must be many of them. In fact, for a species to perpetuate itself and not go extinct, it needs to have enough members to sustain what scientists call a breeding population. This is the minimum number of animals required to provide sufficient genetic variation to keep a population healthy over time. The minimum breeding population varies from animal to animal, but typically zoologists estimate that there would need to be tens of thousands of a given species to sustain a wild population.

While it's romantic to imagine one or two of these magnificent creatures somehow existing in remote areas of North America and only being sighted every decade or so, it beggars belief to think that tens of thousands—or even just hundreds—of these supernaturally large animals are soaring in the skies above New Mexico and across the country all the time, yet remaining unseen. In fact, advances in modern technology have made the likelihood that these animals exist even smaller; satellite images (such as those found on Google Earth) have such high resolution that they can capture an object only a few feet wide. Surely, flying animals with thirty-foot-plus wingspans would have been incidentally photographed by now by the unblinking, all-seeing eyes in the skies.

Even if thunderbirds could somehow remain hidden from prying human eyes and satellite optics, the enormous size to which they are believed to grow in and of itself is problematic. Recent scientific research suggests that wingspans of twenty feet or more may be physically impossible for any modern animals. Zoologically, great body size comes at a high cost in terms of both how much food is required and also simply how an animal's body must function. Massive wings are heavy, and their maximum feasible size may fall well below the estimates made by eyewitnesses.

Jennifer Viegas (2010), writing for Discovery News, noted:

> It's now thought that seventeen feet may be close to the maximum wingspan that can be achieved by a flying bird. Prior wingspan estimates for pelagornithids [a prehistoric bird] went up to twenty feet, but they were

> based on more fragmented fossils. "Most likely, evolution of such large sizes was to avoid competition with other birds," Gerald Mayr, a paleornithologist at the Senckenberg Research Institute and Natural History Museum, told Discovery News. "Birds with such a large size can, of course, sail across huge distances and may more easily find prey in the open ocean." However, "there are a number of drawbacks if you become so large," he added. "Chicks would have to be raised over a long period of time, making them more prone to predation [and] bird feathers are quite heavy, so very large birds may have become too heavy."

It seems that the thunderbirds' greatest enemy is not skeptics, nor errant aircraft, nor lightning, but instead Mother Nature. Any bird that grows too large would fall to an Icarian fate; it may be able to escape from gravity, but it cannot escape from evolution and physics.

For millennia, people have looked to the sky and seen curious things: sometimes it's a meteor or an eclipse; other times it's a UFO or an apparent spaceship; and yet other times it's a bird that seems far larger than possible. No matter what is—or isn't—up there, people will forever see what they want to see.

REFERENCES

Allan, Tony. 2008. *The Mythic Bestiary: The Illustrated Guide to the World's Most Fantastical Creatures*. London: Duncan Baird.

Bartholomew, Robert, and Benjamin Radford. 2012. *The Martians Have Landed!: A History of Media-Driven Panics and Hoaxes*. Jefferson, NC: McFarland.

Benedict, W. Ritchie. 2002. "Thunderbirds in Canada." *Fate* magazine, June.

Blackman, W. Haden. 1998. *The Field Guide to North American Monsters*. New York: Random House.

Chorvinsky, Mark. 2002. "Cowboys and Dragons: Unraveling the Mystery of the Thunderbird Photograph." *Strange Magazine*, no. 21. http://www.strangemag.com/strangemag/strange21/thunderbird21/thunderbird1_21.html#.

Coleman, Loren. 2007. "Civil War Dinos." Cryptomundo, February 16. http://www.cryptomundo.com/cryptozoo-news/c-w-dinos/.

Flight Safety Foundation. 2012. "Accident Description." http://aviation-safety.net/database/record.php?id=19621123–1.

Francis, Scott. 2007. *Monster Spotter's Guide to North America*. Cincinnati, OH: How Books.

Gaal, Arlene. 1986. *Ogopogo: The True Story of the Okanagan Lake Million Dollar Monster.* Surrey, BC: Hancock House.

Gerhard, Ken. 2012. Interview by Benjamin Radford, February 29.

Giddings, Ruth W. 1959. "Yaqui Myths and Legends." Anthropological Papers of the University of Arizona, no. 2.

Grahame, John, and Thomas D. Sisk, eds. 2002. "The California Condor on the Colorado Plateau." Canyons, Cultures and Environmental Change: An Introduction to the Land-Use History of the Colorado Plateau. http://cpluhna.nau.edu/Biota/california_condor.htm.

Hall, Mark. 2004. *Thunderbirds: America's Living Legends of Giant Birds.* New York: Paraview Press.

Heinselman, Craig. "Thunderbird." Cryptozoology.com. http://www.cryptozoology.com/cryptids/thunderbird.php.

Kirk, John. 1998. *In the Domain of the Lake Monsters.* Toronto, ON: Key Porter Books.

Lame Deer, John. 1984. "Wankanyan Tanka, the Great Thunderbird." Recorded By Richard Erdoes in 1969. In *American Indian Myths and Legends*, edited by Richard Erdoes and Alfonso Ortiz, 218–22. New York: Pantheon.

McCormick, Annie. 2007. "Big-Bird Encounter One for the Books." KRQE-TV, broadcast, July 19.

Meurger, Michel, and Claude Gagnon. 1989. *Lake Monster Traditions: A Cross-Cultural Analysis.* London: Fortean Tomes.

Moon, Mary. 1977. *Ogopogo.* North Vancouver, BC: J. J. Douglas.

Nez, Noah. 2011. "Thunderbirds." Native Skeptic (column). *Skeptical Briefs* 21, no. 4 (Winter 2011–2012): 7–9.

Polidoro, Massimo. 2002. "A Pterodactyl in the Civil War." *Skeptical Inquirer* 26, no. 3 (May–June): 21–22.

Polo, Marco. (ca. 1300) 1958. *The Travels of Marco Polo.* Translated by Ronald Latham. New York: Penguin Books.

Radford, Benjamin. 2010. *Scientific Paranormal Investigation: How to Solve Unexplained Mysteries.* Corrales, NM: Rhombus Publishing.

Radford, Benjamin, and Joe Nickell. 2006. *Lake Monster Mysteries: Investigating the World's Most Elusive Creatures.* Lexington: University Press of Kentucky.

Roberts, Kathaleen. 2011. "Wings of Power." *Albuquerque Journal*, May 29, F1.

Smith, Mike. 2007. "Bighoot, the Flying Head." Cryptomundo, May 4. http://www.cryptomundo.com/cryptozoo-news/nm-bighoot.

Viegas, Jennifer. 2010. "Prehistoric Bird Sets Wingspan Record." Discovery

News, September 15. http://www.msnbc.msn.com/id/39194076/ns/technology_and_science-science/#.Tz__dpjZekQ.

Whitcomb, Jonathan David. 2009. *Live Pterosaurs in America: Sightings of Apparent Pterosaurs in the United States.* N.p.: CreateSpace.

Zander, Dave. 2007. Interview by Benjamin Radford, July 23.

Zarzynski, Joseph. (1984) 1988. *Champ: Beyond the Legend.* Revised edition. Port Henry, NY: Bannister Publications.

CHAPTER 8

THE HAUNTED OLD CUCHILLO BAR

The small town of Cuchillo, New Mexico (fifteen minutes from Truth or Consequences)—depending on your sense of wordplay—may or may not literally be a ghost town. It's certainly a *near* ghost town, having only a handful of current residents (about three dozen, depending on who's out of town on any given day), down from thousands during its heyday around 1900. Over the past 180 years, the Old Cuchillo Bar and Store served as a post office, gambling house, storeroom, mercantile shop, restaurant, saloon, and boarding house. All that is gone now, although some say that the spirits of countless travelers remain.

The building, like the town itself, has fallen on hard times—especially after a devastating fire in 2000. The building is littered with artifacts from its bygone days: lanterns, antlers, spurs, branding irons, bottles of tonics and drinks that went out of fashion (or out of business) decades ago, and so on.

The ramshackle place is owned by artist Josh Bond, who spends much of his time and money trying to fix up the property and save a piece of history. The structure was built around 1830, when Andrew Jackson was president of the United States, a young Charles Darwin would soon sail toward the Galapagos and begin research on the theory of evolution, and the age of railroads was just beginning.

These days, Bond keeps busy. "I do steel sculpture and painting and construction, photography, websites, graphic design," he told me during my first visit. "I stay pretty creative. . . . I moved to Cuchillo ten years ago, but I bought this place three years ago. Didn't move in, because there were people living here, didn't move in for about two years, then redid the hotel part," he said. There are three or four separate buildings on the property, depending on how you count them.

"I do think there are ghosts here," Bond, thirty-six, says. "I believe you can't have 150 years of a building without having some residual energy from either the previous owners, or the thousands of people who drank at the bar over the years. I have not personally seen a ghost, but I believe I'm not alone in these buildings. My theory is that these roads have been traveled for so long. I don't know that one specific ghost haunts one specific place, there's just energy and spirits moving around the place. . . . Possibly previous owners of the bar."

Bond admits that he has no hard evidence of ghosts. He's an artist, not a paranormal investigator, he tells me. "But I have had many ghost hunting groups out here to investigate, and they've provided me with the evidence." Indeed, in some circles the haunted Cuchillo Bar is famous; it was featured several times on local television stations, appeared in a national news story, and has the distinction of being one of the only (if not the only) haunted houses put up for sale on eBay.

There is no shortage of people working to turn ghosts into gold and spooky stories into silver. Hundreds of amateur ghost-hunting groups across the country offer ghost tours of local areas—supposedly haunted hotels, mansions, cemeteries, and so on. Bond hopes that the interest in ghosts will help draw attention to the crumbling historical buildings he bought. Although educational in its way (and character building, I daresay), fixing them up has been a Sisyphean feat. Bond is forthright about his need to raise funds to restore the buildings to their former glory (or at least fix the roof to protect the adobe walls). To that end, he did what any enterprising entrepreneur would do: he offered one of his haunted buildings for sale on eBay, a three-bedroom, one-bath home built around 1890. The thick adobe walls and hardwood floors are verifiable; the ghosts are another matter. The auction ended, appropriately enough, on Halloween 2009, without a bidder.

INVESTIGATING THE HAUNTING CLAIMS

I was of course intrigued by the story (who wouldn't be?), and I investigated the haunted house twice: once for two days and an overnight in July 2009, and again in October of that year with investigative reporter Larry Barker of KRQE-TV.

Josh and I teamed up; we were both looking for explanations. My interest in the house was not in proving or disproving the existence of

Figure 8.1. *The Old Cuchillo Bar and Store, reputedly one of the most haunted places in New Mexico. Photo by the author.*

Figure 8.2. *Josh Bond in his Old Cuchillo Bar, which served spirits for nearly a century—and may still to this day. Photo by the author.*

ghosts, and I pointed out that if they were really there, then I couldn't debunk them even if I wanted to. My interest is in trying to scientifically explain and understand what is going on, trying to explain the "unexplainable." In my years of investigating paranormal claims, I have managed to find scientific explanations for mysterious events, and I was eager to test my skills and mettle in this old place, with such a rich history.

In preparing to investigate the Old Cuchillo Bar, I began by researching what Bond and others had claimed about the place—the reported ghostly phenomena. For a small, dilapidated bar in a town few had heard of, it had gotten a lot of attention. According to Bond, as of 2010 at least seven different ghost-hunting groups and individuals had conducted investigations there. I was curious to see what others had done, what evidence they had collected for ghosts.

I found five groups who claimed to have looked into the Cuchillo haunting, although the amount of time and effort they had spent researching varied widely. One group calling themselves Wild West Ghosts apparently visited Cuchillo at one point, although there's no record of what they did or what their results were; their website expired long ago. Another group, Southwest Paranormal Investigations, mentions Bond and his haunted location on their website: "Our friend Josh Bond from Cuchillo has invited Southwest Paranormal Investigations to investigate his small town ghost and we have completed this investigation with evidence coming soon!"

Unfortunately, as of early 2014—apparently years after their visit—nothing about Cuchillo appears on Southwest Paranormal Investigations' website, or anywhere else online for that matter. (It is very common for amateur ghost-hunting groups to disband after a few months or a year or two at most after the initial enthusiasm fades and good ghostly evidence proves to be elusive.) One investigator, Debe Branning of the Mesa, Arizona–based MVD Ghostchasers Paranormal Team, spent only an hour or two "investigating" Cuchillo's ghosts in October 2009.

Fortunately, two groups took the topic seriously enough to spend more than a few hours in Cuchillo, and they made their research available: the West Coast Ghost and Paranormal Society (WCGAPS), based in Phoenix, and Ghost Investigations New Mexico.* Both of these

* This is not a complete list of all the individuals and groups who have looked into the Cuchillo Bar; there are others, including KTSM-TV's Ric Dumont from El Paso, Sherry Fletcher, and more.

groups more or less followed the investigation model presented by the Atlantic Paranormal Society (TAPS) on the TV show *Ghost Hunters*. As we will see, this is not necessarily a good thing.

GHOST INVESTIGATIONS NEW MEXICO

The team from Ghost Investigations New Mexico conducted several studies of the Cuchillo Bar starting in July 2009. They would arrive at eight in the evening, set up some equipment (video cameras, lights, etc.), and look for evidence of ghosts. For reasons that will become clear, this is an ineffective and counterproductive technique (for more on this, see Radford 2010, chapter 4).

Although video cameras were set up, the team reported on their website that "video results were harder to quantify and qualify due to a large quantity of floating dust, flying insects and bats" and concluded that they had found nothing they could present as evidence of a ghost or paranormal activity.

Figure 8.3. *The rear of the Old Cuchillo Bar and Store, a prime spot for ghost hunters. Photo by the author.*

The main evidence they sought (and found) was in the form of audio recordings. The team recorded faint sounds that they interpreted as random comments from ghosts, including, "just now," "comment," "it's on," and, perhaps most memorably, "come on you asshole." Audio samples of these recordings were available on the group's website as of this writing. The problem is that it's not clear what the sounds are: ordinary random sounds from the environment, comments spoken by the ghost investigators themselves, or utterances from the spiritual realm. For example, the ghostly voice interpreted as saying "it's on" sounds exactly like a person faintly whispering "hey Von"—Von being the name of one of the investigators. I'll discuss this in more detail later.

THE WEST COAST GHOST AND PARANORMAL SOCIETY

A second investigation was conducted by the West Coast Ghost and Paranormal Society. The WCGAPS team "research[es] and seek[s] out scientific explanations for strange occurrences. In some cases, however, normal explanations cannot resolve what we find. If after capturing evidence we are unable to find a reasonable explanation for a claim, we scrutinize our findings and only then acknowledge it as a paranormal event."

The team claimed to have witnessed the following paranormal activity at the Cuchillo property: "The feeling of a presence, hearing voices plus knocks and bangs in the hotel and store, feeling 'spooked out' in the bar area (won't go in the bar after dark), finding the cabinet doors open after already closing them and seeing shadow figures throughout the hotel and especially in the courtyard area. No particular time of day when experiencing activity, but does notice it more at night."

As is common in ghost investigations, some of these claims cannot be scientifically tested (for example, the "feeling of a presence" is impossible to objectively verify). However, the three primary claims that can be investigated are hearing voices, bangs, and knocks; seeing a shadowy figure; and finding cabinet doors unexplainably opened.

Like the Ghost Investigations New Mexico group, the WCGAPS team spent time trying to record ghost voices as evidence of a haunting. Their report states, "On audio in the stable area with two investigators, we caught an Electronic Voice Phenomenon (EVP), a voice not heard at the time of recording, saying what we believe to be, 'told you' in between the two investigators having a conversation about the moon.

Also on two different audio recorders at separate times, and on the audio of one of the camcorders, we captured a growl." (There were a few other audible and ambiguous knocks, taps, etc.)

One reason that the ghost hunting teams have similar methods and protocols is that they are, to a greater or lesser extent, modeled directly on the TAPS team from TV's *Ghost Hunters*. In fact, nearly all amateur ghost-hunting groups are inspired by and modeled after TAPS.

I contacted Andy Rice, founder of the WCGAPS, and asked him to describe the research his team did in Cuchillo. "We send people out with professional audio recorders. . . . We had three different locations we were investigating," Rice told me. "Most of the time we send out two team members to each location: one to the stables, one to the guest house, and one to the bar area. We send them out in twenty- to thirty-minute sessions, and the reason we do this is to control audio contamination. . . . Ninety percent of the places, we're able to debunk," Rice said. "Cuchillo is in the other 10 percent" (Rice 2009). According to the team's report on the case, "After reviewing the claims, eliminating possibilities of reasonable explanations . . . [the] WCGAPS has concluded, for the second time in many years of investigating, that the 180-year-old property in Cuchillo, NM is in fact haunted." Their strongest piece of evidence was something called EVPs.

A CLOSER LOOK AT GHOST VOICES AND EVPS

Electronic voice phenomena (EVP), the attempts of the dead to contact the living through interference on recorded media, has been popular with the paranormal crowd for decades and has enjoyed a new burst of popularity over the past few years among ghost-hunting groups.

After surveying the efforts of various ghost hunters who had visited Cuchillo over the years, it became clear that by far the strongest evidence they found was in the form of EVPs. Most of the other ghostly evidence was ambiguous—minor effects with perfectly ordinary explanations—but all the ghost hunters were very impressed by the ghost voices they claimed to find.

So it seemed important to take a closer look at this evidence. In analyzing the phenomenon, I was equipped with at least two important assets that the previous ghost hunters had lacked: a degree in psychology (from the University of New Mexico) and a background in science.

In their simplest form, EVPs (also known as Raudive voices after early EVP researcher Konstantīns Raudive) are heard as voices and bits of speech hidden among the background noise and static from radios, televisions, and other devices. Ghost hunters claim that such interference is created (or modified) by spirits trying to speak to us from unknown realms.

There are several ways that ghost hunters collect EVP samples; often it simply involves setting up an audio voice recorder in an empty room and then leaving. Other times, investigators will have recorders running as they walk through a supposedly haunted area. Sometimes ghost hunters will try to talk with any spirits they think might be present, asking questions of the empty room and waiting for a reply—any sort of "reply" at all will do, any noise or action from a creak to a tap.

Ghost hunters will later carefully review the tapes or audio files, turning the volume up high and increasing the contrast so that even faint background noises are made more noticeable. Many of the sounds are indistinct at best; repeated listening or extensive computer filtering may be required to discern any faint words. If the person listening to the recording hears anything that sounds strange, that will often be interpreted as a ghost voice. Scientific investigators never use this technique, because it is completely illogical and unscientific.

There is little mystery about what causes EVPs, and it has nothing to do with ghost voices. Psychological research shows clearly that our brains naturally look for meanings and patterns in the world around us; we are so good at finding patterns that we sometimes recognize them where they don't exist. One common example of this is when we see faces in random shapes like clouds. The faces are not really there, of course, but our brains subconsciously seek out dots that could look like eyes, an opening that could look like a mouth, and even a nose and ears. People who see faces in clouds aren't stupid or crazy; they are perfectly normal. Exactly the same phenomenon occurs when people hear EVPs.

Although EVPs can seem mysterious to those who haven't researched them, they arise via a well-understood psychological process called apophenia, which causes people to "hear" distinct sounds in random white-noise patterns such as the background static in an audio recording (or a phantom doorbell or ringing telephone while one is in the shower). James Alcock, a professor of psychology at York University in Toronto, notes that EVPs can be simulated in a laboratory setting: if the test subject is given an expectation of what they will "hear," and if the cadence of those words matches the cadence of the white noise, "then the brain will turn those sounds into those—now clearly discernible—words" (Alcock 2005). EVPs are created in our brains and influenced by our expectations. If a ghost hunter is expecting (or hoping) to hear words or phrases in faint sounds—especially in a place thought to be haunted—then he or she just might.

The problem is that it's not clear what the sounds are—whether they are ordinary random sounds from the environment or even sounds made by the ghost investigators themselves. Ghost hunters can accidentally create EVPs and "ghost voices" through careless investigative techniques. Since the microphones they use are often sensitive, they pick up very faint but ordinary sounds that most people without the benefit of such equipment don't notice. Despite a person's best efforts, it is impossible to be completely silent, even when sitting or standing motionless. Involuntary bodily functions like breathing make sounds, as does a growling stomach (the result of contracting digestive muscles and gas moving through the intestines, medically called borborygmus). Some ghost hunters have even accidentally recorded each other's farts—an evil scent, but not an evil spirit!

Then there are countless faint sounds that we hear but don't notice—fish tank bubblers, refrigerator motors starting up, clocks ticking, dogs barking, the wind howling, and so on. Sometimes an EVP sounds like a voice because it *is* a voice . . . not from beyond the grave, but from someone nearby. I investigated a case in Buffalo in 2003 in which exactly this phenomenon occurred. Amateur ghost hunters tried to record EVPs in a "haunted" house where they were sure that only ghostly voices would be recorded. They indeed recorded EVPs of voices and grew convinced that their house was haunted. But my experiments proved that their recorder was much more sensitive than they realized, and the faint voices were actually coming from passersby on the sidewalk near the house. So I know from firsthand investigative experience that this can be a problem (for more on this case, see Radford 2010, chapter 5).

Scientific investigators do not search for EVPs for several reasons. First, of course, there's no logical reason to think that a ghost or spirit would be able to speak, since speech is created by a physical body. Speech requires physical lungs to take in air and physical vocal cords in the larynx to create vibrations, which are in turn converted into intelligible speech by physical lips, a tongue, teeth, and a palate. If ghosts lack a physical body, then by definition they can't create speech; there's really no way around it.

Second, there are many telltale signs that EVPs are not ghost voices at all; one of the most obvious is that EVP "responses" are almost always nonresponsive. The ghosts who are allegedly communicating don't actually say anything meaningful but instead give random sounds and noises. A ghost saying, "Welcome to my home; my name is Ricardo Sanchez, and I died in 1925 of a gunshot wound," would be especially helpful and compelling for a science-based paranormal investigator. Instead, EVPs are almost always random words, and any meaning or connection to the location or situation is supplied by the ghost hunters' imaginations.

Third, it is virtually impossible to rule out all possible sources of sound contamination in nearly any haunted location. That is, in order to establish definitively that a given mysterious sound has no possible alternative explanation (and might therefore be a ghost), one must be able to prove that there were no other sources of sound anywhere. Haunted houses are often located in neighborhoods, with dozens or hundreds of people living within earshot—not to mention cars, radios, pets, wild animals, and so on.

THE GHOST WHO SAID "TOLD YOU"

Let's take a closer look at the primary EVP evidence offered by the WCGAPS. It's one of the team's most prominent pieces of evidence for ghosts at the Cuchillo Bar, and it appeared in several YouTube videos.* A male and female investigator are heard, apparently in the barn. The woman comments, "That is a pretty moon." Then there's a faint two-tone sound, followed by the man saying to her, "Did you know the moon used to be a lot closer?"

When the two-tone sound is replayed, the team believes that it's a ghost saying, "told you." The validity of this EVP is highly dubious, for several reasons. First, it's merely a brief, low sound that could have been created by anything; there's no logical reason to believe that it's a human or ghostly voice. Second, the sound was recorded in an open barn (figure 8.4); I investigated that barn and saw many potential sources of random environmental sounds, from small animals to wind. It is piled high with lumber, steel pipes, dirt, stones, adobe bricks, and other detritus. Third, the sound could be interpreted as nearly anything; although the team heard the low two-tone murmur as the phrase "told you," it could just as easily be heard as "toad stool," "toe shoe,"

* The "told you" ghost voice can be heard in a YouTube video titled "WCGAPS Investigates the Old Cuchillo Bar Property," available at http://www.youtube.com/watch?v=s2GFHgvlIto.

"cold blue," "old poo," or countless other short words or phrases. Furthermore, even if it were a ghost, why would it throw out a random phrase like "told you" that has nothing to do with anything anyone was saying? The idea that "told you" is an intelligent response by a ghost to the human comment, "That is a pretty moon," makes no sense.

It's also not clear why these two investigators were making random personal conversation during a supposedly serious ghost investigation. Random spoken words and conversations like this are exactly the sorts of activities that lead to false EVP evidence. Mentioning how pretty the moon is, or the fact that the moon's orbit used to be closer to Earth than it is now, is perfectly harmless banter—except when you are recording everything and will later be listening for the faintest sounds and interpreting them as ghost voices.

Figure 8.4. *Investigating the Old Cuchillo barn, where ghost hunters recorded ghostly voices. Photo by the author.*

Despite the lack of scientific validity, the team concluded: "Based on the quality of the EVPs and that they are in direct response to our questions [sic], we feel very confident in stating that the Cuchillo Bar does indeed have paranormal activity by what would appear to be least one male spirit." The team returned in October 2010 to do follow-up research in the form of more EVP sessions. The second session, somewhat predictably, resulted in more ambiguous sounds that were once again interpreted as ghostly voices. What is needed to prove that ghosts haunt Cuchillo (or anywhere else) is better-quality evidence, not more of the same poor-quality evidence.

INVESTIGATING WITH JOSH BOND

I'd heard from the ghost hunters about what they did and what they found, but I wanted to hear more about what Josh had to say. After all, the various ghost hunters only spent anywhere from a few hours to an overnight at the site at a time; Bond lives and works there, so he's around it all the time. It seemed that, to really understand what was going on, it was best to listen to the person who lives there instead of recording random sounds from around the property.

I met Josh at his front door, and he offered to show me around. I interviewed him as we wandered about the property. Josh said that most of the time he doesn't notice any ghosts, and he tries not to go looking for spooky sounds. "You know I notice things, and I hear things, and I write them off a lot of times. I normally have a TV or stereo going, just so I have white noise in the background, because like I said I got a lot of work to do, I don't want to spook myself too bad. And I really think the ghosts are on my side. I've never felt any threatening presences or been scared or anything like that."

"I write shit off a lot," Bond says. "My friends give me shit, because like I was replacing one of the windows and I had this big piece of glass leaned up in the courtyard, and it was against the wall, and there was no wind, there was nothing, there was no way, there was no way this glass could have broken, and it got flipped over and broke. I was bitching about it to a buddy and he was like 'Dude, come on, it's got to be ghosts,' and I'm like, 'I don't know . . . '"

"How many incidents would you say you've experienced?" I asked.

"You know, it really just depends on how I look at it. I'd say at least a hundred different things have happened since I've moved here. I mean since I originally bought my first place over hundreds, because the first house I bought was from the 1880s, and I used to have some pretty strange stuff happen there, so I sold it and bought the one behind it. That's the guesthouse that the investigators looked at. But yeah, I mean there's daily occurrences, but to validate them in my head as ghosts is kind of difficult sometimes. Just because you can't explain it doesn't mean it's a ghost."

Bond acknowledged that most of the "mysterious" sounds may have an earthly explanation. "Due to the conditions of the buildings, they are in a deteriorating state, so there's a lot of noises that happen naturally—roofs clanging and stuff," he said.

I asked Bond when the Cuchillo Bar had its heyday. He replied, "1850 was when this was most active, and then through to the 1900s this was basically the stagecoach stop for the mines and the railroads, so a lot of people would stop here." He was clearly conversant and enchanted by the history. "Cuchillo at that point was two thousand people, now it's down to thirty-five, and it was somewhat of a metropolis for farming communities, and this was the mainstay for this whole area, this stagecoach stop. The fire happened in 2000, so the store part closed in 2000, but the bar stayed open until 2003."

"And are there weird things going on in this particular place?" I asked.

"Yeah, the most recent thing I heard was whistling coming from the bar. I could hear it inside, almost like human whistling, like a song, like an old country song. And I came through the bar, and as soon as I got to the bar it stopped. I didn't find the cause, didn't find out what was making it, why it was happening. That was about a week ago." I looked around the area. Was it a musical, carefree ghost, or a breeze whistling through one of the many crevices in the area? Who knows?

I asked Josh to show me what possibly strange or potentially ghostly things he'd experienced, and he led me through the blackened, fire-ravaged room near the bar. It contained piles of stuff—some antiques that surely had value, some junk, and a lot of stuff in between.

"Whistling, knocks, shadows in the doorway, this doorway here. You know, I'm not here [in this room] a lot at night, for the obvious reason, I have to live here and I try not to spook myself too bad, because I have a lot of work to do ahead of me. So, I write off a lot of shit. I really should start writing stuff down as it happens, but to me, you know, I gotta live here and deal with it."

"And does this happen at particular times or different times?"

"Just different times, this was late afternoon when I heard the whistling. This is the old store, when the fire happened, they built this walkway here so the old lady who ran the store could get from her house to the bar. This got pretty devastated and is still pretty devastated, I have pictures of this in its original state and it's amazing."

We walked into the next room. "This is the bar," Josh said, gesturing with a wave of his arm. Sure enough, a row of eight dusty barstools sprouted from the worn wooden floor (figure 8.5). Across from them lay three wooden benches that were probably much more comfortable after a few drinks. Large, low windows that hadn't tasted Windex since the Nixon administration bathed the room in a hazy glow.

Rusted spurs dripped from the dark green metallic ceiling above the bar; below that were rows of wooden shelves holding innumerable bar items, from four generations of Coors cans to beer glasses, snuff boxes, horseshoes, and tip jars. In fact, there was a little of everything, from a metal scale that might have weighed out a prospector's gold to a tarnished little trumpet. Not everything was old, of course; it had been used as a modern bar fairly recently, after all. The walls, once white (or very light green), were stained and discolored.

Figure 8.5. *The haunted Cuchillo Bar has been the scene of a few spooky sounds including shot glasses being filled with liquor. Photo by the author.*

To my left, past a reach-in cooler (broken, of course), was a door to another room with bathrooms, as the hand-painted wooden sign above the doorframe (and below a pair of unimpressive old antlers) indicated.

"They [past visitors] had some stuff happen in here. I've had glasses fall when I was working in here, I've had things happen. . . . They heard the sound of liquid being poured. Kind of bizarre, I guess not too bizarre for a bar. I've gotten spooked a couple of times, I've had things fall off shelves, when I was over here something would fall over there. I've never heard voices in here, but I don't spend a lot of time in here, maybe since I bought the building I've spent about eight hours in here total, just cleaned it, this is pretty much how it was when I bought it.

"The bar dates back to the 1850s, when these buildings were a stagecoach stop, for the mines. There was constant activity in this town. I was told even by some of the locals that they wouldn't even go to T or C [Truth or Consequences], back then it was called Hot Springs, unless they had to, because everything they needed was right here in this town. . . . I've heard about some amazing fights in here, I've heard about a gunslinger named Bojorquez, who came in and raised all sorts of craziness. If those walls could talk it would be amazing. There's a lot of history here."

He opened the creaky, dusty bar door outlined in turquoise paint, and we stepped outside onto the wooden steps. I followed him about twenty yards toward a half-crumpled barn. "This is the barn, it's two stories, twenty-six feet tall at the peak, its one of the only two-story adobe structures this old in New Mexico still standing, although it's missing the second floor. When the Indians would attack, raid the area to get the horses, the locals here in Cuchillo would gather in the barn here to protect the horses from getting taken."

I wandered into the barn; there wasn't much to see except huge piles of lumber, steel pipes, tumbleweeds, nails, and broken adobes, accented with a dusting of broken glass. I remembered that this was where one of the ghost-hunting groups had recorded an EVP of a ghost saying, "told you." The barn was crumbling and wide open to the elements, of course, and sounds could have come from anywhere. As I kicked at some of the broken adobes, Josh continued, "Unfortunately some of the adobes were sold off, and it's in a deteriorating state, but much history to be had. I also heard at one point that sometime in the 1900s it was used as a whorehouse." I looked around at the small area and tried to picture a few scrabby beds bouncing with randy prospectors and their sweet painted ladies. Josh then led me back into the house to tell me more about the history. I was about ready to begin my own investigation.

THE GHOSTLY CLAIMS

The ghostly activity alleged at the Old Cuchillo Bar and Store is typical fare for a haunted location. It includes an overall spooky feeling; faint, unexplained whistles, knocks, or thumps; objects falling on the floor; and a cabinet door mysteriously opening on its own. Of these claims, only a handful can be investigated (for example, there's no way to prove or disprove the existence of a "spooky presence" or a feeling of being watched). Josh did not keep any record of his experiences, so there's no way to analyze the events to distinguish any patterns (for example, it might be that on the rare occasions that something had fallen off a wall or shelf, that was exactly the time when a heavy truck rumbled by on a dirt road nearby, possibly causing vibrations from the road).

For my investigation, I focused on events for which there was some sort of evidence, something that could be examined and tested, proved or disproved. While stories and anecdotes are interesting, ultimately they have never been useful in providing good evidence for ghosts. Real, hard evidence—like doors opening on their own or objects flying through the air—are much closer to what would be needed to provide proof of the paranormal. Even photos or videos would be *something*—but unfortunately there were no recordings of any paranormal activity. Although a glass fell off a shelf in the bar at one point, it was a long time ago and there's no way to know what caused it. (I've worked in many restaurants and have seen and heard empty glasses fall off bar shelves when no one was around; usually whoever put them there had been in a hurry and left them a little too close to the edge.)

While I investigated all the alleged haunting evidence at the Cuchillo bar in detail, here I will focus on the hard evidence. I couldn't really investigate incidents that had occurred months or years earlier, but I could examine things that were going on while I was there. These came down to three main claims: (1) strange noises; (2) mysterious lights and shadows; and (3) an antique cabinet that mysteriously opens on its own—in classic poltergeist fashion.

GHOSTLY SOUNDS

As I examined the building, I realized that the decrepit place was in perfect condition for creating "unexplained" sounds of all types. Simply standing still and quiet for more than a few moments revealed many creaks, thumps, bangs, whistles, knocks, and even some wheezes that might easily go unnoticed unless one is specifically listening for them. This is hardly paranormal or unexplained; it is a natural and predictable result of a badly damaged building.

Then there are the bats, rats, squirrels, rabbits, tarantulas, roaches, and other vermin that nest under the floorboards, in the ceiling rafters, behind the walls, and elsewhere throughout the building. As I played my flashlight along the walls and ceilings, I was startled by a pair of large bats who dive-bombed me (or at least it felt that way) on several occasions. The animals not only made typical high-pitched squeaks and flapped their wings, but at times made an eerie scratching sound of tiny claws on sheet metal. Although I didn't see any rats or squirrels firsthand, I saw evidence of their presence (droppings and trails in the dust); and Josh confirmed their presence. With so many hidden animals capable of making such a variety of noises—from growls to squeaks and hisses—it would be surprising if people *didn't* report hearing mysterious noises.

Furthermore, there are several jagged holes in the ceiling. During the daytime, of course, these admit erratic spots of light across the worn wooden floor (often revealing hovering clouds of dust); but both day and night they also produce a cross breeze, and air often flows freely through the rooms. In the process, the wind sometimes picks up pieces of debris in and around the holes in the ceiling. Wood, tarpaper, corrugated metal, plastic, and other materials on the roof and exterior walls are not nailed down but instead flap around freely in even a moderate breeze. Because Cuchillo is located in a canyon, the area's geography helps funnel winds over and around the Old Cuchillo Bar.

Josh was quick to admit that even some of the weirdest sounds could easily be the product of his imagination. After all, if it's dark and spooky and cold, almost anything might sound like a ghost. A low wind could create a hum that sounds like low murmuring in a bar, or a banging shutter could be interpreted as a distant gunshot. Without recordings to listen to and analyze, there's no way to know what they were. I finally realized that if ghosts did in fact haunt the building, they only made sounds that normally occur in a place like that. After hearing for myself the wide variety of natural, ordinary sounds the place made, I concluded that the most likely explanation for most of the "odd sounds" was the place itself.

MYSTERIOUS LIGHTS AND SHADOWS

I was more interested in tackling the strange lights and shadows that Josh and others had reported. Again, there were no photos or videos of these phenomena, so there was no evidence to analyze. But just because no one else had recorded the lights and shadows didn't mean that I couldn't, so I got my cameras ready.

I set up one camera on a tripod and turned it on while I walked through the building looking for possible reasons why people might report strange lights or shadows. For example, in previous ghost investigations I have found that unnoticed mirrors often reflect light into unusual places and create mysterious, ghostly effects.

After a few minutes of wandering, I turned a corner to find something bizarre: an eerie red glow on the floor. It was in front of an old chest and an old wooden desk chair. I was startled to see the mysterious light—it was one of the brightest lights in the dim room, and its color made it all the more spooky and mysterious (figure 8.6). I instinctively reached for the digital camera on my belt, wanting to get a photo before it disappeared. I wanted to document the phenomenon, get it recorded, *then* try to figure out what it was. I flicked the switch but the camera didn't turn on. No whirring or clicking. The batteries were dead!

Figure 8.6. *A mysterious blood-red light appeared on the floor at the rear of the Old Cuchillo Store; was it a ghost's way of revealing the location of his foul murder? Photo by the author.*

I rushed out of the room, flashlight in hand to light the way, to my investigation kit in the bar and grabbed my backup camera. I ran back to the room, trying not to stumble over the piles of detritus on the floor, while turning my camera on and steadying my hand for the shot. I turned the corner to capture the strange light—but it was gone!

The room was slightly darker than before; there was a little bit of light above and against a small chest that was coming from a small window on the opposite wall. But the blood-red light stain I had seen just twenty seconds earlier had disappeared. I didn't panic, and I wasn't scared—but I was pretty baffled. A shiver ran through me as I tried to figure out what was going on. Was it my imagination? Were my eyes playing tricks on me? Was there something in the room that I had surprised when I first turned the corner and saw it, but that was camera shy the second time? Did the ghostly crimson light reveal where a bloody murder had taken place, decades or even a century earlier? The gothic scene evoked a verse in my mind from Edgar Allan Poe's haunting poem "Annabel Lee": "The moon never beams without bringing me dreams."

I began to back out of the room, my eyes darting back and forth. I planned to go get my video camera and train it on that room in case the light returned when I wasn't there. At that exact moment, the light reappeared in front of me. I immediately took a photo to capture it. "I got it!" I almost shouted to nobody in particular. The digital camera's processing bar seemed to take years. I watched the little glowing green "busy" bar move from left to right, silently urging it along. I'm sure it took only a second or two, but it felt like hours. Out of the corner of my eye I could still see the mysterious light—it was right there on the floor, not going anywhere (this time). But I wanted to get it on film so other people could see what I saw.

Finally it was done, and I pressed the button to review the photo I had just taken. It came up, and I was in for another puzzling surprise: the light wasn't there. It didn't appear in the picture at all. There was the floor, and the chairs, and the chest, but no light. A split second later I realized why: the automatic flash had gone off and drowned out the faint red light with its harsh white flashbulb light. My blood pressure rising, I furiously thumbed buttons to turn the flash off and reset the camera. I did, and felt relieved when I still saw the red light through the viewfinder screen. I snapped the shutter and waited another eternity, and when the photo appeared I saw that I'd finally captured the ghost. I took a second photo, just to be sure, then I approached the mysterious light.

Now that I was closer to it (and not distracted by Byzantine camera operations), I could see it much more clearly. It wasn't actually blood red as I had first perceived, but more of an orange color. As I approached, a sliver of it disappeared, and I immediately recognized the silhouette of my left shoulder against the light. The strange light spot was coming from above and behind me; but if it was just light coming through the opposite window, why was it that creepy color?

I turned around to look at the window, which was filthy, hazy, and mostly blocked by clutter inside and outside resulting in dim, jagged light. But there, in the far bottom right-hand corner, I saw what was casting that orange light: a colored bottle on the outside window ledge, wedged between the window frame and what looked like a round metal beer sign (figure 8.7). Like the window itself, it was dirty, and indirect sunlight shone through in some places and not in others. That was clearly the source of the light spot, and when I looked at the spot on the floor again I realized why I had originally thought it was blood red instead of orange. My mind had been playing tricks on me, but it had help: the chest just behind the light was painted (or stained) red. When I first glanced at the light, I'd seen the orange, and the darker red behind it, and combined them in my mind.

I chuckled to myself on having been scared—well, not scared but *startled*—by a light from an antique bottle in a window. Yet it had been a real mystery, solved through some detective work. But as I took a photo of the bottle on the window, I realized that there was one nagging part of the mystery I hadn't solved: Why had the light disappeared when I went back to look for it?

The explanation was probably simple (someone or something outside happened to block the light coming through the window at the particular time I looked). I went outside to look; no one was around, but I did notice a ragged piece of black plastic (one of many) about the size of a refrigerator, hanging loosely above the eaves. Josh had placed it there to keep rain out of the damaged roof, and it swayed in the hot desert breeze not far above the window. As I watched for a minute or two I saw the plastic dip down and block the light that was streaming into the window, then rise back up again. As far as I was concerned, this mystery was solved. This kind of circumstance, or something like it elsewhere on the property (this wasn't the only colored glass bottle in front of a window), could explain other reports of odd lights, colored or not, in the building.

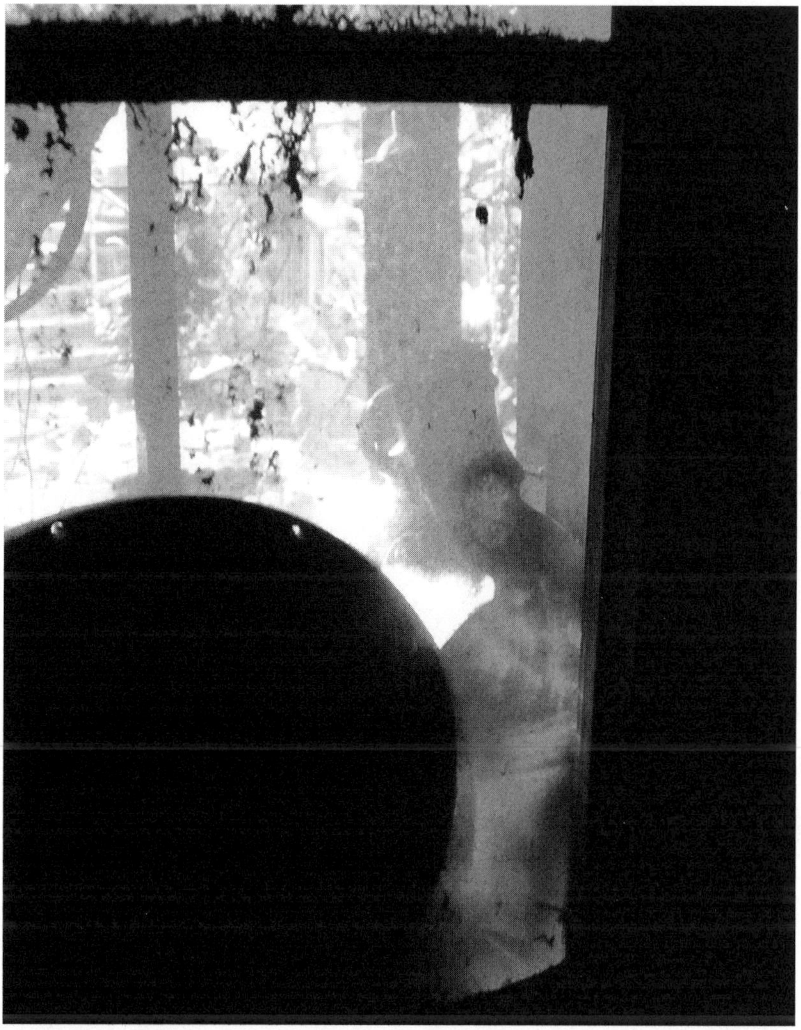

Figure 8.7. *The source of a mysterious ghostly light was revealed upon investigation. Photo by the author.*

SHADOWS HAUNTING THE BAR

Armed with a better understanding of what might create "unexplained" lights around the Old Cuchillo Bar, I continued my search but didn't see any other mysterious luminations, so I turned my attention to the shadows. There is no electricity in the main part of the building; cables and extension cords run from the main house to provide electrical light. In the main room, which used to serve as a general store (and still contains piles of dusty inventory), the only natural light comes in through the glass in the door. It was in this area that shadowy figures had been reported on a few occasions. After spending some time examining the area, I devised a hypothesis that might explain these apparitions.

During the daytime, the area around and just inside the doors is brightly backlit with sunlight glare, making it difficult to see what's there and creating odd shadows (figure 8.8). (This effect is apparent in pictures of people photographed in front of windows or other bright objects in the background.) The sharp contrast also creates an optical illusion of a ghostly afterimage as one's eyes try to adjust from the bright New Mexico daylight to the near pitch darkness inside. Under such conditions, people often see shadowy figures—but it has nothing to do with the netherworld and everything to do with optical illusions.

Figure 8.8. *The front of the old store, where strange, shadowy forms have occasionally been reported; optical illusions may explain some of the ghostly sightings. Photo by the author.*

Why do people report seeing dark shadowy movements that do not really exist? Recent psychological research has interesting answers that explain some ghost reports. It has been proven that certain patterns of light and dark, and patterns of colors, create the illusion of movement. Many examples can be found in books about optical illusions.

Researchers Vilayanur Ramachandran and Diane Rogers-Ramachandran of the Center for Brain and Cognition at the University of California, San Diego, note that scientists do not know exactly why this illusion happens; however, they continue, "What we do know is that the odd arrangements of luminance-based edges must somehow 'artificially' activate motion detecting neurons in the visual pathways. That is, the particular patterns of luminance and contrast fool the visual system into seeing motion where none exists" (Ramachandran and Rogers-Ramachandran 2008).

Thus we have a combination of circumstances that are known to create optical illusions: low light in most of a room combined with bright, glaring daylight coming through full-length windows; and both direct and indirect light coming from odd angles (not above, as we usually experience it, but from the sides and even below). Furthermore, I realized, the room was full of shadows because it is so cluttered. Normally we don't notice shadows in our everyday lives because light sources are above our heads, so the shadows of ordinary objects (furniture, people, pets, etc.) are cast more or less downward, out of sight and unnoticed. But throughout the Cuchillo property—and especially in the old storehouse area where most of the shadows were reported—the light is coming from the side from about knee level upward. This condition is guaranteed to create unusual shadows (and, likely, shadowy figures) as one walks through the room. Try this yourself: put a desk lamp on the floor in a darkened room, turn it on, and watch how ordinary shadows jump into your field of view.

If the shadowy figures had been photographed or videotaped, there would be more evidence to go on. But since they were fairly rare and not recorded, my best guess was that optical illusions combined with the unusual lighting were responsible for the shadows. Having solved (or offered plausible explanations for) two mysteries so far, I was eager to tackle the third and most puzzling phenomenon: the haunted cabinet.

THE HAUNTED CABINET

The only recurring physical phenomenon attributed to ghosts on the property was a kitchen cabinet door (figure 8.9) that Josh Bond said he would sometimes find open—despite the fact that he lives alone and that the cabinet had a metal latch that prevented the door from swinging open. The door simply could not have opened on its own without the help of some entity or force. Bond currently lives in that part of the building, which at various times was used as a guest house.

"This happens a lot. I go to bed and this is open when I wake up in the morning," Bond explained. "And it latches pretty good; it's not something you can just flick open, it takes some pressure. That's one of the weird things that happens in here pretty frequently. I didn't have this part of the house investigated because I live here and because I'm turning it into a vacation rental and I don't want to spook my guests too badly."

Doors opening or closing on their own are common in haunted house reports; the phenomenon is often attributed to poltergeists (German for noisy ghost). Although unusual, there may be natural reasons why a door might open on its own that have nothing to do with ghosts. Having some experience with similar phenomena from previous investigations (including at Louisiana's famously haunted Myrtles Plantation), I got to work.

I examined the latch on the cabinet door. It is of a style called the Hoosier Cabinet Lever Latch (figure 8.10) and consists of a small finger lever on the left plate, which, when lifted, pulls a small metal bar out of a corresponding hook on the right plate. When I saw this, the reports seemed even more mysterious. This type of latch is designed to prevent a cabinet door from opening, for example, from a passing breeze or from the cabinet being tilted forward slightly. It was physically impossible for the door to open without the latch being lifted. Could this be a hoax? Or was there really a prankster spirit nearby?

I then examined the entire cabinet, trying to figure out why *that* door—and only that door—was affected by the ghost. Why didn't any of the other cabinet doors with identical latches open on their own? What was different or unique about that particular door? Like almost everything else on the property, the cabinet is an antique. Various spaces in the piece hold spices, boxes of cereal, peanut butter, and other typical pantry items. The long, tall, haunted cabinet space, on the other hand, is different and unusual. It holds an antique flour dispenser, a device built into the cabinet and popular in the early 1900s.

Since that part of the cabinet was the oldest, one explanation might be that the resident ghost felt more comfortable opening a cabinet that contained something he or she might have used in real life, instead of a cabinet containing Red Bull energy drinks and Frosted Mini-Wheats. Or perhaps there was a more earthly explanation . . .

Figure 8.9. *This haunted antique cabinet is one of the biggest mysteries on the Old Cuchillo property. Does a playful ghost open the cabinet doors when no one is around? Photo by the author.*

Figure 8.10. *The lever latch on the haunted cabinet prevents the door from opening on its own. Some unseen force must be responsible for mysteriously opening the door—but what? Photo by the author.*

Josh left to run errands, leaving me to face the haunted cabinet alone. I waited for a while in the kitchen, silently daring a ghost to open the door in front of me (perhaps out of spite). As the minutes ticked by and nothing happened, I decided to take a more proactive approach.

Testing the latch several times, I noticed some resistance on the finger lift. It opened easily, but unlike the other latches, which hung free and loose, the latch on the large cabinet mysteriously held tension. Following up on this clue, I realized that the slight but continual outward pressure on the door, ordinary vibrations from everyday activities—closing doors, cooking, walking, cars driving by on the road outside, the washer and dryer operating on the other side of the wall, and so on—would cause the latch to very slowly and imperceptibly rise up, a fraction of millimeter at a time, until it finally popped open on its own and swung wide open because of the physics of inertia. There was an unseen force lifting the latch, but it wasn't a ghost.

I tested this hypothesis with a series of gentle knocks on the side of the cabinet. I watched closely, and with each rap the latch twitched up slightly; after three or four knocks, it popped open and the door swung wide. It took less than two seconds.

I realized why it would seem so mysterious and spooky. If this happened when someone was in the room—especially at night, and in a place already thought to be haunted—it would seem mysterious, supernatural, and maybe even terrifying. If, instead, the door opened with no one in the kitchen, to be discovered only later—say, upon waking in the morning and walking into the kitchen to find that someone (or something) had opened the cabinet door overnight—it would seem both unnerving and unexplainable. I had seen similar situations in many other ghost investigations, in which ordinary phenomena were given extraordinary meaning.

While the other cabinet doors and shelves were used regularly, the "haunted" cabinet door was never used. The flour dispenser was empty and probably had been for many years. Because there was nothing inside that cabinet except an empty dispenser, Bond had no reason to open it—and the fact that it would sometimes open on its own was therefore all the more mysterious.

But that didn't really solve the mystery: *Why* was there tension on the door? Was there a mischievous spirit pushing from the inside, trying to get out? Through a closer examination of the Hoosier cabinet, I determined the cause of the outward pressure on the door and its latch. The flour container, which was made of tin or aluminum, did not fit snugly inside the cabinet but instead bowed out slightly at the top. Although the cabinet door would easily close, the metal canister's slightly concave form pushed against the door from the inside. Every few weeks, ordinary vibrations would nudge the latch one tiny, unnoticeable bit higher until finally it would pop open at some random, unexpected moment. Physics, not psychics, solved the mystery of the haunted cabinet.

OVERNIGHT IN THE HAUNTED HOUSE

There was one final investigation I wanted to carry out: conducting an overnight investigation in search of spirits and the supernatural in the building Bond had for sale on eBay. Josh took me to the house where I'd be staying. It was, he said, the most haunted location on the property—partly because a few of the other ghost hunters claimed to have found a lot of activity there. Although I wasn't terribly impressed with the "evidence" that had been collected in that house, I was eager to see for myself. Maybe better investigative techniques would reveal better evidence. Maybe there was nothing going on at all—or maybe this would finally be the place where I'd see my first ghost. I was game. I was joined by Chris Ayles, a colleague who had accompanied me on previous investigations, including into the jungles of Nicaragua in search of the bloodthirsty monster *el chupacabra* in 2009 (see Radford 2011, chapter 4).

We walked through the open screen door and into the kitchen. "So [in] this house I've always felt like there was a presence in this kitchen," Josh said. "Always. There was a woman who died in this house in 1959. It always feels like there's movement in here for some reason. I mean I've had a lot of things happen in this house, a lot of noises. . . . You know, it's a 150-year-old house, so you're gonna have noises, but when I bought the house literally every room was piled so high you couldn't even see into the room. I would sleep in here, spooked as shit. . . . I'd shut every fucking door I could and turn the TV up all night, drown it out, it was pretty creepy."

I put my gear down on the kitchen table and we followed Josh into the next room. "This room had horrid wallpaper all over it. This is the shrine that was in the house when I bought it. . . . But you know, the house was just full. I have wedding dresses and all their [the previous owners'] old stuff. And I'm someone who just can't throw this stuff away. To me it's a part of the history of this place, just all their old clothes."

He showed us two other rooms in the small house and a lumpy mattress that would serve as a bed. I told Josh that I wouldn't be sleeping at all that night, but it would be a good place to nap after sunrise the following day.

"That's it." Bond shrugged. "You're on your own. You wanted to spend the night in the creepiest place I have, so this is the house I offered you guys."

We looked at him. "So if we get so totally scared that we start screaming can we knock on your door?"

Josh smiled a strange smile, like he didn't know if we were joking, and even if *we thought* we were joking, he wasn't so sure that we'd be laughing when the witching hour was upon us. He left, and I looked at my cell phone and noticed that there was no reception; whatever happened—something or nothing—I was completely cut off from the outside world.

Chris and I explored the place, looking around and taking photographs of each of the rooms. One of the ghost-hunting teams claimed to have heard objects moving in an adjacent room, but they didn't see anything when they went to investigate. Unfortunately, they apparently neglected to photograph or film the rooms and their contents beforehand so they could compare before-and-after photographs to see what, if anything, had moved—or if they were only hearing tricks of acoustics. (Whenever possible, I try to learn better investigative techniques from other researchers' mistakes.)

To be honest, the experience was something of a letdown. Chris left around midnight, needing to return home to sleep for work the next day. I stayed up until dawn, passing the long hours walking around, listening for sounds, looking for lights or anything else that might seem strange. Cameras and recorders were on and ready. I did find a stack of old newspapers dating back to the 1940s, and I read those. Josh appeared at one point a little after midnight to check on me; I assured him that everything was fine so far.

Despite the long hours patiently waiting for anything odd or paranormal to happen, the ghosts were a no-show for me. There were a few unnerving moments early in the morning when a slow, low creaking sound echoed throughout the house—followed by a leaden thud, then more creaking. Flashlight in hand, I soon traced the sound to an exterior door swaying in the night wind. Of course it's possible that the ghosts had overheard my conversations with Bond and, knowing that I was a skeptic, refused to appear for me just out of spite. I finally tumbled into slumber at about seven o'clock, slept for a few hours, and then went to find Josh to report back (and get some breakfast).

CONCLUSION

As I left the Old Cuchillo Bar and Store, I reflected on my investigation and realized that, out of at least a half-dozen investigators and ghost hunters, I was the only one who had found rational, logical explanations for the various reported phenomena. I made a sincere, sustained effort to investigate what was going on—I was in the field observing, not dismissing or debunking—and in the end I found no evidence that the place was haunted by anything other than bats, rats, and decades of other people's debris.

I reported my findings back to Josh; I showed him why the cabinet door in his kitchen mysteriously opened on its own. I explained some of my findings about the odd sights and sounds (which he had largely agreed with all along; he always suspected that most of the sounds were normal). Understandably, he was slightly disappointed that I'd found no real evidence of ghosts.

I had begun my investigation by explaining to Josh that I'd approach the case from a skeptical, science-based position. I'd do my best to understand what was going on, without really caring if the answer turned out to be good evidence for ghosts or no evidence for ghosts. Josh accepted my conclusions with good nature; after all, to him I was only one of several investigators who had examined his property, and the others had concluded that his place was indeed haunted. The fact that I had solved most or all of the mysteries there (and could explain why the EVP evidence was in fact worthless) was irrelevant.

To Josh, the fact that I brought more science and research to my work (and was therefore a better-qualified investigator) probably didn't matter. He had already posted quotations and testimonials on his website from ghost-hunting groups concluding that the place is haunted; one more investigation (albeit a more in-depth and scientific one) suggesting the opposite wasn't going to change that. My research at the Old Cuchillo Bar was featured on the local news station KRQE-TV in October 2009. As of the time of this writing, five years later, the Old Cuchillo Bar's website does not have a link to the KRQE broadcast (which is posted online), nor is there any mention of my investigation or its conclusions.

Josh believed that his building was probably haunted, if only because it's so old. I agree with him, in a way. The same things that are characteristic of (and reported in) a haunted house (cold spots, mysterious lights and sounds, etc.) are characteristic of (and reported in) old houses and buildings in poor condition. The list is virtually identical. So in order to establish if there's anything genuinely odd going on, one must rule out phenomena that are ordinary in crumbling buildings.

There's a strong correlation between how old a house is and what condition it's in. With the exception of buildings that have been professionally restored because of their historical value, older houses are almost always in worse shape than newer houses. And when a building is half-destroyed by fire, rain, and other agents, odd sights and sounds are guaranteed. The other part, of course, is psychology. Our minds and eyes can play tricks on us, and—as I personally experienced—it's easy for our imaginations to create mysteries where none exist, especially in a dark, cluttered, spooky old building.

There's a difference between an investigator *expecting* to find ghosts (based on a location's reputation as being haunted) and *being open* to finding evidence for ghosts. Launching an investigation with the assumption (conscious or unconscious) that ghosts are there is just as detrimental to an objective conclusion as starting out assuming that no ghosts are there. Keeping an open mind can be difficult, but it's essential for distinguishing truth from fiction. I was there and reviewed all the evidence that Josh Bond and other investigators had collected. In this case, based on the evidence I saw and my own investigation, I found nothing supernatural, paranormal, or unusual; all the strange phenomena were almost certainly due to the condition of the buildings and the environment, not ghosts. (Previous ghost hunters came to more or less the same conclusion.)

So why had I found answers where others had failed? I think there are several reasons. One is that I investigated Josh's original claims instead of trying to generate my own claims and evidence. Second, from my background in science and psychology, I recognized that the ghost voice recordings had no scientific validity, and therefore I didn't waste my time pursuing a dead end. Third, I didn't give up; I kept working until I solved the various mysteries. Often the difference between something "mysterious" and something "explained" is longer hours, better logic, and harder work. When ghost hunters call some phenomenon a mystery or an enigma, it simply means that *they* can't figure it out, given the information they've collected from whatever effort they put in.

It doesn't mean that the phenomenon defies explanation or that someone else may not be able to solve it (as in the case of the haunted cabinet). I also spent more time investigating at Old Cuchillo than previous ghost hunting groups had.* My visit was one of the most complete and in-depth investigations at the Old Cuchillo Bar ever conducted. Although other teams had shown up with more team members and more equipment, they had failed to find plausible solutions to the mysteries and in fact often ended up generating new mysteries (such as the EVPs). Often, well-meaning but scientifically misguided ghost hunters will accidentally create new "evidence" that they fail to debunk, while not fully addressing the original claims.

Whether or not I think that ghosts haunt the Old Cuchillo Bar is irrelevant. Josh Bond is convinced that some unknown presence or energy lives alongside him on his ramshackle property. For Josh and many ghost hunters, the mystery—and the ghosts—will remain. It is possible that resident or transient spirits do in fact haunt the Old Cuchillo Bar, despite little or no evidence. Like many spooky places in the Land of Enchantment, if it's not haunted, it should be.

ACKNOWLEDGMENTS

I thank Chris Ayles, Josh Bond, and all the ghost hunters who shared their knowledge and experiences.

REFERENCES

Alcock, James. 2005. "Electronic Voice Phenomenon: Voices of the Dead, or Just So Much Static?" Press release, Committee for the Scientific Investigation of Claims of the Paranormal, January 6. http://www.prweb.com/releases/2005/01/prweb194167.htm.

Associated Press. 2009. "Ghost Hunters Inspect 180-Year-Old Hotel." May 11. http://www.foxnews.com/story/2009/05/11/ghost-hunters-inspect-180-year-old-hotel/.

Bond, Josh. 2009. Interview by Benjamin Radford, July 9, 10.

* According to their report, the WCGAPS group only spent about six hours actively investigating the haunted location (starting at 9:00 p.m. and ending at 3:00 a.m., with the balance of the time spent sleeping, looking at archives, or setting up gear). In contrast, I spent over twenty hours at the location over the course of two visits, looking for evidence of ghosts or the paranormal.

Hopper, Kevin. 2009. "N.M. Ghost Town/Bar Convincingly Earns Its Title." *Local IQ*, July 30–August 12.

Radford, Benjamin. 2010. *Scientific Paranormal Investigation: How to Solve Unexplained Mysteries*. Corrales, NM: Rhombus Publishing.

———. 2011. *Tracking the Chupacabra: The Vampire Beast in Fact, Fiction, and Folklore*. Albuquerque: University of New Mexico Press.

Ramachandran, Vilayanur, and Diane Rogers-Ramachandran. 2008. "A Moving Experience." *Scientific American Reports*, Special Edition on Perception.

Rice, Andy. 2009. Interview by Benjamin Radford, July 29.

West Coast Ghost and Paranormal Society. 2013. "Old Cuchillo Bar and Store." http://www.wcgaps.com/investigations/2009-investigations/2009-06-old-cuchillo-bar-cuchillo-nm/.

Wierima, Brian. 2011. "Bringing Science and Technology into the World of the Paranormal." November 10. http://www.dl-online.com/event/article/id/64169/.

CHAPTER 9

MIRACLES OF THE HOT EYE

OJO CALIENTE'S HEALING WATERS

Highway 285 is a picturesque road that winds through the low hills of northern New Mexico, not far from where the Chama River joins the Rio Grande. The road connects Santa Fe and Taos, but those in too much of a hurry to get between the two might accidentally miss one of the state's hidden treasures. Nestled along the Rio Ojo Caliente is the town of Ojo Caliente with its famous springs.

Ojo Caliente, about two and a half hours from Albuquerque, is said to be America's oldest spa. Many come from around the state and indeed from around the world to soak in its famed healing waters. According to the Ojo Caliente Mineral Springs Resort and Spa, "Our sulphur-free, geothermal mineral waters have flowed from a subterranean volcanic aquifer for thousands of years. Ojo Caliente is the only hot springs in the world with a remarkable combination of four different types of mineral water: lithium, iron, soda and arsenic. Over 100,000 gallons per day come to the surface, revitalizing those who soak in the long believed healing waters. Our ten pools are filled with different types and combinations of waters with temperatures ranging from 80 to 109 degrees."

THE HISTORY OF OJO CALIENTE

Although the town of Ojo Caliente (the name means "hot eye" in Spanish) is more than just its famous hot springs, its rich history is closely tied to what is now the Ojo Caliente spa. The official history is provided to visitors in the spa's brochure:

Steeped in myth and legend, these ancient springs have been a gathering place and source of healing for hundreds, even thousands of years. The use of the waters can be traced back to the earliest human settlements in the region. Ancient people, believed to be the ancestors of today's Native American Tewa tribes, built large pueblos and terraced gardens overlooking the springs. Posi or Poseuinge, "village at the place of the green bubbling hot springs" was home to thousands of people [and] a vibrant center of activity in the fifteenth century. Surrounding the springs today is substantial evidence, including clay shards and arrows, of prehistoric civilization in the ruins of the cities populated before the birth of history. In the 1500s the Spaniards, in their quest for gold and the Fountain of Youth, also discovered the Springs. One explorer's record cites, "The greatest treasure that I found these strange people to possess, are hot springs which burst out at the foot of a mountain. . . . So powerful are the chemicals contained in this water that the inhabitants have a belief that they were given to them by their gods. These springs I have named Ojo Caliente."

Enter explorer Zebulon Pike (Pike's Peak discoverer), who, while under arrest in 1807 for exploring New Spain without permission, was marched to Santa Fe, passing through Ojo Caliente. He observed the hot springs as "the greatest natural curiosity." Antonio Joseph, a man prominently connected with the history of New Mexico and recognized as one of the most influential citizens of the Territory, next noticed these unusual waters. Born in Taos in 1846, his parents moved there from Missouri and opened the first general mercantile establishment in that area. Enduring hardships, the family remained, but sent Mr. Joseph to be educated by Bishop [Jean Baptiste] Lamy in Santa Fe, New Mexico. . . . In 1868 . . . Mr. Joseph moved to Ojo Caliente, where he opened Ojo Caliente Mineral Springs as the first natural health spa in the country. Joseph's Ojo became a hub of activity by providing overnight lodging, a Post Office, and a general store where historical ledgers show Kit Carson frequently purchased supplies.

At Ojo, Mr. Joseph built a sanitarium, which soon became known throughout the country as a place where thousands of invalids were annually cured. . . . The famous and the infamous have taken these waters. Volumes of testimonials filled with declarations of miracle cures abound. Whether unproven folklore or not, generations of the faithful continually make the pilgrimage back to these special waters.

What began as a simple stone and wood bathhouse has grown over the years. A hotel was built in 1916, and it is now listed on the National Register of Historic Places. In the 1970s and 1980s Ojo Caliente had the look and feel of an old hippie commune, although by the 1990s the owners had begun to embrace the lucrative and burgeoning upscale New Age–oriented spa business model (figure 9.1). The spa even has a labyrinth on the property (see chapter 10), where people are encouraged to walk, meditate, and heal. The Ojo Caliente hotel used to have a bulletin board just inside the front door where travelers left testimonials about their healings and experiences. That bulletin board is long gone, and it seems that the miracle cures that were once abundant and nationally known are rarer (or at least less publicized).

Figure 9.1. *The Ojo Caliente Mineral Springs Resort and Spa, where sacred waters have bubbled up for millennia. Photo by the author.*

HEALING WATERS

Water, of course, has long been a symbol of cleansing, purification, renewal, and rebirth. Many religious rituals involve water and incorporate the liquid in important rituals; for example, in Christianity baptism washes away spiritual sins, and in Islam water cleansing is performed before prayer (and after sex). There are countless legends of healing and curative waters all around the world—indeed, the source of eternal life and youth was said to be a water fountain.

Figure 9.2. *Bathers at the Ojo Caliente cliffside pool, coming for healing and relaxation. Photo by the author.*

Water is the basis of all life, and it's not surprising that the handicapped and the sick would be drawn to it. Stories of miracle cures and healings are an integral part of Ojo Caliente. What special healing properties do the waters hold? The different types of water are used to treat different types of health problems, according to signs placed near each spring:

THE LITHIA SPRING: Located at the heart of the springs, the historic pump has been dispensing this unique water since the nineteenth century. Lithium is believed to relieve depression and aid digestion.

THE IRON SPRING: A Native American legend tells that the giant rock in the iron pool guards the place where the ancient people of the mesa once received food and water during times of famine. The warm, iron-rich water bubbles up from the natural pebble floor, providing hot spots to discover in this mystical outdoor cliffside pool. Iron is considered to be beneficial to the blood and immune system.

THE SODA SPRING: The rock walls in the enclosed soda "steam" pool create a soft echo providing a sense of calm and relaxation. Water from the Soda Spring is said to have been used to relieve digestive problems.

THE ARSENIC SPRING: The arsenic water is believed to be beneficial for relief from arthritis [and] stomach ulcers and to heal a variety of skin conditions. Water from the iron and arsenic springs is blended in various pools throughout the property.

"During most of the early part of the 20th century," one source says,

> Ojo Caliente was best known as a sanitorium, where sick people journeyed to "take the waters" and seek a cure. Indeed, the New Mexico Bureau of Immigration claimed in 1900 that "these wonderful fountains of health cure the most dreadful of blood diseases: kidney and stomach disorder; paralysis; rheumatism; malaria and many forms of female complaints." Nowadays, people still benefit from both drinking and bathing in the waters. Some visit for a few days—while some devote much longer. The idea is that the waters help to eliminate excessive acids and other toxic impurities from the body, encouraging better health and more energy. The three types of springs are tapped and named after their differing origins. The Iron waters are thought to be beneficial to the blood. In trace amounts, Arsenic is thought to be relieving to arthritis, rheumatism, stomach ulcers and even helps to heal burns and eczema. Last but not least, the Soda and Sodium Lithia springs are good for over-acidic stomach problems and assist with depression, sluggish kidneys and excess stomach gas. (Hotelbook 2011)

I have visited Ojo Caliente almost a dozen times since the 1970s and fondly remember the days before the healing waters freely mixed with aromatherapy-scented commercialism. In the past, the primary activity was to soak in the hot waters and take in a "milagro wrap" (being wrapped like a mummy in towels, fresh from the steaming water). Since that time, much has been added on, including luxurious cliffside suites, new cottages on the north and south ends of the property, and even an RV park.

These days, a wide variety of treatments and classes are available, including yoga; woga (water yoga); hot stone therapy; an Ayurvedic "herb formula of neem, lotus, and gotu kola" said to heal "prematurely aged hands"; reflexology; deep-tissue massage for $150; an "energy-balancing" foot massage; and even a special four-day "Ojo Escape" for $899 per person (which includes many of the above services plus a free tote bag). As of 2014, lodging costs between $120 and $449 per night, and reservations are recommended.

What is the secret behind the stories and legends of healings, cures, and restorative treatments offered at Ojo Caliente? To find out, I examined the treatments offered at the spa, the baths at the hot springs, and the characteristics of the waters themselves. A full investigation of all the treatments available at Ojo Caliente is far beyond the scope of this book, but I'll touch on the three most popular: energy balancing, reflexology, and sweat therapy.

ENERGY HEALING AND BALANCING

There are many alternative medicine therapies that claim to "balance" human energy fields, such as Therapeutic Touch, Reiki, and some types of yoga. Today, many people go to New Age and holistic practitioners to get their chakras, chi, or auras balanced. The idea of health being a state of balance has a long history, much of it mired in antiquated medical practice and belief. Medieval medicine held that disease was caused by an imbalance of bodily fluids called humors. There were four humors: yellow bile, black bile, phlegm, and blood. Working under this premise, physicians treated patients by trying to restore harmony and balance among the humors. Bloodletting was a common treatment (veins would be opened with knives and leeches applied to sick patients), along with the use of emetics, laxatives, and purgatives.

There is an attractive simplicity to the humor model, although it was thoroughly debunked with the advent of modern medicine a few hundred years ago. No medical doctor these days will search for an imbalance of the humors in a sick patient. Yet many modern alternative medical treatments, including those offered at Ojo Caliente, rely on just such a theory of equilibrium, seeking to balance not humors but other energies that are likewise unknown to science and medicine.

Reiki, for example, is offered at the spa and is claimed to relax and heal by balancing a universal energy (called *reiki*) in the patient. However, Reiki has never been proven effective (see, for example, Lee, Pittler, and Ernst 2008), and mainstream medical organizations such as the American Cancer Society and the National Center for Complementary and

Alternative Medicine have found no evidence supporting claims that Reiki is effective for treating any condition or illness. Even a review in the generally pro–alternative medicine *Journal of Alternative and Complementary Medicine* found that "serious methodological and reporting limitations of limited existing Reiki studies preclude a definitive conclusion on its effectiveness" (vanderVaart, Gijsen, Wildt, and Koren 2009).

Indeed, the entire premise behind Reiki rests on unproven theory and speculation instead of established fact. Repeated scientific studies have failed to show that a human energy field even exists (whether one calls it aura, chi, ki, prana, etc.), much less that this hypothetical energy field is subject to disease-causing imbalances. Many Reiki healers admit that there is little or no scientific evidence for their claims, but they insist that they "feel the energies" and defensively assert that they don't need the Western "medical establishment" to validate their approach.

It is medically true that "imbalances" can cause disease in some cases, but not in the way usually assumed. You can view a correctly functioning organ as being "in balance" if you like, but it is not a medically accurate or useful label. A kidney or lung that is not working properly or is cancerous is simply that; there is no "imbalance" of substance or energy that need be—or can be—corrected. A person with the flu caught the disease from a flu virus, not from having an energy imbalance.

The underlying promise of these "energy balancing" therapies also implies a "normal," baseline state of affairs—but how do we know what that state of affairs is? With a concept as elusive and subjective as "balance," how does one really know when one is balanced? If achieving such a balance leads a person to become perfectly happy and healthy, this ideal is unnatural and unsustainable. Just because you're feeling good one week and bad the next doesn't necessarily mean that something is out of "balance." Normal life has ups and downs, good and bad, joy and sorrow. Real life is not "balanced." I suppose that one could somehow try to strike a balance between the good and the bad, the happy and the sad, but how would that be done practically? Wouldn't that suggest that a person who had just enjoyed a wonderful experience ought to immediately seek out a depressing one to keep it all in balance? Like many things, the idea of energy balancing has a certain intuitive, superficial appeal. But once you scratch the surface and start asking some simple, logical questions, problems arise.

REFLEXOLOGY

The Ojo Caliente spa also offers reflexology treatments. Robert Todd Carroll, chair of the philosophy department at Sacramento City College, explains the premise:

> Reflexology is based on the unsubstantiated belief that each part of each foot is a mirror site for a part of the body. The big toe, for example, is considered a reflex area for the head. Reflexology maps the body with the feet, the right foot corresponding to the right side of the body and the left foot corresponding to the left side of the body. Because the whole body is represented in the feet, reflexologists consider themselves to be holistic health practitioners, not foot doctors. . . . Practitioners of reflexology claim that they can cure a variety of aches and pains by massaging the correct reflex points on the foot. It is said by those who practice it that reflexology can cure migraine headaches and relieve sinus problems. It can restore harmony to hormonal imbalances and cure breathing disorders and digestive problems. If you have a back problem, a massage on the right spot on the right foot (which might be the left foot in some cases) can alleviate your suffering. If you suffer from circulatory problems or have a lot of tension and stress, reflexology promises relief. (Carroll 2003, 328)

One of the most popular reflexology products of the past decade are Kinoki brand foot pads. The manufacturer's promotional literature describes how the large, adhesive bandages work: "Formulated in Japan using all-natural tree extracts and powerful negative ions to rid the body of harmful toxins, this foot pad works on the principle of foot reflexology. Simply place the pads on the soles of your feet (or a targeted body part such as the shoulder or knee) before going to bed. By morning the pad will have absorbed toxins accumulated in your body from pollution, radiation exposure, etc., turning the white pad to a shade from gray to black." The Kinoki pads remove "heavy metals, metabolic wastes, toxins, parasites, chemicals, and cellulite" from the body. According to reflexology, there's no need for expensive liposuction or plastic surgery: the pads remove cellulite. And since they absorb radiation, they can apparently also be used in the event of nuclear accidents, like the one that devastated Japan in 2011.

How, exactly, this is done is never explained. How do the pads know which of the body's countless chemicals (many of them crucial for good health) to remove? Furthermore, even if the pads worked as described, they couldn't leach out enough toxins or heavy metals to make a difference. For those not impressed by the plentiful testimonials, perhaps the most effective sales tool is the pads themselves, which do indeed turn to an unappetizing color within a day or two of putting them on your body. All that disgusting black color must be toxins coming from *somewhere*, right?

Well, maybe not. One writer, Chris Woolston (2008) of the *Los Angeles Times*, conducted a little, "not-quite scientific experiment: I put a few drops of sterile saline solution on a fresh pad. The result: a dark-gray, unsightly mess that looked exactly like the pads I'd been pulling off my feet. Either moisture alone can discolor the pads or the saline industry has some explaining to do. The pads also turned dark after a few minutes near a warm fireplace."

If people feel better after using the Kinoki pads, it's for the same reason that people feel better after using other discredited devices and therapies: the placebo effect. People subjectively report feeling better after getting any treatment, whether genuine or sham. Indeed, academic physician and researcher Edzard Ernst concluded that "the best evidence available to date does not demonstrate convincingly that reflexology is an effective treatment for any medical condition" (Ernst 2009). Although there's no evidence that reflexology does anything medically beneficial, there's plenty of evidence that having your feet rubbed produces smiles!

SWEATING OUT TOXINS

While New Age treatments such as Reiki and reflexology have not been shown to heal or cure anything, the most popular spa treatment at Ojo doesn't involve imaginary body energy or theoretical links between one's feet and one's organs. It involves a much more down-to-earth (and indeed earthy) process: sweating.

Sweat lodges in various forms have been around for millennia. The purification that people seek in sweat lodges is partly physical and partly spiritual. Most people who visit sweat lodges and steam rooms do so because they want to "sweat out the bad stuff" or "sweat out the toxins." Indeed, this is exactly what the Ojo Caliente springs are claimed to do: "The idea is that the waters help to eliminate excessive acids and other toxic impurities from the body, encouraging better health and more energy." (Of course just being in a hot spa feels nice, but you can get essentially the same experience in a really hot bath.) Indeed, as one Ojo Caliente spa brochure touts, their mud pool helps detoxify the body: "Slather mud all over your body and bake in the sun until done. As our special blend of clay dries, toxins are released from the pores of your skin and you come away feeling cleansed and refreshed" (Ojo Caliente 2006).

The idea that the body can sweat out toxins is widely believed and accepted. Hot springs and pricey spas around the world offer "sweat wraps" and sweat lodges, promising to detoxify and purify the body. Steam rooms can be warm and relaxing, but there is no scientific basis for the idea that people can "sweat out" toxins or impurities from the body.

Sweating is the body's method of regulating its own temperature. Because humans are warm blooded, our bodies need a way to control excess heat (generated either internally through a fever, or externally, as on a hot summer day). When the body gets too hot, it releases water via sweat glands, which in turn cools the skin and body through evaporation.

Organs such as the liver help the body collect and get rid of toxins, but sweat glands do not. Sweat, which is mostly water with some dissolved minerals and urea, is nontoxic, and therefore the idea of "sweating out the toxins" is simply wrong. Sweating will make you cooler, but it won't cleanse or purify your body. Human physiology simply does not work that way. Family physician Jeffrey Cain, president of the American Academy of Family Physicians, explains: "Sometimes when someone has a fever they think that if they pile on the pajamas and get under a lot of blankets they will sweat out the virus. There's no science to it. When you break a fever, you will sweat, and as your fever goes down, you'll get chills. But you can't sweat out a virus" (Mahany 2012). Similarly, while the mud and clay in the Ojo Caliente mud pool may be relaxing and fun, the clay does not "release toxins from the pores of your skin," as advertised. A steam bath or sweat wrap can be relaxing, but it is no more "cleansing" than a hot bath—and a hot bath can be far safer than a sweat lodge.

Indeed, sweat lodges can be harmful—and even deadly. On February 3, 2011, New Age motivational speaker James Arthur Ray was charged with three counts of manslaughter for his actions during an October 8, 2010, sweat-lodge ceremony he held near Sedona, Arizona. After an hour inside a small, steam-filled tent, some participants collapsed and others began vomiting. Ray encouraged them to stay and endure the discomfort as a form of cleansing that would make them stronger. In the end, three people died, eighteen were hospitalized, and several others were sickened. Ray was later convicted of three counts of negligent homicide and sentenced to two years in prison. Exposure to conditions that one typically finds in a sweat lodge can lead to heat stroke, dehydration, smoke inhalation, or suffocation.

The Ojo Caliente spa does post disclaimers about potential health dangers: "Hot water and sudden body temperatures can be stressful to your body. If you are pregnant or have chronic health problems, please consult your healthcare professional. The consumption of alcoholic beverages may impair judgment and/or cause loss of consciousness and is strongly discouraged."

THE ROLE OF PLACEBOS

This analysis leads us to another puzzle: If scientific medicine shows that these treatments and therapies are not effective, how can we explain the fact that thousands of people are convinced that they were healed or cured by them? The answer lies in psychology.

It is well known that many patients pursue (and often swear by) treatments that do not work. Many alternative treatments have no scientific proof that they work, including homeopathy, ear candling, faith healing, and vibrational or energy healing. The problem is that it's often not clear whether something "works" or not, especially when it comes to health issues.

That's partly the result of the well-known placebo effect: in some cases, people will feel better because they *think* that a treatment will make them feel better. That does not mean that a patient's beliefs about a certain treatment, in and of themselves, have any amazing healing powers. The placebo effect appears in a limited number of medical situations, usually involving subjective measurements such as pain relief. Believing that a pill or treatment will cure cancer or regrow a lost limb won't make it happen, and believing that a treatment is effective does not make it so. As mentioned earlier in the case of balancing humors, both patients and doctors were convinced for centuries that disease was caused by an imbalance of imaginary fluids in the body called humors, and that bleeding was really an effective cure. After all, the treated patients (those who didn't die of the disease or the treatment) usually did get better.

Although the treatments offered at the spa don't appear to have any special curative or restorative powers, perhaps there's a special benefit to soaking in the waters themselves; after all, when "thousands of invalids were annually cured" by Ojo Caliente's waters in the late 1800s, none were offered New Age treatments!

Despite the centuries-old reports and claims of miracles, cures, and healings, it seems that many of the treatments offered at Ojo Caliente have little or no basis in medicine. That doesn't mean that they may not feel great and be worth every penny—it just means that there's very little science underlying many of the treatments. Perhaps there's more to the mystery . . .

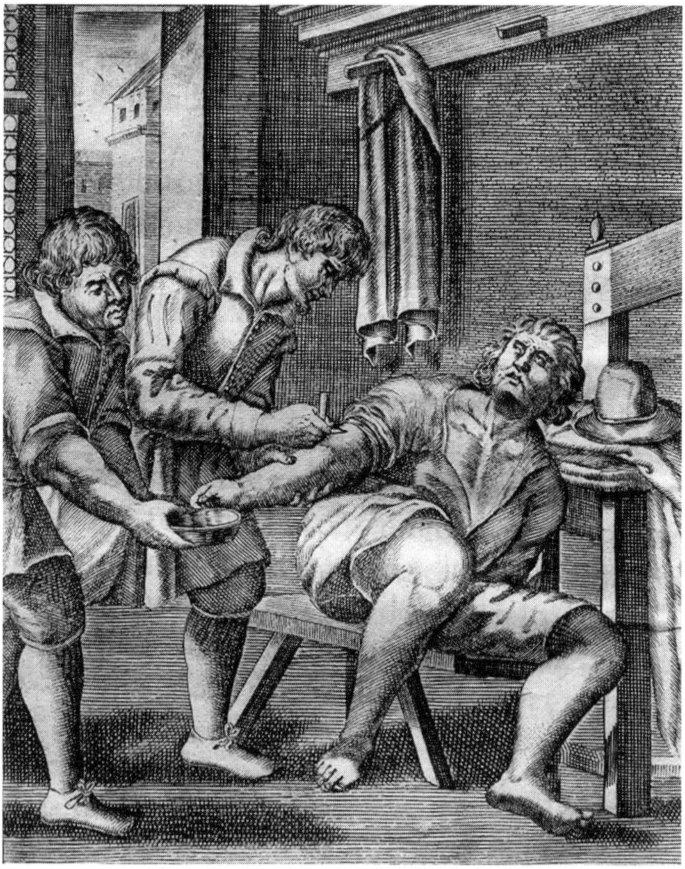

Figure 9.3. *"Bloodletting Scene," by Cintio d'Amato. Medieval Italian physicians treat a patient by bloodletting in this 1671 woodcut. (In* Nuoua et vtilissima prattica di tutto quello ch'al diligente barbiero s'appartiene *[Naples: G. Fasulo, 1671]. http://www.nlm.nih.gov/exhibition/horse/blo_bloodletting2.html.)*

INVESTIGATING THE HEALING WATERS

As we have seen, there is a long history of claims about the healing and curative properties of the sacred waters of the Hot Eye. Is it possible to find any truth to these stories? What do we know about the famed waters of Ojo Caliente from a scientific and geochemical point of view? Could they somehow cure a person who soaks in or drinks the water?

Well, the waters bubble up from four to six thousand feet below the earth's surface, rising through the Ojo Caliente geological fault zone, which runs roughly in a northeasterly direction. The water itself does not come from the earth's interior (at least not directly); instead, the flow comes from snow and rain runoff from highlands in northern New Mexico. That water seeps into the ground through leaching and geological fractures, finally making its way toward Ojo Caliente, where it is brought to the surface by geothermal activity. James Witcher (2002) of the Southwest Technology Development Institute at New Mexico State University notes: "The hot springs at Ojo Caliente are associated with calcium carbonate deposits of tufa [a variety of limestone] or travertine. The Ojo Caliente fault zone has many tufa deposits along its trace in the region from Ojo Caliente to La Madera as well as some warm springs. A shallow, 87-foot deep, hot well produces 128 to 132 degree Fahrenheit water. The Ojo Caliente springs range in temperature from 95 to 111 degrees." Aside from heat, the waters contain many minerals and elements: "The well and spring waters have total dissolved solids between 3,600 and 3,700 milligrams per liter."

When discussing the benefits of a soak in hot springs, it's important to recognize up front that a big part of the healing and curative qualities of the water is of course its temperature. Soaking in a hot bath or sauna feels good; it relaxes muscles and relieves tension. Many medical conditions and injuries use heat therapy (thermotherapy) to reduce pain and inflammation, relieve joint stiffness, and increase blood flow.

Because of this, many conditions and ailments will be temporarily relieved by soaking in hot water. That's hardly mysterious or miraculous; but what of the stories of amazing healings and cures? Could there be something special in the water, some curative element that medical science should explore?

To find out, I visited Ojo Caliente several times (I wish all my investigations involved soaking in hot springs!). I interviewed people, examined records, and collected samples from two of the most popular wells and springs: iron and lithium.

I submitted the samples to Albuquerque's Hall Environmental Analysis Laboratory, an accredited lab that routinely performs tests for soil, water, air, and environmental contaminants. The waters were analyzed for levels of beryllium, calcium, iron, lead, potassium, sodium, arsenic, and lithium.

TABLE 9.1

Iron Well

Element	Quantity (ppm)
Beryllium	0.031
Calcium	25
Iron	0.038
Lead	ND
Potassium	36
Sodium	950
Arsenic	0.26

ND: not detected

Lithium Well

Element	Quantity (ppm)
Beryllium	0.030
Calcium	26
Iron	0.47
Lead	ND
Potassium	34
Sodium	920
Arsenic	0.28
Lithium	3.01

ND: not detected

MINERALS AND MIRACLES

There's something quaint and appealing about the idea of absorbing nutritive or nourishing minerals while you soak in a natural hot springs. After all, you get to relax while toxins are leached from your body and replaced with all-natural minerals from deep inside the earth. (Of course, if the toxins are released from your body into the hot springs' pool water, they would then be floating around to be absorbed by everyone else in the pool—yuck!)

However, there's no truth to this idea. Human skin acts as a very formidable barrier to many things, from bacteria to toxins.

Indeed, according to the field's standard reference, *Casarett and Doull's Toxicology*, "Human skin comes in contact with many toxic agents. Fortunately, the skin is not very permeable and therefore is a relatively good barrier for separating organisms from their environment. . . . The absorption of toxicants through the skin varies, depending on the condition of the skin." Another factor is the hot water itself: water plays a very important role in skin permeability. Ordinary skin is about 7 percent water by weight, and when the skin absorbs water (such as occurs during a long hot soak), this results "in an additional two- to threefold increase in permeability" (Klaassen 2001, 656).

So hot springs do make the skin more likely to absorb various minerals. However, minerals in water are not absorbed through the skin except in barely detectable, negligible amounts. And the concentration of these elements in water is quite low. For example, the lithium well water contains 0.47 parts per million of iron, so out of two million units, less than one of them is iron. Even with the increased absorption through waterlogged skin, it's clear that little if any of these minerals will actually enter a person's body. People get far more of these elements and nutrients from a daily multivitamin, or an apple. The human body takes in nutrients by eating and drinking them, not soaking in them.

Thus, when the signs around Ojo Caliente state, for example, that "water from the Soda Spring is believed to relieve digestive problems and arthritis symptoms" and "the arsenic spring water is believed to be beneficial for relief from arthritis [and] stomach ulcers and to heal a variety of skin conditions," they are not referring to sitting or soaking in the water but instead drinking it—and perhaps not even then. While we all need vitamins and minerals, most people get all the minerals they need from their diets; even multivitamin supplements are usually unnecessary. Although the average person "taking the waters" won't get any additional minerals during their soak, many visitors to Ojo Caliente bring empty bottles to collect the well waters to drink. So let's turn to the benefits of drinking the waters. Of the eight elements tested (beryllium, calcium, iron, lead, potassium, sodium, arsenic, and lithium), the two that would have a noticeable effect on health in the quantities present are lithium and iron.

THE LITHIUM LIFT

One ingredient of the waters that could possibly heal or cure (at least temporarily) is lithium, which acts on the central nervous system to reduce the symptoms of mania and is widely thought of as a general, all-natural mood lifter.

The lithium well, located in the courtyard of the spa, is an especially popular place to pump drinking water with an old-fashioned crank handle (figure 9.4). A placard on the well states: "The lithia spring water is believed to produce positive effects in mental health balance, relieve depression, and aid digestion."

While there is some truth to this, it's important to realize that there's little evidence that lithium does anything for people not suffering from mental illness: "Lithium has no effect on normal mood but reduces the tendency toward mood swings in about 70% of the people with manic-depressive illness" (Berkow 1997). Thus, any "positive effects" on mental health will only be seen in those with preexisting mental illnesses such as depression and bipolar disorder. If you're just having a bad day or need a mood lifter, lithium won't help.

Figure 9.4. *A sign touts the famous healing waters of Ojo Caliente's hot springs. Photo by the author.*

Indeed, according to Emory University School of Medicine psychiatrist Charles Raison,

> although lithium is not FDA approved as an augmentation strategy for treating depression, there is probably more evidence supporting the efficacy of lithium in this regard than for any other strategy, except for perhaps some of the newer anti-psychotics like Abilify. . . . Lithium is primarily known for its use in bipolar disorder, where it has been shown to be quite effective in treating manias and moderately effective in preventing/treating depression and in keeping people's moods stable over long periods. But it also has been known for years to rapidly convert antidepressant non-responders to responders and to do so at doses lower than are required for optimal treatment in bipolar disorder. No one knows for sure how it works as an augmenting agent, but many scientists suspect that its effects may trace to an ability to increase activity of the neurotransmitter serotonin. (Raison 2010)

Furthermore, "because lithium takes four to ten days to work, a drug that works rapidly, such as haloperidol, is often given at the same time to control excited thought and activity" (Berkow 1997). Thus any perceived mood lift within the first few hours (or days) of visiting Ojo Caliente is not the result of the lithium itself but the expectation of the benefits—essentially the placebo effect—or simply the relaxation of visiting such a beautiful place.

The other issue is medicinally effective dosages; while the exact amount of lithium prescribed by a doctor will vary by patient and circumstance, the typical oral dosage for adults with acute mania is 600 milligrams or 10 milliliters three times a day, and half those doses for long-term treatment of mania (Mayo Clinic 2011). The amount of lithium present in the waters from the lithium well is 3.01 milligrams per liter. Therefore, a person would have to drink two hundred liters (more than fifty gallons) of the water to see any effect. Common brand names of lithium include Lithobid, Eskalith, and Eskalith-CR (controlled release). There are also some risks associated with using lithium: "Possible adverse effects of lithium include tremor, muscle twitching, nausea, vomiting, diarrhea, thirst, excessive urination, and weight gain. Lithium can make acne or psoriasis worse, can cause the blood levels of thyroid hormone to fall, and rarely can cause excessive urination. A very high level of lithium in the blood can cause a persistent headache, mental confusion, drowsiness, seizures, and abnormal heart rhythms. Adverse effects are more likely to be found in the elderly" (Berkow 1997, 402–3)—although, again, the levels are so low compared to the typical therapeutic dosage that a person would be unlikely to be able to take in that much. Still, the lithium well sign notes: "This is not an EPA or NMED approved drinking water source. Drink at your own risk."

IRON WELL

Aside from lithium, another mineral present in (relatively) high quantities at Ojo Caliente is iron, which, along with iodine, is the mineral that people most commonly suffer from deficiencies of. Most people, however, do get enough iron in their diets, usually from meat, beans, peaches, and other foods. Surprisingly, there's more iron in the lithium spring water than in the iron spring water—ten times more, in fact.

As it does with lithium, Ojo Caliente promotes the health benefits of iron: according to a sign posted at the cliffside pools, "iron is considered to be beneficial to the blood and immune system, prevent fatigue, and promote healthy skin tone." This is basically true, but the sign is misleading. Iron is indeed an important mineral and plays a crucial role in the body's processes. Iron deficiency can lead to a condition called anemia, which in turn can lead to physical weakness, impaired muscle and motor control, intestinal problems, impaired learning ability, skin discoloration, and other unpleasant effects.

The sign implies that the iron content in the waters will increase the iron content in the body through soaking (otherwise, what's the point of posting the sign in the bathing area?), which, as we have seen, is not true. Unless one is anemic or eating a very poor diet, neither soaking nor drinking the waters will provide any additional useful source of iron. Furthermore, Ojo Caliente clearly caters to an upscale clientele; people who aren't getting enough to eat (or a balanced diet) likely won't be spending much time in the spa's pools or visiting the well-apportioned wine bar.

In the final analysis, although the hot spring waters do contain the minerals claimed (such as iron and lithium), the minerals can only be taken by drinking the waters, not soaking in them. Most people already get all the minerals they need, and in any event there is simply not a high enough concentration in the waters to a make difference. One exception may be the calcium that's present in the water, which has been used as a digestive aid for millennia; it's possible that ingesting some of the calcium-rich waters might help an upset stomach.

ARSENIC AND THE OLD PLACE

The test results do raise an important caution: the arsenic levels in the two samples suggest that neither should be ingested. In 2006 the National Drinking Water Standards (NDWS) set 10 ppb (parts per billion) as a safe limit for arsenic content; the Ojo Caliente iron well has twenty-six times that amount, at 260 ppb, and the lithium well has twenty-eight times the safe amount, at 280 ppb. Arsenic is a tasteless and odorless element, which makes it difficult to know when you're drinking it. It has been used for centuries as both a medicine and a poison. Short-term effects, which can occur within hours or days of ingestion, can include headaches, confusion, severe diarrhea, and drowsiness. Long-term exposure to arsenic has been linked to cancer of the bladder, lungs, skin, kidneys, liver, and prostate.

If the Ojo Caliente waters were the only potential source of arsenic, drinking the waters wouldn't be that worrisome; however, because arsenic occurs naturally, many people are already exposed to elevated levels in their everyday environments. If one drinks a lot of the water or is not in good health to begin with, arsenic is a concern. After all, a place known for its healing and curative waters will attract the unhealthy and infirm for exactly that reason. Those who are sick or desperate for treatment may be exactly the people most likely to drink as much of the water as they can if they believe that it holds the potential for a cure.

As with anything, moderation is key; drinking a few glasses of the Ojo waters probably won't hurt you. From a scientific and medical point of view, the issue comes down to potential harm versus potential benefit: there are no known health benefits to drinking the water at Ojo Caliente, but there are known potential harms. Simply soaking in the hot springs is enough to relax and rejuvenate anyone.

As I researched and visited Ojo Caliente, I kept hoping to come across some modern documented cases of miracle cures and healings. What about the early reports of the disabled walking after visiting the springs, or tuberculosis-ridden bodies returning to health after a soak in the waters? Such reports seem to be the stuff of legend. Like many of the miracle healings at Chimayo (see chapter 2), there are many stories and testimonials but few if any proven cases.

To be fair, Ojo Caliente is no longer actively promoting its history of (alleged) healings and miracle cures. The spa is careful not to make any outright false statements about the medical benefits of its waters that might trigger complaints, peppering their signs and literature with qualifiers such as "is believed to," "is considered to," and "is said to." Fair enough; Ojo Caliente is a hot springs, not a hospital. People go there to relax and soak in the waters, to meditate and refresh—not to cure cancer. And, of course, it is possible that true miracles have occurred there. Miracles or not, skeptics and believers alike can visit this picturesque retreat and ponder the mysteries of the Land of Enchantment as they look up at a blackboard sky from the soothing waters.

REFERENCES

Berkow, Robert, et al., eds. 1997. "Depression and Mania." In *The Merck Manual of Medical Information: Home Edition*, 402–5. Whitehouse Station, NJ: Merck Research Laboratories.

Carroll, Robert. 2003. *The Skeptic's Dictionary: A Collection of Strange Beliefs, Amusing Deceptions, and Dangerous Delusions*. New York: John Wiley and Sons.

Ernst, Edzard. 2009. "Is Reflexology an Effective Intervention? A Systematic Review of Randomised Controlled Trials." *Medical Journal of Australia* 7, no. 191: 263–66.

Hotelbook. 2011. Review of Ojo Caliente Mineral Springs Resort and Spa. http://guides.hotelbook.com/sisp/index.htm?fx=event&event_id=34616.

Klaassen, Curtis, ed. 2001. *Casarett and Doull's Toxicology: The Basic Science of Poisons*. New York: McGraw-Hill.

Lee, M. S., M. H. Pittler, and E. Ernst. 2008. "Effects of Reiki in Clinical Practice: A Systematic Review of Randomised Clinical Trials." *International Journal of Clinical Practice* 62: 947–54.

Mahany, Barbara. 2012. "Keeping the Doctor Away, Through Folk Wisdom." *Albuquerque Journal*, January 2, C1.

Mayo Clinic. 2011. "Lithium (Oral Route)." December 1. http://www.mayoclinic.com/health/drug-information/DR600869/DSECTION=proper%2Duse.

Ojo Caliente Mineral Springs Resort and Spa. 2006. "Soothing Body, Mind and Spirit Naturally . . . for Centuries." Promotional brochure, November.

Raison, Charles. 2010. "Is the Use of Lithium Common in Depression?" CNN Expert Q&A, June 15. http://edition.cnn.com/2010/HEALTH/expert.q.a/06/15/lithium.depression.raison/index.html.

VanderVaart, Sondra, Violette M. Gijsen, Saskia N. de Wildt, and Gideon Koren. 2009. "A Systematic Review of the Therapeutic Effects of Reiki." *Journal of Alternative and Complementary Medicine* 15, no. 11: 1157–69.

Witcher, James. 2002. "Ojo Caliente: America's Oldest Spa?" *Geo-Heat Center Bulletin*, December.

Woolston, Chris. 2008. "Kinoki Foot Pads' Detox Claims Don't Stand Up to Science." *Los Angeles Times*, September 22. http://www.latimes.com/features/health/la-he-skeptic22-2008sep22,0,2825052.story#axzz2nr32fNoo.

CHAPTER 10

LABYRINTHS

SACRED SYMBOLS IN THE SAND

The middle-aged woman in the flowing, earth-tone dress moves simply; her arms and hips swing wide in fluid motions as she steps ahead lightly but purposefully. She's not in a ballroom or a nightclub; she's tracing her way into the center of a giant labyrinth. For her, the pattern at her feet is a spiritual path as much as a physical one. Her rhythmic humming slows as she nears the center, and she delicately steps into the flower-shaped space. I watch, with interest and a touch of reverence, as she bows long and deep in four directions, stretches, closes her eyes in meditation for a few moments, then begins to retrace the path out. Although she's only about thirty feet away from the outside of the labyrinth, her journey out will take nearly five minutes.

The woman is one of several people drawn one sunny spring day to walk a labyrinth just outside Santa Fe—part of a growing worldwide movement devoted to using the pattern for meditation and spiritual renewal. Hundreds of labyrinth books, websites, videos, and seminars have appeared in recent years, and organizations all over the world promote them, including several in the Land of Enchantment.

Labyrinths are designed in grass fields, inlaid in beautiful floors, and painted on giant canvas sheets. Unlike a maze, there is only one path to follow, leading to the center. While most people are content to simply walk the labyrinth, some take the opportunity to actually dance it. The joyous and rhythmic movements enhance the experience for some: "Often the labyrinth is symbolized by a spiral drawing on the ground . . . along which the dancers wind inward, left to center in the direction of death, and out again right, in the direction of life" (Grimble 1970).

Figure 10.1. *A classic Cretan-style labyrinth. Illustration by the author.*

Usually, the walking itself is pretty straightforward: follow the path in, and follow the same path back out again. Unlike a maze, which has different paths and choices, one cannot get lost in a labyrinth. Courtesy dictates that one remove one's shoes for indoor labyrinths, and loose clothing seems to be the norm. More than one person can walk the path at the same time, slipping silently by each other as they pass. While at the center (the "rosette"), some people give thanks to deities or meditate. Some leave offerings; at a shrub labyrinth in Lily Dale, New York, for example, I found fifty-seven cents in change, a small black feather, a few leaves, and a half-finished cigarette. (I've always wondered whether the smoker resolved to give up the habit then and there.)

On the way back out, walkers are encouraged to focus on any revelations, healings, experiences, or answers that may have come to them. Although labyrinths are often used for meditation and relaxation, they are also employed for various ceremonies such as graduations, coming-of-age rituals, and so on. Sometimes the walks are accompanied by chanting, drumming, or other music. The journey can take a surprisingly long time to complete, especially in large patterns.

I first heard about labyrinths from my mother. On a visit to her house one dark fall day I saw a pattern laid out with fist-sized stones in the sandy dirt near her small garden not far from the Rio Grande. Years later when she got married, the ceremony was conducted in the center of a larger labyrinth, and the bridesmaids and others walked the design. Curious about my mother's new interest, I decided to do a little research. The philosophical roots of the labyrinth revival were more Byzantine than I had imagined, tracing back in some cases to Freud, feminism, and even theories rejecting science and logic. My inquiry became a personal investigation that eventually drew me to hundreds of labyrinths on three continents.

A HISTORY OF LABYRINTHS

The labyrinth is an ancient symbol, and although its exact origins are murky, early versions have been found in Crete and Italy. Many cite Egypt as the source of the labyrinth (Grimble 1970), where it "was the scene of religious dramas involving the god-king in the shape of a bull" (42).The bull motif carried over into later incarnations; the most famous legend involving a maze or labyrinth is that of Theseus, who slew the bull-headed Minotaur inside a maze and found his way out with a line of thread. The labyrinth design is clearly laden with symbolic meanings, many of them involving universal themes of death and rebirth.

In their book *Labyrinths from the Outside In*, Donna Schaper and Carole Ann Camp (2000) tell of fishermen in Sweden, Finland, and Estonia building labyrinths as good-luck tools. They "walked them before going out to sea to ensure a good wind and a good catch. The fishermen would walk into the labyrinth slowly, presumably with trolls, who represented ill-fated intentions, following them. Then they would run out of the labyrinths quickly and jump in their boats, leaving the slow-thinking trolls behind stuck in the labyrinth" (4).*

Labyrinths have also been found in the American Southwest: the Hopi Indians used classical seven-circuit labyrinths, a symbol that appears on pottery and jewelry. Although many writers (e.g., Middendorf 2000; Schaper and Camp 2000) claim that the giant earthen Nazca Lines in Peru are labyrinths, this is not true. Like labyrinths, the designs—some clearly of animals such as monkeys, spiders, and birds—are unicursal (made with one continuous, uncrossed line), but they completely lack any labyrinthine pattern (figure 10.2).

* This theme of confusing or confounding pursuing evil spirits is common in folklore around the world. Some traditions hold that one way to escape pursuing vampires is to throw a handful of rice behind you; the vampire must stop and count each of the grains of rice before continuing the chase, allowing the lore-savvy would-be victim a chance to escape.

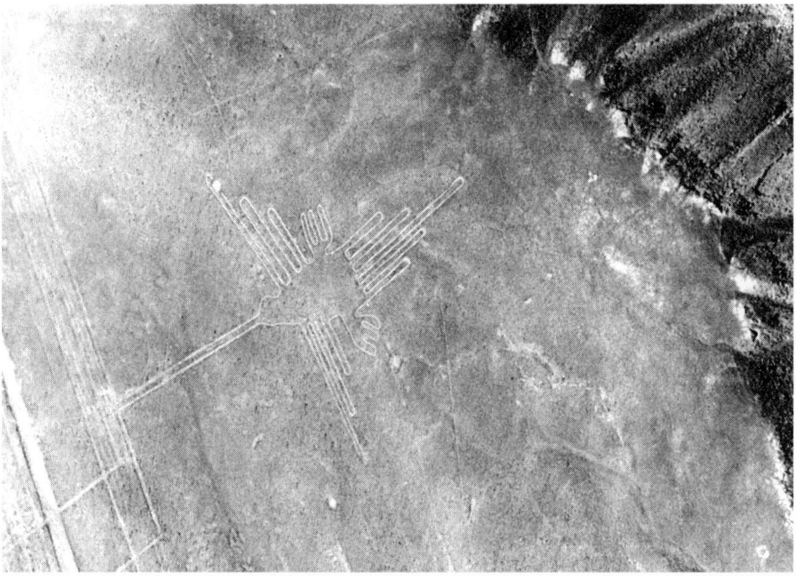

Figure 10.2. *The huge Nazca Lines in Peru are often claimed to be labyrinths; however, they are not, as they lack the distinctive labyrinth pattern. Photo by the author.*

Figure 10.3. *This design is found on the floor of the Chartres Cathedral in France, one of the best-known and most beloved labyrinths in the world.*

The surge of interest in labyrinths since roughly 2000 is largely credited to Reverend Lauren Artress, author of *Walking a Sacred Path*, widely regarded as the bible of the labyrinth "revival." Her 1995 book crystallized much of the interest in labyrinths for the New Age world and beyond, and she remains a popular speaker and activist.

There are several types of labyrinths; one of the most common is the seven-circuit form. The most influential labyrinth design is inlaid on the floor of France's Chartres Cathedral (figure 10.3); that pattern has been duplicated on hundreds of floors, walls, and canvases. Labyrinths can be made of chalk, cloth, stones, or well-placed shrubbery; others, like one in downtown Toronto, are cultivated in grass. Still others, like the Labyrint Waalkade in Nijmegen, Holland, are created from stone and water.

NEW MEXICAN LABYRINTHS

Taos, New Mexico, is one of the top labyrinth destinations in the world, containing more than two dozen public and private labyrinths. The town and its environs likely have among the highest labyrinths-to-residents ratios of any municipality in the world, and it seemed like the perfect place to explore labyrinths more deeply.

In May 2011 my mother and I joined a labyrinth tour of Taos, hosted by a nonprofit educational group, Living Labyrinths for Peace. The tour began at Kit Carson Park and took the better part of the day, visiting nearly a dozen different labyrinths in the region. The tour was led by John Acker, a longtime labyrinth devotee and development director for Living Labyrinths for Peace. I asked him how he had gotten involved with the labyrinth movement. "In 1999 I built a labyrinth at Kit Carson Park," he told me. "We took the elements of a dream that I had had, and played them out in a public art way, and had people walking through it and interacting with this dream enactment." The purpose of the Living Labyrinths for Peace project, he said, "is to unite all the human disciplines in a way to bring inner peace into world peace through the labyrinth . . . and to promote labyrinths and education."

Much of the labyrinth's power lies in the design shape itself, he explained. "There are between four and six basic designs, but new ones can be created. For the most part they move from the outer to the inner, which is a metaphor for moving from the outer world to the inner world of yourself. People use them for all sorts of prayer work, affirmation work, getting answers to questions, meditation, prophecy, and so on. . . . In Native American lore the spiral of life is the archetype of the labyrinth, which is the outer to inner and back again; it's a metaphor for the life journey and transformation."

We began with one of the most remarkable labyrinths in the area, located at a cozy place nestled just off the road called the Adobe and Pines Inn. It's a seven-circuit design, sixty-six feet in diameter and laid out in slate, with a water fountain bubbling peacefully at the rosette (figure 10.4). The outer ring is lined with a variety of native plants, "spaced so that there's blooming all year long," Acker noted. "For example the blue flax comes up, then the artemis and others, it blooms all the way into October, it makes it really nice."

I walked the labyrinth and immediately noticed something unusual about it. Each labyrinth is unique; I've walked hundreds of different designs, but there was something peculiar about this one. What felt different? I wondered as I wandered.

A few turns later I figured out what it was: it wasn't some mystical cosmic energy but something more earthly, at my feet in fact. I looked down at the unusual light-brown textured surface I was treading upon.

Figure 10.4. *This sandstone-and-shrub labyrinth at the Adobe and Pines Inn in Taos, New Mexico, has a water fountain in the center. Photo by the author.*

I leaned down and scooped up some in my hand: crushed pecan shells. They created a pleasant, buoyant effect with each step—very different from pavement, tile, grass, or any other surface we usually walk upon. It was a brilliant touch to an already impressive labyrinth.

When I completed my path out, Acker told me more about the design. "As you walk each labyrinth the energy that you experience is very different. This particular one is a very unique design; it's actually a combination of two different designs. There's the concentric circle, which is the first half of the labyrinth, then it goes into a spiral of life, which is the traditional Native American design." The two types of labyrinths reflected the designer's parents' ancestries: European and Native American.

Acker pointed to a rectangular stone receptacle holding some small rocks near the entrance. "As you begin you take a stone and put your intention into it and as you come to a place where you feel resolution, that's where you put your stone down, as a mark that something happened for you there. The pond in the center with a waterfall is wonderful because you hear it as you're walking the labyrinth, but when you get to the center and you're standing over the top there's this rush of natural sound and connection that takes place."

I took notes and photographs as others took their turns, and I sat in the grass to reflect on my walk. As with previous labyrinths I'd walked, I did not experience any transcendental connection to the universe; I didn't feel any of the mystical earth energies or healing vibrations that Acker, Artress, and others had mentioned. Then again I'm a generally practical, skeptical, science-minded type.

But I did have a wonderful time. It was a peaceful, calming, meditative walk in the sunshine and fresh air. Each person's experience is different, and just because I didn't feel some cosmic connection doesn't mean that no one else did. In a way, that's the whole point of the labyrinth: the experience is what you make of it. After some light refreshments—including foil-wrapped chocolates that I pocketed a handful of—we were off to see more.

PHILOSOPHIES BEHIND THE LABYRINTH

As we drove, we discussed the fact that each person experiences a labyrinth differently, that it's a very subjective experience. In her book, Artress discusses the value of the imagination at length; it's clear that imagination is very important to experiencing the powers of the labyrinth. "The labyrinth is an evocative tool. It works through the imagination and the senses" (Artress 1995, 97). In other words, the more imagination you have, the more likely the labyrinth will work for you.

Artress believes that the spiritual crisis and environmental decay that she sees in our society is partly the result of a lack of imagination. New Age feminism plays a prominent role in labyrinth literature, often denigrating "rational, male-centered thinking" in favor of feminine, nurturing, "intuitive" thought. For the woman who spawned the current movement, labyrinths are more than just an interesting design; they are a tool for reconnecting with both imagination and femininity. *Walking a Sacred Path* frequently portrays our modern world as too rational, unimaginative, and out of touch with wisdom, and the twelfth and thirteenth centuries as the good old days of unreason, when our connection to the Earth was strong and women were valued. (Artress ignores the fact that, during the time she claims women were more valued, they were actually considered to be the property of men, denied education, and so on).* "We are beginning to realize that Western civilization—held together by rationalism, empirical research, and man's control of nature—is coming apart," Artress writes. "As we in the West learned to use our rational minds, we developed a sense of superiority that denied our intuition and imagination their rightful place among the human faculties we need to survive" (Artress 1995, 106). (Non-Western cultures might find Artress's implication that they never learned to be "rational" insulting.)

Although this paradigm is appealing to many, it is also simplistic and somewhat contradictory. Barbara G. Walker, writing in *Skeptical Inquirer*, cautions against taking the male/female paradigm too far:

* It is interesting that much of the feminist-influenced theory behind the labyrinths is rooted in Sigmund Freud, whom many believe to have been sexist and even misogynistic. It was Freud, after all, who developed the theories of penis envy (that women, lacking a penis, secretly felt inferior to men) and hysteria (the "wandering uterus"—that women have a condition in which subconscious emotional conflicts are manifested as severe mental dissociations or physical symptoms; the underlying anxiety is assumed to have been "converted" into a physical symptom, and this was considered to be a female disease brought about by movement of the uterus). One labyrinth source, www.sacredwalk.com, notes that "it is important to express these [painful] feelings so that we move through this to the next place in our lives, without taking the baggage of hurt with us." This message, common in labyrinth literature, is Freudian through and through: our current problems won't be resolved until we deal with their causes and begin a transition. Some feminists have come full circle from deriding Freud for his antiquated and sexist notions of women to embracing him for his insight in resolving issues for transition.

> We [feminists] are in danger of going too far into our own brand of dualism, when we label patriarchal and bad everything that is modern/scientific, while declaring matriarchal (or natural) and good everything that is primitive/magical. At the same time, we accept with off-handed ingratitude the gifts of technology that are made available to us every day: electric light, radio, television, telephones, trains, airplanes, cars, [and] computers. . . . Only science, with its objective, "linear" approach, could have discovered bacteria, viruses, [and] antibiotics. . . . Almost everything that we can claim to know with any certainty about our world has been learned through science and not by subjectivity, instinct, or insight. (Walker 1993)

While this false "Paradise Lost" nostalgia theme is common, other writers see labyrinths not so much fulfilling a void of imagination as serving as a kind of user-friendly spirituality. Donna Schaper believes that many people are shunning the traditional, rigid rituals of religion and "widening their claim to worship in nature—hiking a mountain, for example, rather than sitting in a designated worship space" (Schaper and Camp 2000, 31). In this way, labyrinths are a more accessible path to God or enlightenment. Labyrinth walkers can take a spiritual journey on their own terms, when they wish, how they wish, and more or less where they wish.

Perhaps responding to a desire for easy spirituality, many churches have embraced labyrinths and built them on their grounds. The best-known church labyrinth in the United States is at the Grace Cathedral Church in San Francisco, where Lauren Artress serves as canon for special ministries; it follows the same pattern as the famous Chartres labyrinth.

SYMBOLS AND VISIONS

What happens in a labyrinth depends entirely on the person walking it. Some experience nothing more than a pleasant stroll; other walkers' reactions to the labyrinth can be quite dramatic. Some weep, while others claim to have seen visions of God or dead loved ones. The labyrinth is in many ways a giant ink blot onto which its users project their hopes, fears, and dreams. One gets out of it what one puts into it. It can mean anything to anybody: those hoping to connect with a hidden, inner world might just do so; those hoping to hear the voice of God or dead loved ones may hear just that. But because an integral part of the labyrinth experience is suspending judgment, and because of the subjective nature of this experience, we must approach the topic with caution.

Artress tells us, "Experiencing our feelings and inner thoughts without judgment is part of developing spiritual maturity" (1995, 98). But if we use the labyrinth as a tool to clarify or explain, hopefully when we walk out we will have arrived at some sort of answer, and that process by definition involves judgment: perhaps not rational, logical judgment, but judgment nonetheless. If we seek to know what is good or bad about our lives or our situations, that in itself is a question of judging.

This message, however, leads to a bit of a contradiction: on one hand we are told not to be judgmental in the labyrinth, but we are also supposed to judge whether the messages we receive are to be accepted or not. There is clearly some danger in suspending judgment and reason while at the same time using one's imagination to look for answers. What if a spouse leaves a faithful marriage because some "message" from the labyrinth hinted that his or her partner was cheating? If one suspends all rational judgment, who's to say?

Labyrinth guru Artress cautions against reading too much into labyrinth experiences and messages: "Like the symbols in dreams, I would not encourage anyone to take the symbols they receive on the labyrinth literally. . . . One woman walked the labyrinth and felt she had been told to sell everything she owned." Others, notes Artress, may feel that "he or she has been selected to carry out a mission that hinders or hurts others" (1995, 166).

On rare occasions, labyrinths can induce visions and hallucinations. One man saw Jesus while he walked the labyrinth; another saw angels (Artress 1995, 94–95). Artress also mentions one woman who saw "beings of light-blue in hue, faceless but human in form" (96). Some claim to hear God's voice as they walk (22, 37, 42); others hear angelic voices (95) or sense the presence of the dead (76).

One woman, Marylin Arrigan, was walking on a labyrinth on the bank of the Saint Mary's River in Maryland in 1999; she related, "I was [suddenly] in a very bright light. I had a vision of an Indian face with long straight hair, blowing in the wind. He had uplifted arms. He kept telling me to look up. I kept looking up. I was engulfed in light. He asked if I was committed to walking the labyrinth. I said yes. He said 'If you are, you must leave a footprint.' When I got to the center, I left two deep footprints. As I was walking out he said, 'Now you are walking out, you must go out in the world and leave a footprint'" (Quinn 1999).

No one else saw the figure. The area around the labyrinth is well known as ground that is sacred to Native Americans (that's one reason the labyrinth was sited there), and it is not surprising that such a vision (or hallucination) might appear to someone expecting a spiritual experience. It is also noteworthy that the Native American whom Arrigan saw closely matches a popular stereotype. The noble Indian with windblown hair and uplifted arms could be taken from any number of classic images, from wood carvings to television commercials. What would be remarkable would be to have a spiritual vision of a modern (yet equally full-blooded) Native American, working on a telephone line as a repairman, arguing in a Santa Fe court as a lawyer, or dressed in jeans and fixing a car on a reservation. Yet those images do not carry the romantic notions of Indian nobility and thus are unlikely to appear in personal visions.

The sometimes dramatic reactions of labyrinth walkers are not surprising, since many who use the labyrinth as a spiritual tool are, by their very presence in the labyrinth, seeking answers or a "higher knowledge"; moreover, they may be emotionally troubled. Indeed, as Artress writes, "the labyrinth is particularly helpful to those of us in transition" (1995, 73). For the most part, those who aren't expecting (or at least hoping for) some sort of mystical experience are less likely to walk the labyrinth. And, because of their expectations and even their very nature, those who do walk the labyrinth are predisposed to having strong emotional responses. This is important to keep in mind when hearing about dramatic, spiritual moments involving labyrinths. Artress gives many striking testimonials in her book, but the vast majority of people walking the labyrinth probably experienced only a short, somewhat relaxing walk. Yet of course their lukewarm experiences were not notable enough to be solicited or included in labyrinth books. Many labyrinth enthusiasts are reluctant to oversell and hype the benefits of labyrinths because first timers may then be disappointed if they don't hear God, find themselves healed, or have some life-changing revelation.

THE MAN IN THE MAZE AT FRED BACA PARK

Back in Taos, we moved on to a very different type of labyrinth, this one located at Fred Baca Park. Instead of rock and dirt, this "man in the maze" design was outlined with twine and sticks in green grass. In the center near the entrance was the stylized outline of a man in red chalk or paint. At different places in the labyrinth a wire stuck out of the ground, topped with a small red plastic surveyor's flag.

"Each of these flags represents an environmental disaster," Acker explained. I looked at what was written on the little red flags: one read, "Trinity Site, NM, First Atomic Bomb"; another read, "Prince William Sound, AK, Exxon-Valdez Oil Spill"; still another read simply, "Destruction of Old Growth Forests." On and on, each tag paid tribute to one contamination after another. The intended goal was to commemorate each environmental disaster the walker passed (and presumably to resolve to not continue or repeat the events), although many walkers were ignoring the flags.

As we took turns walking the labyrinth, a small crowd of curious onlookers gathered. Our guides happily and patiently explained what labyrinths were. Many were eager to walk the design and see for themselves what it was about. One woman called her young son over to walk the labyrinth, and he happily wandered through, being careful not to trip over the thin ropes and wires. The grass labyrinth was a nice change from the stone and earth designs, although after about forty minutes the heat bore down on us and we moved on.

After we left Fred Baca Park, our tour visited several more labyrinths in the area, including at Ojo Caliente Mineral Springs Resort and Spa (figure 10.5), San Geronimo Lodge, and elsewhere. Another famous New Mexico labyrinth is at the Temple of New Atlantis at Stardreaming, "a place for people to open their hearts to the stars and experience the magic of

Figure 10.5. *This stone-and-sand labyrinth greets visitors to the Ojo Caliente Mineral Springs Resort and Spa in northern New Mexico. Photo by the author.*

Oneness," according to its "neo-visionary artist" and creator, James Jereb. The eleven-circuit labyrinth is composed of forty-two tons of chipped stone of thirty varieties and is 130 feet in diameter. The twenty-two-acre site, containing two dozen other temples and sacred sites, is located near Santa Fe.

LABYRINTH AS THERAPY

As we left, Acker told me about the reputed physical healing power of the labyrinth. Like at other New Mexican healing sites such as El Santuario de Chimayo and Ojo Caliente, there are reports of miracle cures in labyrinths. He related a story from several years earlier in which "one person with multiple sclerosis had to go into the labyrinth with assistance but then once they got to the center they were able to walk out without any assistance at all. There have been spontaneous healings . . . definitely, emotional healings occur within the labyrinth."

Several people claim to have been cured by walks in labyrinths, although to what degree that is attributable to the placebo effect or to religious fervor is hard to determine. Artress admits that the medical evidence that labyrinths can heal physical diseases is shaky, although "there are people that [suggest] the labyrinth heals Parkinson's and it does this and it does that" (Artress 1995, 126).

Some labyrinth advocates, including educator Judy O'Brien (director of the children's program at Maryland's Sotterley Plantation), believe that the seven-circuit shape of the labyrinth may help to enhance children's learning capacities, including those with attention deficit hyperactivity disorder. O'Brien planned to design experiments in which elementary school children walk labyrinths, testing their reading and comprehension skills both before and after. Although her tests were to have begun in 2000, O'Brien has not yet released her results, if there are any, and she did not respond to my requests for an interview for this book.

O'Brien may have a tough time proving her theories. Several years ago, similar claims arose surrounding the use of classical music for children. The claim was that classical music—and Beethoven in particular—helped young children to learn. In 1998 Georgia governor Zell Miller planned to use public money to buy classical music cassettes and CDs to distribute to every mother of a baby born in that state. Other states including Florida were considering similar measures. Yet it turned out that the principal study claiming to support the theory had examined college students and was unrelated to child development. A review of the literature showed no good evidence whatsoever that mere exposure to classical music had any effect on children's intelligence (McCutcheon 1998). After being criticized for its lack of scientific validity, Miller's initiative was quietly scrapped.

Although churches were among the first institutions to embrace the labyrinth, some medical programs have also incorporated them. The first medical facility to install a labyrinth on its grounds was San Francisco's Pacific Medical Center. Artress claims that cancer support groups walk the labyrinth, as well as any other patients wanting to relax and reduce stress. Artress suggests that a patient's stress may be reduced in the secure knowledge of a beginning and an end (in the labyrinth), although it's unclear why that would be a factor. *Any* activity can have a beginning and an end, whether it is limited by a fixed time period or by simply walking to a predetermined destination and back.

Little has been written about labyrinth therapy in medical journals. One of the few articles appeared in the *Annals of the American Psychotherapy Association* (Harris 1999). The piece, "Off the Couch: An Introduction to Labyrinths and Their Therapeutic Properties," is not a study or a survey but simply a short introduction to the topic by psychologist Neal Harris. Harris has used the labyrinth in his practice as a "vehicle for assisting mental focus, group cohesion and spiritual connection." Harris cites the work of psychiatrist Wayne London, which suggests a short-term increase in mental clarity in some people with Alzheimer's, schizophrenia, and dyslexia after following a labyrinth with their fingers. Harris admits that the research is anecdotal and that any long-term effects have not been studied. Harris reports that he himself devised a wooden finger labyrinth (called the "Therapist Board"), and he concludes on a strangely commercial note: "Discover for yourself why many throughout the world consider a labyrinth to be 'Sacred Space,' a locale where the physical and esoteric worlds meet. I encourage therapists to begin to utilize finger labyrinths (especially the Therapist Board) in their practices." Harris then goes on to provide a telephone and website address for orders.

The research that Harris cites, it turns out, was not published in a peer-reviewed medical journal but instead came from Dr. London's 1998 book *The Spiritual and Healing Aspects of the Classical Seven Path Labyrinth*. In a video titled "Journeys into Healing," London points out that the labyrinth "corresponds to the seven chakras" and that walking it is a "balancing procedure." London has continued studying the benefits of labyrinth therapy, working with Judith M. Joyce, vice president of the Labyrinth Society (and dowser and Reiki practitioner). Their collaboration explores not only neurological disorders but also "the healing effects of the labyrinth on the land" (Joyce 2001). (How exactly the soil, rocks, and trees surrounding the labyrinth are "healed" is not explained.)

A few psychotherapists advocate the use of labyrinths in their therapy. Some claim that patients do not even need to actually walk a labyrinth to get benefits; they can simply trace a labyrinth pattern with their finger on a piece of wood or even follow it with their eyes. (For more on labyrinth therapy, see Radford 2004–2005.)

From a scientific and medical point of view, it's clear that labyrinths can have a calming and meditative effect; just about any action done with the intention of relaxing will be relaxing. In this regard, the labyrinth is just one of many mediation devices and techniques, all of which are as nurturing and relaxing as the participant makes it. There is no evidence, however, that the labyrinth is any more effective than, say, yoga, tai chi, or just a leisurely walk to clear the mind.

THE LABYRINTH AND SACRED SPACE

Many labyrinth enthusiasts insist that there is something mystical about the shape of the labyrinth. People have long believed that certain shapes hold special powers and mystical qualities; circles, pyramids, and pentagrams, for example, are widely used in occult ritual. This belief is of course not rooted in science but instead in mysticism and magical thinking—the only meaning these or other symbols have is what is given to them by humans—and it gets into the realm of what New Agers call sacred space. "Sacred space is by definition the place where two worlds flow into each other, the visible with the invisible. The finite touches the infinite. . . . Sacred space can be anywhere, is everywhere, especially when we are able to remain in an open, receptive consciousness" (Artress 1995, 155). As Artress notes, sacred space is therefore more a state of mind than a physical place.

As Artress notes, "Sacred geometry is based on ancient, sacred knowledge that was articulated in architectural forms. It is a lost art that developed a balanced and serene climate for the human psyche and soul. Through proportion, placement, and position of stone, wood, and mortar . . . the mind can find rest, comfort, and harmony. This leaves the mind open to other levels of awareness" (48). Numerology, the belief that certain numbers have magical properties or supernatural significance, is also present in labyrinth lore. Different numbers of circuits (seven, eleven, or thirteen, for example) supposedly have different mystical meanings.

Dowsing, the practice of using divining tools (such as a forked stick or an L-shaped metal rod), is another paranormal activity frequently associated with labyrinths. Labyrinths are often sited according to dowsing principles; for example, people wishing to find a "sacred" or "powerful" piece of earth upon which to create a labyrinth may consult dowsers, who use their tools to best situate the labyrinth pattern so as to tap into maximum "Earth energies."

Indeed, Acker explained, "a lot of labyrinths are laid out by dowsers. . . . Basically one of the things that people who build labyrinths do is they look for the ley lines, look for the energy spots, so that they locate the labyrinth on those particular places." Despite years of research, however, there is no scientific evidence that dowsing is an effective method for finding water, oil, ley lines, lost treasure, or anything else (Radford 2011).

CONCLUSION

The claim that labyrinths have a long tradition of spirituality and are "ancient wisdom" rediscovered is a distinctly modern spin with little basis in truth. While modern pilgrims claim (and like to believe) that they are walking the same paths and patterns of other spiritual seekers centuries and millennia ago, there is no evidence for this. There are no records of people walking labyrinthine designs in a quest for spiritual transformation before our own times; the truth is that we simply don't know what significance labyrinths held for ancient peoples aside from having an interesting design. Although common to many places and cultures, there is little or nothing in the historical record to support the deep, mystical, and spiritual traditions often claimed for them.

The goal of Living Labyrinths for Peace—nothing less than world peace—is an admirable if lofty goal, and one widely shared by other labyrinth devotees. Reverend Artress sees the designs as in some ways a panacea and suggests that "labyrinths, in their many forms, should be spread across the planet. They should be in cathedrals, parks, conference centers, hospitals, and prisons" (1995, 181). Other labyrinth writers, however, caution against unrealistically high expectations: "Labyrinths will not solve our economic or ecological problems, but they will give us the strength to return to the center of ourselves so that we can go back to the task of saving children and saving the air and water on which we depend" (Schaper and Camp 2000, 150).

Can labyrinths bring about world peace? Probably not; if all it took to cast off human anger, evil, and hatred was a few minutes' walk through a labyrinth, the world would be a very different place. Despite close ties to many scientifically dubious and disproven New Age ideas, the labyrinth itself is harmless. The labyrinth's function is meditative, not physically healing or world-peace-making. It's a symbol, and like all symbols the labyrinth's true meaning is not external but internal, instilled by its user.

I encourage people interested in labyrinths to ignore the mystical bells and whistles and enjoy the experience for what it is. Go to a local labyrinth, wait your turn, walk the path. Do it on your own, without expectations. If you see God or feel a cosmic oneness, or if your arthritis clears up, good for you. If not, at least you're getting some relaxing exercise and fresh air in a beautiful setting.

REFERENCES

Acker, John. 2011. Interview by Benjamin Radford, May 7.

Artress, Lauren. 1995. *Walking a Sacred Path.* New York: Riverhead Books.

Grimble, June. 1970. "Maze." In *Man, Myth, and Magic: An Illustrated Encyclopedia of the Supernatural*, vol. 13, edited by Richard Cavendish, 42–45. Tarrytown, NY: Marshall Cavendish.

Harris, Neal. 1999. "Off the Couch: An Introduction to Labyrinths and Their Therapeutic Properties." *Annals of the American Psychotherapy Association* (March–April): 7–8.

Joyce, Judith M. 2001. "Spirit Matters Consulting Services." www.spirit-matters.com/labresume.htm.

Labyrinth Resource Group. 2000. Promotional brochure, Santa Fe.

McCutcheon, Lynn. 1998. "Beethoven's Babies: Much Ado About Nothing?" *Skeptical Briefs* 8, no. 4 (December).

Middendorf, Bobbye. 2000. "Labyrinths Renew Ancient Spiritual Connections." *Conscious Choice*, September, 18.

Quinn, Sally. 1999. "The Light and the Labyrinth." *Washington Post*, December 22, C1.

Radford, Benjamin. 2004–2005. "Labyrinths and 'Alternative' Medicine." *Scientific Review of Alternative Medicine* 8, no. 2 (Fall–Winter): 74–78.

———. 2011. "Dowsing: Dubious, Discredited, and Dangerous." *Skeptical Inquirer* 35, no. 5 (September–October): 36–38.

Schaper, Donna, and Carole Ann Camp. 2000. *Labyrinths from the Outside In.* Woodstock, VT: Skylight Paths.

Walker, Barbara G. 1993. "Science: The Feminists' Scapegoat?" *Skeptical Inquirer* 18, no. 1 (Fall): 68–72.

"Swarm." Photo by Joshua Hoffine, used by permission. JoshuaHoffine.com.

CHAPTER 11

LA LLORONA

WAILING WITCHES HAUNTING THE DITCHES

One sweltering day in 1931 a little girl named Guadalupe visited the Santa Fe River with her two brothers and a few friends. It was a lazy summer afternoon, and the children sought refuge from the high desert heat in the low river's cool waters. The boys laughed and splashed as Guadalupe played near the bank. Suddenly, she recalls, "a strong gust of wind enveloped me[,] and the surrounding cattails and tall weeds swayed violently. Then I heard the sweet tinkling sound of bells. Captivated by the ringing I stopped playing and listened." She noticed that her brothers seemed to hear the bells as well, "for they were standing silently just gazing at the sky." The bells grew louder, and Guadalupe suddenly realized that she was paralyzed, rooted to the spot like a tree: "I could not move a muscle," she remembered. "I was mesmerized by the sound of the bells for at least a minute." The ringing soon faded, replaced by a woman gently sobbing and calling, "mija, mija" (my daughter, my daughter). The little girl's paralysis vanished as quickly as it had come, and Guadalupe stood up and called to her brothers. Terrified by their experience, they all raced four miles back to their home, sensing that they had been in the presence of some supernatural evil.

Once home, they told their parents what had happened, and Guadalupe's brothers offered a chilling revelation: they had not heard, "mija, mija," but instead, "mis hijos, mis hijos" (my sons, my sons). The family decided to return to the spot where the children had encountered something seemingly supernatural. Indeed, Guadalupe recalled, "As my father was getting the horses ready, I heard my mother whisper to him,

'La Llorona.'" Fear and apprehension clung to the family like tar as they headed back down the dusty trail. As they approached the riverbank, they heard a woman's voice wail, "mis hijos, mis hijos." Her father called out, demanding to know who the voice belonged to and what she wanted. Receiving only the aqueous trickling of the river water for a reply, Guadalupe's mother shouted, "Leave my children alone, daughter of the devil!" She then made the sign of the cross and they all turned to leave. As they left, Guadalupe says, "One of my brothers shouted for us to look at the river. We all turned and saw the apparition of the woman walking toward us with her arms outstretched. The setting sun had cast a deep red, orange, gold glow on the river, and we clearly saw this woman walking on its surface." The family then hurried to the safety of their home and told all the neighbors about what had happened and the danger that awaited unwary children at the river.

This story was collected and reported by Antonio R. Garcez in his book *New Mexico Ghost Stories* (2008). Guadalupe is a real woman, seventy when interviewed about her personal encounter with one of the most terrifying—and best-known—evil spirits said to reside in New Mexico. Hers is only one of many encounters with La Llorona, as we will see.

Who is La Llorona and why was she calling to Guadalupe and the other children? There are many stories about La Llorona, but the most common version tells of a beautiful young woman born into a peasant family who married a local man and bore him three children. Sadly, her husband soon died, leaving the poor woman alone to raise the family. She soon caught the eye of a rich and handsome suitor, but he could not accept her children, so she drowned them in a river to be with him. However, her grief and guilt drove her mad, and since then she can sometimes be heard wailing sadly near the river, calling and weeping for her babies. Some say that she snatches misbehaving and careless children from the ditches, either drowning them as she did her own babies or abducting them as replacements.

A somewhat different La Llorona appeared in Mexico City a half century ago: "The Wailing Woman had drowned all her children in the canals of Mexico City. Finally repentant, she began to haunt the streets at night, 'weeping and wailing,' clad in white. Meeting a watchman or a lonely traveler, she would cry out for her children, then disappear" (Leddy 1950, 364–65). There's no mention of unrequited love, no reappearance at the site of her crime (she's seen on a city street, not in a river ditch), no apparent reason for drowning her children, and no particular threat to other children. She's merely an infanticidal mother who later felt guilty and expressed that remorse through weeping.

A group of anthropology students in Mexico City collected various stories about La Llorona in that city in 1949, reporting:

> There are several versions of the legend circulating in the city. The most popular one presents the apparition as a beautiful woman who wanders the streets of Mexico at night, weeping and crying, *Ay! Mis hijos! Ay! Mis hijos!* According to this account, the ghost [had been] a woman of humble origin who, after being forsaken by her rich lover, stabbed her two children as they lay sleeping and then killed herself. Ever since, she wanders the lonely streets in the dead of night crying for her sons, her mournful voice singing in the wind. . . . According to some sources, she is *La Sirena*, the siren. She appears in this form in villages of the highlands of Chiapas [Mexico] just after dusk when the men are returning from the fields. She tries to lure them to their doom by leading them to high cliffs, often calling in the familiar voices of their wives or sweethearts. Or, at times, she tries to throw her victims into one of the gigantic cacti common to that region. In other sections of the country, she haunts lakes and canals where she lures children to their deaths. (Leddy 1950, 364–65)

Not only does La Llorona's story vary greatly in time and place, but her appearance varies as well. Some say that La Llorona appears as a nine-foot-tall woman dressed in white. Some say she appears at the local dump—but only on Saturdays. Her face is sometimes described as incredibly beautiful and almost angelic; other times she appears as an ugly, haggard crone with withered features. Others say she has no flesh at all, wrinkled or otherwise: her face is merely a terrifying, grimacing skull. Still others describe her visage as more demonic, or even equine. Sometimes her features are shrouded with a veil, hat, hood, or nun's habit. She is usually thin instead of fat, with long dark hair instead of short, light-colored hair (an evil witch with a fashionable blonde bob doesn't seem to inspire soul-wrenching dread). Her hair is often wet—perhaps fresh from drowning her children in their watery grave. In the classic witch tradition of familiars, La Llorona is said to be able to change into animals—most often an owl but sometimes a cat, wolf, raven, or coyote. Sometimes an owl seen by a villager in a tree or loft is thought to be La Llorona, who doesn't turn into her human form until she lands on the ground.

Nor is La Llorona confined to Hispanic cultures; in fact she has become a worldwide phenomenon. As Domino Renee Perez writes in her book *There Was a Woman: La Llorona from Folklore to Popular Culture*, "La Llorona is no longer strictly confined to oral narratives, songs, or plays. . . . La Llorona permeates almost every genre of popular culture and even adorns many consumer products" (Perez 2008, 19). Indeed, "La Llorona is used now around the world to sell or promote everything from coffee and women's underwear to films and academic conferences. . . . Her tragedy is used to promote tourism in New Mexico and sell T-shirts on the Internet. La Llorona has made appearances on the short-lived ABC television series *Cracker* (1997–1998), on the PBS family drama *American Family* (2002–2004), and in a commercial for the California Milk Processors Board, in which she is crying not for her children, but for milk. . . . La Llorona has not yet reached the commercial status of the Virgin of Guadalupe—we have not seen La Llorona night-lights, dashboard figurines, or rear-window decals—but I suspect she soon will" (Perez 2008, 3).

THE BIRTH OF LA LLORONA

One researcher, Luis González Obregón, "tells us that the Weeping Woman was first heard in Mexico City about 1550, especially on moonlit nights. She was dressed in white, went through the streets wailing in great anguish, and disappeared into a lake. Among the various explanations offered was the suggestion that she was the infamous Doña Marina, who had repented of her Quisling cooperation with [Spanish conquistador Hernán] Cortés and who, as La Llorona, now wept for her sin" (Leddy 1948, 273).

Although it is widely thought that La Llorona is a Mexican legend, it is not. While the classic image of La Llorona was likely taken from an Aztec goddess named Cihuacoatl, the narrative of her legend has other origins. As Bacil Kirtley (1960) wrote in *Western Folklore*, "During the same decade that La Llorona was first mentioned in Mexico, a story, seemingly already quite old, of 'Die Weisse Frau' ('The White Lady')—which reproduces many of the features consistently recurring in the more developed versions of 'La Llorona,' was recorded in Germany"; references to "Die Weisse Frau" date back as early as 1486. The story of the White Lady follows a virtually identical plot to the classical La Llorona story: "(a) a girl of humble origin is ruined and abandoned by a young aristocrat; (b) she murders her bastard infant(s); (c) she goes insane and dies violently; (d) she returns as a malign ghost, sometimes a beckoning temptress; and (e) those unfortunate enough to meet her die shortly afterward" (Kirtley 1960). Although there are some minor differences, the resemblance is unmistakable; indeed, there are more differences between common variations of the La Llorona story than between the standard La Llorona story and that of the White Lady.

Furthermore, Kirtley notes, "the events of the 'La Llorona' story take place in a Europeanized milieu, and the characters' values, their responses, are thoroughly Spanish, not Indian. Outside of a European social system, with its insistence upon a particular and devious kind of sexual propriety, the story becomes incomprehensible." In other words, preconquest Indians did not have a culture in which the La Llorona story would have occurred, and therefore it almost certainly originally came to Latin America from Europe with the Spanish explorers (Kirtley 1960, 161).

NEW MEXICAN REPORTS OF LA LLORONA

Widely reported and retold, the La Llorona story has a strong presence in the Land of Enchantment. Almost every community of any size with a significant Hispanic presence has at least one story of an encounter with her. Two Santa Fe authors, Edward Kraul and his wife, Judith Beatty, interviewed dozens of people from their hometown and throughout New Mexico about La Llorona. They collected nearly fifty accounts for their book *The Weeping Woman: Encounters with La Llorona.* For a supposedly fictional spirit, she's apparently sighted quite often.

A review of *The Weeping Woman* reveals fascinating variations in the legends. In some cases, people claim to have encountered not La Llorona herself but one of her children, very much alive (which seems to undermine the whole premise of La Llorona's story). Others say that she is not a ghost or spirit at all: "Lately, very little is said about La Llorona, because most people want her dead. But the fact is, she is still very much alive and very real" (Kraul and Beatty 1988, 8).

What happens to her children is a detail that varies greatly; most often they are drowned. Other times they are stabbed, burned, or even dismembered. In some cases, La Llorona's children were not drowned at their mother's hand but merely died near a river. For example, one man from Las Vegas, New Mexico, reported that his father had told him that La Llorona was a woman who was married to an abusive drunk. One night while her husband was out at a bar she decided to leave him for good; she took their two little children and hid them under a river bridge for safety while she returned to their house for the rest of her belongings. But she was gone too long, and the night grew bitterly cold. When she returned for her babies, she found both of them frozen to death; since then, she walks along the river weeping for her children.

La Llorona stories circulated in the small, rural New Mexican town of Corrales, where I grew up. Many longtime residents remember their mothers and friends telling them that La Llorona could be heard wailing along the irrigation ditches (figure 11.1).

Figure 11.1. *An irrigation ditch in the farming village of Corrales, New Mexico, where La Llorona is said to be heard crying for her children. Photo by the author.*

Efforts to verify these La Llorona legends have met with little or no success; it's like trying to grab a ghost or wrangle a wraith. I had hoped to find and interview people who had had first-person experiences with La Llorona, but this became a fruitless task. Almost all the accounts in *The Weeping Woman* and elsewhere date back many decades—often nearly a century ago—and are not accounts told by witnesses reporting what they personally saw or heard, but instead are accounts of what *someone else told them had happened to another person*—what in urban legend research are called friend-of-a-friend (or FOAF) tales. For example, one person identified as Yvonne Roybal told her version of what happened near a prison in the 1930s: "My grandmother told us that one night, one of the guards, a guy named Tafoya" had had a weird encounter with an owl in a graveyard that he believes was La Llorona (Kraul and Beatty 1988, 1). The problem, of course, is that this is (at best) a fourth-hand story (and likely much further removed): the authors are telling us what Yvonne Roybal says her grandmother told her about what had happened to a man named Tafoya. It's not even clear how her grandmother heard the story; she may have simply repeated a neighborhood rumor or legend, but it can hardly be considered a valid eyewitness account of a true event.

As folklorists (and anyone who has played the children's game of Telephone) know, even simple and accurate information usually get badly garbled in its telling and retelling from person to person and generation to generation. It's not that anyone is lying, pulling a prank, or being intentionally deceptive; instead it's simply how rumors, gossip, and legends get started and are perpetuated.

Many of the La Llorona stories are obviously folklore and cannot literally be true. For example, one of the oldest and most popular elements of ghost stories is a person's hair turning white from fright. The idea that psychological trauma leaves a physical mark is an ancient one. It is in fact a well-known traditional international folk narrative motif (labeled F1041.7 in the *Motif-Index of Folk-Literature* [Thompson 2001]). It is also featured prominently in many urban legends, describing the results of, for example, encounters with hook-handed serial killers freshly escaped from local insane asylums.

Sure enough, this theme turns up in many "true" La Llorona stories. For example, a story from Julian Grace of Santa Fe relates that one person who saw La Llorona "developed a white patch on his hair after the experience. Later, all of his hair turned snow white" (Kraul and Beatty 1988, 3). As spooky at this detail is, the phenomenon is medically impossible;

hair cannot spontaneously turn white, either suddenly or overnight. Despite cosmetics companies' claims that their products can restore life and body to hair, hair is dead. The main shaft of a hair follicle is extruded, expired biomass no longer influenced by any physiological processes in the body. Even if an illness, fright, or sudden shock could somehow turn hair white, it would be weeks before the effect would be visible because only the root would be affected. The same principle is involved when a fingernail is injured near the cuticle and the damaged part gradually grows out. It's no more possible for the whole hair shaft to suddenly turn white than it is for a dead tree branch to sprout leaves.

In another story, a gambler said that a beautiful young woman walked into a gambling saloon in the 1940s. It was mostly populated by rough-and-tumble men, and her presence caused quite a stir. This supposedly innocent novice was invited to play poker, whereupon she played with amazing skill, winning hand after hand. The gambler was impressed by this woman, who was sitting next to him, and he soon felt a tap on his foot under the table. At first he thought it was an accident, but he soon came to realize that she was flirting. When he looked under the tablecloth to peek at her teasing, shapely leg, he saw to his horror not a woman's foot but instead a hoof—a cloven hoof, unmistakably a sign of Satan! Most people would have run off in fright, but this steel-nerved man calmly finished playing his hand, collected his winnings, and left, never looking back. Chancing upon a sign of the devil (usually hoofs or horns) is another legend element well known to folklorists, told for centuries around the world.

For this reason and many others, we must take the *cuentos* of La Llorona with a grain of salt, recognizing that even "true" stories are not always so.

LA LLORONA: FOLKLORE HITCHHIKES THROUGH HISTORY

Although La Llorona has roots all over the world, her story can still be found in some very unlikely places. La Llorona stories—even the supposed real-life, eyewitness encounters—usually follow a standard urban legend formula. One common element of the La Llorona stories (and a hallmark of folklore) is the "reveal," a climax that involves a surprising twist or some proof that the experience was real and not a dream, misperception, or misunderstood natural phenomenon.

Take, for example, Guadalupe's story that opened this chapter. We have the identification of the ditch witch (both implicit from the phrase La Llorona spoke and explicit from the name whispered between her parents) and the final twist in which the previously unseen Weeping Woman appears plain as day walking on the water—a feat that of course would be impossible for any human. Before this final twist, it could be argued that Guadalupe had merely seen a real woman out in the water and mistaken her for La Llorona; after all, anyone can call out "mija, mija" and "mis hijos, mis hijos." But this final reveal proved to Guadalupe and her family that what they had seen could not have been of this earth.

We can identify another element of stereotypical folklore in Guadalupe's story. As folklorist Jan Harold Brunvand (1981, 14) notes, a "typical pattern common in many types of folk narratives is the three-fold repetition, with the climax at the third stage." Indeed, we see this pattern; Guadalupe encounters La Llorona three times—once with her brothers and friends, later with her parents, and a final time (when they see her actually walking on water) as they turn to leave the river.

So what's going on? Are these people who report encounters with La Llorona lying or telling tall tales? Not necessarily; sometimes we incorporate legends and folk stories into our own personal histories without even knowing it. Many New Mexican families have extensive oral traditions, stories passed down through the generations of events that happened decades or centuries ago.

Brunvand notes, "Legends can survive in our culture as living narrative folklore if they contain three essential elements: a strong basic story-appeal, a foundation in actual belief, and a meaningful message or 'moral.' . . . In legends the primary messages are quite clear and straightforward; often they take the form of explicit warnings or good examples of 'poetic justice.' . . . Legends survive by being as lively and 'factual' as the television evening news, and they tend to concern deaths, injuries, kidnappings, tragedies, and scandals" (Brunvand 1981, 10–11).

Urban legends and folklore are often told as a true personal experiences (sometimes by the teller, but more often by an acquaintance)—indeed, that's one of the hallmarks of urban legends. It's not surprising—in fact, it's to be expected—that tales of La Llorona encounters are often related as historical fact. "Urban legends belong to the subclass of folk narratives, legend, that—unlike fairy tales—are believed, or at least believable, and that—unlike myths—are set in the recent past and involve normal human beings. . . . As with any folk legends, urban legends gain credibility from specific details of time and place or from references to source authorities" (Brunvand 1981, 3). In other words, people believe it because a seventy-year-old grandmother says that it happened to her. The specific details and locations add authenticity to the story. La Llorona sightings do not occur in fantastic, far-off places populated by genies and magic lamps but instead in the region where the stories are told—sometimes just down the dusty, cactus-lined road, in fact.

LA LLORONA AND THE VANISHING HITCHHIKER

The vanishing hitchhiker story is perhaps the best-known and most-discussed contemporary legend. It is also unique among urban legends in that it involves the supernatural. The basic story goes something like this: during a road trip, usually at night, a lone figure is seen standing by the side of the road. A driver stops and offers the person a ride; the drive proceeds either in total silence or with only a few words spoken. The driver later arrives at a destination and turns to the hitchhiker, only to find that the mysterious guest has vanished. Sometimes the story ends with the driver speaking to someone at the destination who identifies his departed passenger as the spirit of a person who had died nearby. As Brunvand notes, "The specific 'proof' in the story of the hitchhiker's actual presence in the car and her status as the ghost of a particular individual is always a key motif. Besides the book she leaves behind . . . the object may be a purse, a suitcase, a blanket, a sweater, a scarf, or some other item of clothing, or simply footprints or water spots in the car" (Brunvand 1981, 27). There are countless variations around the world, all of them told as true stories.

A man named Ray Lucero, from Pecos, New Mexico, described his encounter with La Llorona:

> During the winter of 1953, I stopped at Joe's Ringside in Las Vegas, New Mexico, to watch the strip show and have a few beers. It was cold, and I was tired of driving. I was on my way home from La Joya to Denver. . . . Around 11:00 or 11:30 p.m. I left Joe's and continued to La Joya. As I was driving down the hill toward Tecolote, the bright lights from my Ford illuminated the figure of a woman standing on the side of the road. In those days, the road was a single lane, one way, and not the big freeway that there is now. I thought to myself, "What is that nun doing on the highway in the middle of the night?" Her dress was a habit of the Catholic nuns I was familiar with. I pulled the car over to a stop and reached over to open the door on the passenger's side. I asked her if she wanted a ride, and she got in the car

> without saying a word. I could see now that it wasn't a habit she was wearing but a dark cloak that covered most of her face. I really couldn't even see if she was old, young, or what. We passed through Bernal, San Juan, San Jose, all without her opening her mouth. I tried to be polite a couple of times and ask her some questions, but she never answered me. She sat completely still, much like a mannequin in a store window, with one hand on her knee and the other hidden under her cloak. When we got to the Pecos cutoff, I was starting to get uncomfortable. . . . As if that wasn't enough, I began to imagine the smell of sulphur,* like after you've lit a match, but stronger. That was enough for me. I stopped the car in front of Adelo's store and turned to tell him or her to get out of the car, but she had disappeared into thin air. Without opening the door. Then I heard this blood-curdling yell, very high-pitched—terrible. It raised the hair on my neck; that's the truth. Even the dogs ran off. I told this story to some guys at the Sunshine Bar, and one of them said the exact same thing happened to him and some other sucker a couple of weeks before. Then he said to me, "That was La Llorona, *mula*!" (Kraul and Beatty 1988)

This is a clear blending of contemporary and urban legends: La Llorona is the vanishing hitchhiker.** Several details in Lucero's story (particularly La Llorona's nun-like appearance and her distinctive folding of her hands) are not new and likely date back to at least the 1920s, when a twenty-one-year-old man in Tucson said that "when he was young he was told that 'she appeared as a nun, all in white, she wore a large cross [crucifix] and walked with her hands folded in front of her. People called her *La Llorona Monja*'" (Leddy 1948, 277).

Of course, Lucero is repeating a well-known urban legend as a personal, firsthand experience. Note also that in his narrative there's no reason to associate his experience with typical renditions of La Llorona (other than that someone later told him it was her). There are no missing children, no association with a ditch or waterway, no plaintive cries of "mis hijos, mis hijos!" It's an ancient ghost story blended with a New Mexican La Llorona twist.

* The smell of sulfur or brimstone has long been associated in folklore with the appearance of the devil.

** In many versions of this legend, the vanishing hitchhiker is eventually identified as a specific person, usually a local who died tragically years earlier. In vanishing hitchhiker legends in Hawaii, the ghost is sometimes said to be the fire goddess Pele.

LA LLORONA THE CHAMELEON

Many people only know of La Llorona from one or two stories they've heard and aren't aware of different versions. By closely examining La Llorona legends, however, we find not a single, homogeneous evil entity but instead many distinct weeping women under her ghastly guise. Of course, these versions are not mutually exclusive; different elements and characteristics may be combined into one story.

The first version describes the weeping woman; in most stories, she's grieving because she's killed her children, although sometimes she weeps for her dead husband or for unrequited love. Indeed,

> While La Llorona is often connected with infanticide, there are also other explanations for her grief. In Nogales [Mexico] it is told that she is a girl whose mother "caused the curse of weeping to be put on . . . [her]." The story is used to impress the sadness that results from disobeying children. Another Nogales report indicates that the "weeping one" is "a wife of Cortes weeping over the grave of Cortes." In Patagonia she is also a sailor's widow, who stands nightly atop a hill, gazing seaward; at midnight she comes down and spends the rest of the night seeking him, weeping. (Leddy 1948, 276)

Thus we see that guilt and grief over the death of a murdered child—seemingly an important, core element of the La Llorona story—is in fact not universal. In some versions, La Llorona is not only weeping for her children but also *searching* for them, although it's not clear why; the location of her dead babies would scarcely be a mystery, since she would presumably know where she had drowned them.

A second version of La Llorona is that of a siren, a woman who lures men to their doom with sound—sometimes beautiful, melodious singing, other times "bloodcurdling" shrieks or long, mournful wails. As Meri Lao describes in her book *Seduction and the Secret Power of Women: The Lure of Sirens and Mermaids* (1998), sirens date back to antiquity, depicted in mythology as beautiful women perched on rocks in the sea whose irresistible songs lured sailors to their death. The sirens would enchant men to steer their ships toward the singing—and the dangerous rocks that were sure to sink them. Homer's *Odyssey*, written around 800 BC, tells the tales of brave Odysseus, whose naked ears were tortured by the sweet sounds of the sirens (figure 11.2). The siren has many faces; Irish legends tell of the banshee, a woman whose terrifying wail is a portent of death and doom. Like La Llorona, she appears as either a beautiful young woman or an ugly old hag.

Guadalupe, whose story opened this chapter, said that the haunting wail of La Llorona had the power to temporarily paralyze her; others report being spellbound and enchanted. There are other parallels to these mystical sounds as well: "Desert sands throughout the world are occasionally said to make mysterious sounds—sometimes singing, sometimes buzzing, sometimes moaning. In Arab and Muslim countries, these haunting noises are often attributed to the jinn [genies]. Marco Polo, writing in the thirteenth century, also attributed such sounds to evil spirits" (Lebling 2010, 102). And like La Llorona, the sirens, and countless others, these desert sounds signify ill intent, as the wailing and calling are intended to lure hapless travelers off the known path and into the feral wilds, where they become hopelessly lost and die. The idea that wailing sounds near water are actually the voices of drowned souls (or those who weep for them) has roots in ancient superstition; indeed, "in many parts of Europe the drowned dead are thought to wail in storms. In Norfolk [England] they can be heard crying their own names in the noise of the wind" (Hole 1961, 143).

Figure 11.2. *Early versions of the La Llorona story can be found in legends of the sirens, reflected in this illustration by Spanish artist Juan Joffre in 1520.*

A third version of La Llorona is the child abductor or murderer, the constant threat to precious children against whom responsible parents must remain ever vigilant. This La Llorona is evil through and through; she is merciless and will give no quarter in her quest to steal their offspring. The idea that an evil woman or female entity would abduct another person's children and take them as a replacement for her own is not unique to La Llorona. In fact, it is common in the mythology of the changeling, in which a fairy, troll, elf, or other fantastic creature abducts a human baby or child (Silver 1999, 59-80). Lilith, the childless she-demon from Jewish mythology, was said to harm both mothers and their babies. Even the jinn of Arabic culture are believed to occasionally snatch human children for their own purposes (Lebling 2010, 90).

A fourth version of La Llorona has emerged among some feminist and women's studies writers, who interpret the tale very differently. To them, the weeping woman is a victim of society deserving sympathy and pity. Domino Renee Perez, for example, criticizes folklorists for "failing to interrogate the stories that inform our worldview, leaving unchallenged classist, sexist, or homophobic ideologies attached to and conveyed by artifacts like those featuring La Llorona" (Perez 2008, 39). For her, La Llorona is not an evil woman but a victim of a misogynistic, patriarchal society that left her with no other option but to drown her children. In fact, "many Chicana cultural producers keep [La Llorona's infanticide] as a focal point of their productions, but radically alter the content or expose mitigating or hidden factors that contributed to the infanticide" (42). The goal is to make La Llorona seem more sympathetic and to justify—if not outright excuse—the murder of her children.

Through this Chicana feminist prism, for example, one modern version of La Llorona can be seen as a single unwed mother on welfare who has had an abortion and whose status as a mother is denied not because she drowned her children but because a man "does not view her as his legitimate partner. Her usefulness to men lies in her ability and willingness to provide them with extramarital sex" (Perez 2008, 50). Another writer, Cordelia Candelaria, suggests that La Llorona's infanticide should be viewed not as a murder of innocents but as a noble and revolutionary act of "political euthanasia, a woman's conscious attempt to save her beloved and cherished children from their parents' awful fate" (Perez 2008, 81). Of course, with the weeping woman encompassing such rich and varied lore, one can easily find examples to support just about any position, agenda, or viewpoint; folklore, like art, can be interpreted in countless ways.

LA LLORONA THE BOGEYWOMAN

La Llorona's most important role, however, is that of the bogeyman—the evil monster and social threat. Monsters, from Bigfoot to sirens to lake creatures, have long been used as agents of social control.* For example, in my book *Lake Monster Mysteries: Investigating the World's Most Elusive Creatures*, I discuss how Champ, the monster of Lake Champlain, is used to frighten misbehaving kids; and on the island of Zanzibar in East Africa, the skeptic-raping bat-demon-ghost Popobawa has been used for political purposes (Radford and Nickell 2006; Radford 2010).

The question of what an encounter with La Llorona means depends on what message the person in the story takes from his experience with her. The most obvious is the warning to kids about staying away from ditches and waterways, since that's where she's said to seek victims. Although the stories of La Llorona, like most legends, are usually handed down in informal settings (such as around campfires and from parents to unruly children), in some places local governments have embraced and exploited the La Llorona "bogeyman" story in the interest of public safety. In Albuquerque, New Mexico's largest city, for example, officials searched for ways to keep kids out of the arroyos and ditches. Especially in the sweltering desert summertime, irrigation and drainage ditches around the state are very inviting to children, teens, and even adults. Sudden storms can cause flash flooding down concrete-lined arroyos in urban areas and elsewhere, leading to drownings. In response, various organizations including the Albuquerque municipal government mounted "a public safety education campaign to teach children to stay out of ditches and arroyos. Brochures, bumper stickers, and signs give the message: 'Ditches Are Deadly—Stay Away' and 'Expect the Unexpected.' The Ditch Witch and Water Monster characters visit schools and events" (Kelly and Rivera 2012). The "ditch witch" is an obvious incarnation of La Llorona.

Many kids, of course, roll their eyes at the idea of being told not to do something by a cartoon witch (did any teens really swear off trying pot because their school was visited by a guy in a McGruff the Crime Dog costume?). Still, the message may find purchase with young children and follows a time-honored tradition.

* Although evil characters are often used as threatening figures, sometimes the threat is reversed such that a good character will withhold good things—Santa Claus is a famous example.

But La Llorona is not just for children. Her message is also aimed at parents, telling them of the consequences of not looking after their babies properly. Most often, La Llorona serves as a moralistic bogeyman, warning people tempted by sin or carelessness to do the right thing. Sometimes it's a warning about personal hygiene (one Santa Fean said that her great-grandfather always refused to bathe, until one day in 1865 La Llorona appeared and scared him into taking a bath—once a week); other times it's a caution against infidelity (a philandering man is warned by his wife not to go out looking for girls or he'll meet up with "bad people"—and he does, after being tempted by a vision of La Llorona, whose face turns into a skull as he tries to kiss her); or the dangers of drink (a Santa Fe man repeated a story he'd heard about an alcoholic named Juan who encountered La Llorona while on a binge—she told him that if she ever saw him drunk again he'd be beaten up. He of course was scared straight and never touched another drop of liquor for the rest of his days). To hear some tell it, La Llorona has a record of encouraging sobriety that Alcoholics Anonymous would be envious of.*

Other times, La Llorona reminds people to go to church, repay their debts, keep the Sabbath holy, be kind to strangers, avoid profanity, and so on. It seems there's no sin or vice that La Llorona hasn't at some point warned, frightened, or threatened people against. Indeed, one could argue that this baby-slaughtering Satanic spirit spends much of her time doing the Lord's work.

As New Mexican Chicano writer Rudolfo Anaya notes, there is far more to La Llorona than a simplistic monster: "What incredible power lies in this woman of legend that we have dismissed as a bogey woman of the river. We've used her to frighten children, when we should be using her to raise them—the new children of a new era who understand that each one carries the hope of the future" (quoted in Perez 2008, 179). To that end, his 1997 children's book *Maya's Children: The Story of La Llorona* focuses on cultural stories and narratives. Anaya's La Llorona is not an evil monster but instead a sympathetic victim who was tricked into killing her children by Father Time.

* Note that this aspect of the story makes an assumption that many health care professionals and drug addicts would disagree with: namely, that the addiction is a choice instead of an illness. One can be "scared straight" out of a vice, but one cannot be "scared straight" out of a disease.

MODERN ENCOUNTERS WITH LA LLORONA

While the vast majority of La Llorona stories are old legends retold as FOAF tales, a handful of people from our own era claim to have had encounters with the weeping woman. A close analysis, however, reveals that very few of them report actually seeing the woman; instead, they experience a strange but possibly natural phenomenon that they interpret as being a sign of her presence. For example, Ernest Lucero of Albuquerque heard "a very sad kind of howling, very drawn out but real loud," coming from a wooded area in the darkness. It could of course have been many things, from the wind to a coyote, but he believes that it was La Llorona (although he didn't see her or report her signature phrase, calling for her children).

Folklorist Betty Leddy (1950, 363) traces one La Llorona story to February 13, 1730, when, according to a family history, a Mexican man named Enrique Mondragon encountered the apparition. Mondragon was crossing a bridge and, by his own account, heard "a very long, drawn-out and painful cry which made [him] very nervous" and sickened him almost to death—which he apparently attributed to La Llorona for reasons that aren't clear. Almost three hundred years later, a woman from Santa Fe "felt a presence" in her home and thought it was La Llorona (although it's interesting to ask why she assumed it was La Llorona and not just some vague feeling—or even a different ghost!). Another Santa Fe resident wrote about "a terrible, eerie, plaintive wailing that seemed to travel from underneath the bridge and up the sides of the arroyo. . . . It sounded [exactly] like a woman wailing. It was the wind, of course, and I'm sure a meteorologist or physicist could explain the dynamics of that to me now, but at the time we much preferred to believe that it was La Llorona we were hearing" (Kraul and Beatty 1988, 91).

All of us, believers and skeptics alike, love a good story. Even the most scientifically minded of us—knowing full well that odd howls or wails are probably not coming from an unseen, mourning La Llorona—secretly like to pretend. Sometimes our eyes and ears fool us; other times we fool ourselves, scared yet eager to actually catch a glimpse of the terrifying legend herself.

As we have seen, many people not only believe in La Llorona but claim to have actually encountered her. I have investigated many urban legends, including organ theft and kidney snatching legends, ghost stories, and others. There are several ways to analyze the La Llorona story and judge whether or not it is true—whether the weeping woman is a myth (as many believe) or instead could be a genuine threat to the unwary.

One way to examine the truth behind the La Llorona story is to work backward; instead of beginning with the reports of her appearances and trying to verify the details (a near-impossible task, for reasons I've described), let us instead assume for the purpose of analysis that she is real and see if we can find evidence of her sinister presence. We might note, for example, that all the stories of her attempts to abduct children are near misses. For an entity whose main purpose for existence is often said to be the abduction of unwary children, she may be terrifying but she's completely incompetent; she always fails. She never *actually* abducts anyone—she only threatens to.

If a child goes missing, parents and police don't assume that the youth must have been taken by La Llorona. The child could be a runaway, or lost, or even abducted by unknown but real persons. Of course, both children and adults drown in ditches, streams, and rivers every year, but those deaths are not investigated as homicides committed by La Llorona. Police know that ordinary drownings are common enough without accusing witches from old legends.

Imagine the outcry if a police chief called off the search for a missing boy, explaining: "Eyewitnesses reported that La Llorona was heard in the area earlier in the week; we assume she has killed the boy, or taken him as her own somewhere in the spirit world." La Llorona is simply not a plausible explanation for a missing child; perhaps she was considered so centuries ago when belief in witchcraft and the supernatural was more common, but not at the dawn of the twenty-first century.

The most likely reason there are no known abductions or deaths attributed to La Llorona is the same reason there are no known abductions or deaths attributed to Bigfoot, leprechauns, or dragons: despite family lore, legends, and first-person sightings, she simply does not exist outside the context of campfires, family stories, and folklore. Yet we must not be too quick to dismiss La Llorona, for she—or, more accurately, *her story*—is incredibly powerful. If a scary story might keep a child out of trouble, most people won't look at it too closely; the value of a story often has little or nothing to do with its literal truth.

Some suggest that Santa Fe's Public Employees Retirement Association building is haunted by La Llorona, although several sources, including *Haunted Places: The National Directory* (Hauck 2002), list the building as haunted but make no mention of La Llorona as among the resident spirits. In fact, the ghosts there are claimed to be Native American spirits from a nearby Indian burial ground.

REAL-LIFE LA LLORONAS

Of course, real-life events can mirror myths and legends. The process by which people act out legends they are familiar with is called ostension, and it is not uncommon. In 2010 twenty-nine-year-old Shaquan Duley smothered her toddler sons, strapped them in a car, and drove them into a South Carolina river. Orangeburg County sheriff Larry Williams said at a news conference that Duley had explained that "she just wanted to get rid of the children, as sad as it may be" (Radford 2010). Several murderous mothers have been dubbed modern-day La Lloronas, including Susan Smith, a South Carolina woman who drowned her children in a lake after claiming that she had been the victim of a carjacking in 1994. Several Hispanic women in Houston, Texas, drowned or tried to drown their children in Buffalo Bayou at one time or another; one—Juana Leija—even announced during her criminal trial, "I am La Llorona."

As much as we may not want to admit it, mothers murdering their children is far from rare. Statistics show that the vast majority of crimes against children are committed not by strangers but by the victims' own families, church clergy, and family friends. According to the National Center for Missing and Exploited Children, "based on what we know about those who harm children, the danger to children is greater from someone they or their family know than from a stranger." A 2000 report by the Office of Juvenile Justice and Delinquency Prevention reported that over three-quarters of child kidnappings were committed by family members or acquaintances of the child. Indeed, children are in far more danger of being abused, kidnapped, or killed by their parents than by a random stranger on the street (or a wandering witch in a ditch). According to a report titled "Homicide Trends in the U.S." issued by the Department of Justice's Bureau of Justice Statistics, of all children under age five murdered between 1976 and 2005, 31 percent were killed by their fathers and 29 percent were killed by their mothers. A 2000 study conducted by Marlene Dalley analyzed trends in Canadian child murders and concluded that "both mothers and fathers kill infant children at the same frequency, though when all (victim) age groups are considered mothers and step-mothers killed more children than fathers and step-fathers." A 2003 study published in the *Journal of the American Medical Association* found that, of thirty-four North Carolina newborns who were killed or left to die, at least 85 percent of them were killed by their mothers (usually by strangulation or drowning). Sadly, mothers who murder their children are hardly the stuff of folklore; it is a regular occurrence in the United States and around the world.*

Folklorist Ed Walraven, in discussing modern reports of La Llorona, notes that the spirit has come a long way from haunting ditches around Mexico City (or the Santa Fe River). As we have seen, La Llorona stories, like all urban legends, adapt to the cultural—and physical—environments in which they are told. In 1991 Walraven noted a new urban twist on the story: just as the weeping woman blended with the vanishing hitchhiker story years earlier,

> evidence exists to suggest development of a new, non-traditional location for La Llorona sightings, the municipal landfill or city dump. . . . What may be occurring are the first signs of a merging of the traditional La Llorona legend and the contemporary stories of babies found abandoned in trash dumpsters, a more modern method for disposing of children than drowning. . . . One could argue successfully that placing an unwanted infant or infants in the trash, not drowning, may have become the preferred method of ridding one's self of them. For several reasons, this approach neatly addresses the shift in population to urban areas. It must be recalled that the population which has shifted to urban areas was a few generations ago rural in nature, not only in the United States, but also in Mexico and most of Central and South America. It is hard to drown one's children in the bustle of a city without being noticed. (Walraven 1991, 209)

* According to a 2002 study published by the Centers for Disease Control and Prevention, a person's first day on Earth is also the day he or she is most likely to be killed: the risk of homicide for newborns is ten times greater than at any other time in life. For the vast majority of the newborn victims, the killer is the child's own mother. If an average of one child per day were intentionally killed by any other cause, there would be a national outcry, yet the public takes little notice of parental killings except in high-profile cases. In fact, according to figures released by the United Nations Children's Fund (UNICEF), between 2000 and 2010 more than twenty thousand American children are believed to have been killed in their own homes by family members. That is nearly four times the number of U.S. soldiers killed in Iraq and Afghanistan during the same decade, and saddles America with the worst record of child abuse in the industrialized world (Radford 2011).

For a legend to linger in circulation, it must remain relevant to those who tell the stories. "The folklore pump seems primed: the La Llorona legend is deeply ingrained in the Hispanic culture; the growing Hispanic population is moving to more urban settings; those hearing stories of a La Llorona–like mother wanting to rid herself of her children will find abandonment in a corner dumpster in the city much more believable and appropriate to the surroundings than drowning; if La Llorona is looking for her dead children, she should turn up at the city dump if their bodies were left in a trash dumpster" (Walraven 1991, 211). It is quite likely that, hundreds of years from now, La Llorona may be sighted on a spaceship or even a colony on another planet.

In the end, saying that a person saw "La Llorona" is meaningless, for there is not one La Llorona but many. Like other legends, she appears in countless guises and forms, depending on the social context and personal beliefs of those who see her. She is both impossibly beautiful and horribly hideous; she is dressed in both black and white. She is intent on harming children, yet her image and story keep children safe. She can be anything and everything. She is at once both nowhere and everywhere. She is not real, yet she has haunted humans for half a millennium, and she will surely live on. That is the timeless riddle of La Llorona.

REFERENCES

Anaya, Rudolfo. 1997. *Maya's Children: The Story of La Llorona*. New York: Hyperion Books.

Brunvand, Jan Harold. 1981. *The Vanishing Hitchhiker: American Urban Legends and Their Meanings*. New York: W. W. Norton.

———. 2001. *The Encyclopedia of Urban Legends*. Santa Barbara, CA: ABC-CLIO.

Garcez, Antonio. 2008. *New Mexico Ghost Stories*. 3rd ed. Placitas, NM: Red Rabbit Press.

Hauck, Dennis William. 2002. *Haunted Places: The National Directory*. New York: Penguin Books.

Hole, Christina, ed. 1961. *The Encyclopedia of Superstitions*. New York: Metro Books.

Kelly, Susan, and Craig Rivera. 2012. "Ditch and Arroyo Safety." Albuquerque's Environmental Story. http://www.abqenvironmentalstory.org/topics/s5safe.html.

Kirtley, Bacil. 1960. "'La Llorona' and Related Themes." *Western Folklore* 19, no. 3 (July): 155–68.

Kraul, Edward Garcia, and Judith Beatty. 1988. *The Weeping Woman: Encounters with La Llorona*. Santa Fe, NM: Word Process.

Lao, Meri. 1998. *Seduction and the Secret Power of Women: The Lure of Sirens and Mermaids*. Rochester, VT: Park Street Press.

Lebling, Robert. 2010. *Legends of the Fire Spirits: Jinn and Genies from Arabia to Zanzibar*. Berkeley, CA: Counterpoint Books.

Leddy, Betty. 1948. "La Llorona in Southern Arizona." *Western Folklore* 7, no. 3 (October): 272–77.

———. 1950. "La Llorona Again." *Western Folklore* 9, no. 4 (October): 363–65.

Montaño, Mary. 2001. *Tradiciones Nuevomexicanas: Hispano Arts and Culture of New Mexico*. Albuquerque: University of New Mexico Press.

Perez, Renee Domino. 2008. *There Was a Woman: La Llorona from Folklore to Popular Culture*. Austin: University of Texas Press.

Radford, Benjamin. 2008. "Popobawa." *Fortean Times*, October.

———. 2010. "How Rare Are Female Child Killers?" Discovery News, August 17. http://news.discovery.com/human/mother-killer-murder-child.html.

———. 2011. "U.S. Worst in Child Abuse." Discovery News, October 24. http://news.discovery.com/human/us-worst-child-abuse-111023.html.

Radford, Benjamin, and Joe Nickell. 2006. *Lake Monster Mysteries: Investigating the World's Most Elusive Creatures*. Lexington: University Press of Kentucky.

Silver, Carole. 1999. *Strange and Secret Peoples: Fairies and Victorian Consciousness*. New York: Oxford University Press.

Thompson, Stith, ed. 2001. *Motif-Index of Folk-Literature: A Classification of Narrative Elements in Folk Tales, Ballads, Myths, Fables, Mediaeval Romances, Exempla, Fabliaux, Jest-Books, and Local Legends*. 7 vols. Bloomington: Indiana University Press.

Walraven, Ed. 1991. "Evidence for a Developing Variant of 'La Llorona.'" *Western Folklore* 50, no. 2 (April): 208–17.

CHAPTER 12

MURDER ON THE MESA

THE BONE COLLECTOR SERIAL KILLER

February 2, 2009, began like any other day for New Mexican Christine Ross. She and her playful dog, Ruca, left their quiet suburban home on Albuquerque's west side to go for a walk. They wandered through a vacant, sandy lot near where new homes abruptly meet desert sands and scrub brush.

Ruca, as dogs do, sniffed here and there while the pair wandered, and at one point found a whitish bone. At first there seemed nothing unusual about it; the West Mesa is a scrubby, desert area where animal bones are not uncommon. Coyotes, rabbits, birds, dogs, and other animals have lived and died there for centuries under the scorching sun.

But as Ruca pawed at the partly buried bone, Christine realized that it was larger than those of most animals she'd expect to find in the area. Could it be a cow or horse bone? Vast, arid swaths of New Mexico are used for ranching—but there are no cattle this close to the West Side, near the recently minted subdivisions.

There was something odd—almost familiar—about it. Christine peered closer; it looked almost human. *Or human*, she realized.

She took out her cell phone and texted her sister, a registered nurse. She took a photo of Ruca's prize bone and sent that as well. A few minutes later, Christine Ross got a chilling response: her sister said that the bone resembled a human femur. She and Ruca may have stumbled upon a dead body.

Christine immediately called the police, not knowing that she was standing on what would become one of the largest crime scenes in the country. She hoped it was all a mistake, that the bone wasn't what it seemed to be, but the police examined the bone and confirmed that it was indeed human. A lost hiker, perhaps. But when the police dug the skeleton up, they found more and more bones. Over the course of several weeks, they uncovered the bodies of a dozen women and one fetus.

It eventually became clear that a serial killer was at work. The killer was dubbed the West Mesa bone collector by the popular television show *America's Most Wanted*, and the revelations set Albuquerque—and indeed the entire state—on edge. Someone had been abducting people, probably locals and perhaps at random, killing them, and dumping their bodies (figure 12.1). That was chilling enough, but when did it all happen? Was it decades ago, or weeks ago? Was the killer still on the loose?

I've investigated serial killings before (see, for example, Radford 2010, chapter 6), but the West Mesa murders struck close to home for me—literally. The bone collector's grisly graveyard is less than fifteen miles from where I live.

It's one thing to see news reports about a murder, or even a mass

Figure 12.1. *Albuquerque's West Mesa, where a serial killer buried his victims, is the largest crime scene in New Mexico. Photo by the author.*

murder or serial killing, in a far-off place. One might expect it in a big city like New York, Vancouver, or Atlanta. But this was different; it was not some abstract body-dumping ground somewhere in the wooded Pacific Northwest or the New Jersey shore. The Southwest's most prolific serial killer had repeatedly committed these gruesome murders not far from where my family and I live, where I buy my groceries—in short, where I call home.

Evil had truly struck home; it was unnerving to watch the national news programs and see slickly shot and edited images of an area so familiar to me and my neighbors, and where I could visit on a short drive.

THE GRAVEYARD

The sheer scale of the crime scene was far beyond anything that the Albuquerque police had ever encountered before. The investigation area covered over a hundred acres of land (approximately seventy-five times the area of a football field), mostly scrub brush and desert sand. Police had to meticulously move and search over forty thousand cubic yards of dirt, sand, plant and animal matter, and trash. It was an enormous, exhausting, expensive, and time-consuming task that would tax any police department to its limit.

The size of the area made it hard to manage, but the location of the bone collector's yard also troubled investigators. It is only a few minutes away from one of the most widely traveled highways in the state, Interstate 40. Only a few miles away, near downtown Albuquerque, I-40 meets Interstate 25, creating a perfect nexus of busy roads potentially allowing a quick and clean getaway.

Mobile serial killers are especially difficult to catch. For example, serial killer Robert Rhoades, a Texas long-haul trucker, kept a mobile torture chamber in the cab of his rig. He crossed the country kidnapping, torturing, and killing people in the early 1990s. It's not known how many victims he may have had, although he pled guilty to killing at least three people, including a newlywed couple in 1990 (Ng 2012).

The killer could be a New Mexican local living alongside other seemingly innocent, law-abiding folks yet harboring a terrifying, dark secret. Or the killer could be an occasional visitor to Albuquerque, perhaps someone from a neighboring state who brings evil to town with him. Or the murderer might be someone who's constantly on the road, whose job brings him to Albuquerque on a regular basis—perhaps a truck driver or someone in the military.

FORENSIC CLUES

The victims were long dead, and the killer unknown. The only clues that could bring justice would be the hardened calcium that even the killer couldn't dispose of. Identifying the bones was a Herculean task. "Complicating the dig has been work that property owner KB Home had done there in anticipation of a housing development. The developer's heavy equipment moved a lot of earth and unknowingly broke and shattered many of the bones," wrote *Albuquerque Journal* reporter Jeff Proctor (2009a). "Reconstructing the skeletons has been difficult because many of the 206 bones that belonged to each person had to be pieced back together. For example several leg bones were in as many as four or five pieces, and several of the skulls had been broken into shards." The bones had been exposed to wind, rain, dirt, and even animals, deforming and discoloring them. It seemed that luck and Mother Nature had conspired to shroud the killer's methods. Unlike many murder scenes, there was little to go on—the animals and elements had long ago stripped away crucial flesh and other evidence.

Although bones were by far the most important discovery, at least two other pieces of forensic evidence were recovered. One of the victims had been wearing an acrylic fingernail with a distinctive pink design resembling the top part of a heart. This may be an important clue because the police believe that this type of nail art was not commercially available in Albuquerque at that time—therefore she may have been from another, perhaps larger, city such as Los Angeles or Phoenix.

Another clue came in the form of teeth—or, rather, false teeth; one of the victims had had dental bridge work done. Police circulated X-rays of the woman's teeth, hoping that a dentist somewhere might be able to identify the victim from the dental work done. In the end, this clue allowed Wendy Honeyfield of the Office of the Medical Investigator to positively identify Syllannia Edwards, the only African American woman buried there. She was last seen in Lawton, Oklahoma, in August 2003, when she was fifteen years old. When her remains were identified in November 2009, police said that they were "cautiously optimistic" that her discovery would solve the case.

THE SUSPECTS

As the investigation lumbered on month after month, the public grew impatient. What was going on? Was the killer still on the loose? Even if no arrests had been made, were there at least some suspects?

In fact, the police had identified a few suspects after a couple of months of work. Six months into the investigation, they narrowed down the list of suspects to five people. Of the five, at least two were already in prison on unrelated charges.

One suspect was a man named Fred Reynolds, a pimp who knew at least one of the missing women and reportedly possessed photos of other missing prostitutes. The police soon realized that they would not be able to question Reynolds about the killings, as he had died in January 2009.

A second man, Lorenzo Montoya, was also a strong suspect. He lived less than two miles from the crime scene, and there was some evidence suggesting that tire tracks led from his home to the site. He, also, could not be questioned by the police; he had been shot to death in December 2006 by a pimp after assaulting a prostitute.

In June 2009 the police revealed a new twist to the case: Chief Ray Schultz stated in an interview with the *Albuquerque Journal* that the bodies had been found naked. "Why were they buried without clothing?" he asked. "It's a fact that really intrigues our investigators and the FBI profilers who are assisting us on this case. It's very unique to find this number of remains all unclothed. Usually when you have remains found unclothed there has been a sex crime associated with the homicide. There's no specific evidence to suggest that here, other than the lifestyle" that the victims had in common—namely, involvement in drugs and prostitution (Proctor 2009b). The chief also acknowledged what many had suspected from the beginning but what had never officially been confirmed: that they were looking for a single person, one serial killer, instead of a gang.

The case got colder and colder, until August 2010, when it seemed there was finally a breakthrough. A photographer in Joplin, Missouri, was questioned about the homicides. Acting on a tip about a series of photographs in the man's possession of women who seemed to be dead, sleeping, or unconscious, the police confiscated tens of thousands of his photos. As it turned out, he had visited Albuquerque several times for the annual International Balloon Fiesta, which draws people from around the world.

The Albuquerque Police Department held a press conference on December 9, 2010, to display the photos and request the public's help in identifying the women in the images. Most of the women seemed to generally fit the profile of the killer's victims in terms of age (early twenties) and race (mostly Caucasian or Hispanic). The police refused to say how the photographs came to their attention or what their connection was with the Joplin man, but the news was widely reported and raised many New Mexicans' hopes that the case would soon be closed.

It was not to be; the Joplin photographs turned out to be a dead end. One photographed woman was recognized by her family, who told the police that she had died several years earlier of natural causes; at least two other women were identified as alive and well. The police concluded that the Missouri photographer was innocent, or at least that there wasn't enough evidence to charge him in connection with the serial murders. Later that year, convicted Colorado serial killer Scott Lee Kimball was questioned in connection with the bone collector murders; he denied killing the women, and there seems to be little evidence that he did.

Around that time, realizing that the public was growing impatient with the lack of details and progress in the investigation, Police Chief Schultz granted an interview and said that investigators had determined a cause of death for the women: asphyxiation. "There were no outward signs of trauma on any of the remains. That leads us to believe they were either strangled or suffocated," the chief said (Proctor 2009c). The police believed that the murders had been committed between 2003 and 2005 and that the killings had taken place during the state fair, when people come to Albuquerque to see the sights—and to engage in prostitution.*

The body count had reached a dozen by April 2009, when investigators realized they'd made a mistake: one of the bones believed to have been of the twelfth victim turned out to be from one of the earlier, identified women. In many ways, it was a relief—one fewer victim meant one innocent life saved. But in another way the discovery was a minor setback because there would be no new information gleaned from that piece of evidence. The detectives knew that with each new victim identified there was the potential for more information. Any new piece of evidence could be the clue that breaks the case.

* Street prostitution increases all across the country at events like state fairs, as authors Steven Levitt and Stephen Dubner (2007) note in their book *SuperFreakonomics*.

Still, they had succeeded in identifying two more victims, Monica Candelaria and Veronica Romero. Like the rest, they had been involved in drugs and prostitution. The ninth and tenth victims, Virginia Cloven and Evelyn Salazar, were identified in 2010. Both had been reported missing in 2004, when they were twenty-three years old. By 2010, forensic investigators had identified all of the adult victims. They were Jamie Barela, Monica Candelaria, Victoria Chavez, Virginia Cloven, Syllannia Edwards, Cinnamon Elks, Doreen Marquez, Julie Nieto, Veronica Romero, Evelyn Salazar, and Michelle Valdez.

The bone collector killings made national news when the grave site was first discovered, and the story was featured several times on high-profile television shows including *America's Most Wanted* in 2009 and *Dateline NBC* in 2010. Although many, including the police and the victims' families, were uneasy about the exploitation and sensationalism inherent in such television shows, they cooperated because they got something in return that they desperately needed: publicity. Police often rely on tips from the public, and the more people who know about the case, the more likely it is that someone with information will step forward. The tip that solves the crime might come from anyone—maybe a local who hadn't been following earlier news reports, or maybe a retired schoolteacher living in California who had visited Albuquerque as a tourist in 2003 and remembers seeing something suspicious. With families desperate for answers and a serial killer possibly on the loose, the police were ready to try anything.

Several family members of the victims grew upset at the news media's characterization of their missing sisters, daughters, and friends as "merely" drug users and prostitutes (although undeniably most or all of them were just that). Regardless of what they did for money or what choices the women had made in their lives, they were fellow humans. They had hopes and dreams, plans and wishes, and friends and families that cared about them. Surely it was not the intention of the police or journalists covering the story to denigrate these women and treat them as less important than anyone else—although the families' defensive sentiments are surely understandable. Some victims' advocates even hinted—probably inaccurately and unfairly—that the Albuquerque police were not doing everything they could to solve the crime because the victims were associated with drugs and prostitution.

While there's no substitute for careful, on-the-ground detective work, some clues are hidden at ground level and can only be revealed from a higher vantage point. The police used satellite imagery to locate nearby areas of desert that had recently been disturbed. They also looked at archived satellite images from years past to see if they could find any trace of who had been there and when.

PSYCHIC DETECTIVES, MISSING PERSONS, AND POLICE INVESTIGATIONS

So far, despite the best efforts of the FBI, the police, and the families themselves, the killer (or killers) have escaped justice. Year after year goes by with no real progress—only false clues, failed promises, and red herrings.

When conventional methods fail, many people turn to unconventional methods—and that was certainly the case with the West Mesa bone collector murders. When the police and the media asked for the public's help in providing information, dozens of psychics were among the hundreds of tipsters who offered assistance.

Some were established in Albuquerque and making their living as part-time or full-time psychics. Others were ordinary men and women (although mostly women) who didn't necessarily consider themselves psychic but nonetheless felt that they had some potentially relevant information that might help solve the case. Some had had a hunch, a dream, or a vision in the days or weeks after hearing about the murders on the news; others had consulted tarot cards or astrology charts. Maybe they heard a rumor *about something*, or just had a vague premonition about the crimes. Could these psychics and "sensitives" help crack the case and bring the West Mesa murderer to justice?

This was, of course, not the first high-profile homicide case in which psychic detectives offered information. Far from it, in fact: after many murders and missing person cases are reported—especially in the national news—police receive at least a handful of tips from psychics. In cases that get a lot of sustained publicity, the police often receive hundreds or thousands of diagrams, messages, and descriptions of visions from psychics.

In order to judge the likelihood of success in this case, it is useful to briefly examine the history of psychic detectives and their track records. What follows is a brief survey of high-profile missing persons cases tackled by both local and internationally known psychics.

Laci Peterson

In what would become one of the most famous missing person cases in U.S. history, pregnant Modesto, California, woman Laci Peterson went missing on Christmas Eve 2002. The disappearance made national news as her husband, Scott, desperately appealed to the police and the public to help find his beloved wife. More than a thousand psychics contacted the police offering clues and information; in February 2003 well-known psychic Noreen Renier (author of several books including *A Mind for Murder: The Real-Life Files of a Psychic Investigator*) was hired by the family to locate Peterson. In an interview with Greta Van Susteren on the Fox News show *On the Record*, Renier discussed her involvement in the case. Scott Peterson's mother, Jackie, had sent Renier three items Laci had owned or been in contact with: an envelope, a sweatshirt, and a shoe. "I'm a psychometrist, which means I touch items and get vibrations, energies from the items," Renier said. (The process by which shoes and envelopes emanate vibrations and energy is unknown to science but apparently familiar to Renier.)

In her psychic visions, Renier claimed that she saw "the rocks, the park, the bridge, the bumpy road, [and] a bunch of numbers," and "someone, a male, hitting [Laci] on the head, and I could see a door there, and I knew that a rug was missing" (Posner 2003). Unfortunately, no information ever surfaced about a door, a rug, a park, a bridge, a bunch of numbers, or a bumpy road. Other guesses, such as those associated with rocks, are obvious given that most likely a body will be found near some rocks somewhere—in a grave, in a bay, or anywhere else.

In the end, Renier said that she gave "a lot of information" to detectives about Peterson. Yet Renier's information was useless to the Modesto police; Laci Peterson's body was discovered not by Noreen Renier (nor by any of the thousand other psychics who offered their assistance in the case)—nor even by police investigators—but instead by a passerby who found it washed up on a bay shore five months later on April 14, 2004. In the end, Scott Peterson was convicted of his wife's murder and sent to death row.

Elizabeth Smart

Elizabeth Smart was a beautiful, blonde, fourteen-year-old girl abducted from her home in Salt Lake City on June 5, 2002. Her case was widely publicized, and more than a thousand psychics, including famous ones such as Allison DuBois (the inspiration for the 2005–2011 NBC television series *Medium*) and Carla Baron (of the 2005–2007 Court TV television series *Haunting Evidence*), contacted the Smart family and the police, offering their visions, information, and other evidence. They offered wildly varying descriptions of Elizabeth's abductor, her location, and her condition; psychics couldn't even agree on whether she was alive or dead. These tips, like all the rest, were carefully investigated whenever possible by the police. Not a single piece of information from all those psychics led to Smart's recovery; instead, she was recognized from news reports by two couples in a Salt Lake City suburb ten months after her abduction. She had been abused and raped daily by her captors.

Chandra Levy

After Washington, D.C., congressional intern Chandra Levy disappeared on April 30, 2001, police detectives received fifty to eighty tips each day, resulting in thousands each month. Hundreds of psychics offered information, but none of it was fruitful. In an interview with the *Washington Post*, the city's executive assistant police chief, Terrance Gainer, said: "The psychic ones, frankly, I don't think we give much credence to. I don't mean to start a war with all the psychics, but they haven't proven very useful." In fact, Gainer said that many of the leads the psychics offered not only contradicted each other but often contradicted known information. "You got 100 different psychics, and they've got 100 different places. They've got her in a cave. Some have her in Nevada. Some have her in water. How can all these psychic radars be all over the country? Who's right?"

Psychic tipsters claimed that Levy was hidden in a mansion; held hostage by a boxer; stuffed in a California storage locker; buried at a military base in Fort Lee, Virginia; drowned in the Potomac River; and abused in thousands of other ways and places. At least one person contacted the police claiming that Levy had been abducted by extraterrestrial aliens. The late psychic (and convicted felon; see Lancaster 2008) Sylvia Browne offered her psychic information in an interview with Paula Zahn of Fox News, saying that Levy's body was located near "some trees in a marshy area . . . but this girl is not alive." When Zahn asked how she knew that, Browne snapped, "because I'm a psychic."

However, Browne, for all her bluster and confidence, was wrong:

Levy's remains were found by accident by a man looking for turtles on a steep hill in a heavily wooded area of Washington's Rock Creek Park—perhaps near "some trees" but clearly not "in a marshy area," since a marsh located on a hill is physically impossible. Browne was wrong but was not alone in her errors: none of the other hundreds of tips from psychics led the police to Levy's body, either.

Lisa Stebic

In June 2007 several psychics offered information in the case of Lisa Stebic, a thirty-seven-year-old Illinois mother of two, who had been missing since April 30 of that year. One psychic claimed that Stebic would be found in Silver Springs State Park in Illinois. The family, desperate for any news or information, grew hopeful and endured a "roller coaster of emotions" as police and volunteers searched the park for Stebic's remains. The news was grim but good—bones were indeed found, just as the psychic had predicted. Sadly, the police soon realized that the bones were those of deer, not a woman. The Stebic family's hopes for closure were raised—then shattered—by a psychic's false information. Despite information given by more than a dozen psychics, Lisa Stebic has never been found.

Shawn Hornbeck

In one of the most dramatic and emotionally devastating psychic errors in history, in 2002 Sylvia Browne told the parents of abducted child Shawn Hornbeck, on *The Montel Williams Show*, that their son was dead. His body, she said, would be found in a wooded area near two large boulders. The boy, she said, had been kidnapped and murdered by a very tall, "dark-skinned man" who wore dreadlocks. The family was devastated—one of the most famous and credible psychic detectives in the world had confirmed their worst fears, that their beloved Shawn would not be coming home. Yet the family was in for another shock when Hornbeck and another boy were found alive five years later in the home of a light-skinned, nondreadlocked Missouri man named Michael Devlin, who had kidnapped and sexually abused them.

Browne made the same grievous error in the case of Amanda Berry, a sixteen-year-old Cleveland girl who went missing in 2003. For nearly two years after her disappearance, Amanda Berry's mother, Louwana Miller, held out hope that her daughter would be found alive and returned to her. That hope evaporated when, again on *The Montel Williams Show*, Browne told Miller that Amanda was dead. "She's not alive, honey," Sylvia Browne told her matter-of-factly. But she was alive; Berry, along with two other missing women, Gina DeJesus and Michelle Knight, was freed after being held captive in a home for nearly a decade by a man named Ariel Castro. Castro was arrested and died in jail in 2013; tragically, Louwana Miller died before Amanda was rescued, still believing that her daughter was dead (Radford 2013).

Jaycee Dugard

The case of Jaycee Dugard is an even more horrific example of the failure of psychics to solve crimes and locate missing persons. In 1991 Dugard, a young girl, was kidnapped off the street on her way to school. For eighteen years no one knew the girl's fate, but in late August 2009 she was discovered living in a virtual prison in the backyard of a couple's home in Antioch, California. She had been confined and raped, even giving birth to two of her captor's children. There are thousands of self-proclaimed psychics and psychic detectives in the world who claim to be able to find missing persons—and dozens of psychics offered information about Dugard. Yet not a single psychic was correct. How can psychics claim such extraordinary powers while they've never once led police to rescue these innocent young victims within hours or days of their abductions? And why did Dugard have to wait nearly two decades for her rescue—by suspicious neighbors, not psychics—while being subjected to continual sexual and physical abuse, if psychics had the power to find her?

Holly Bobo

A young blonde nursing student named Holly Bobo was abducted in April 2011, last seen apparently being forced into the woods near her Tennessee home by a man wearing camouflage. Despite extensive searches, police found neither Bobo nor her abductor. The case garnered more publicity with each passing week and month as the search intensified. Was she alive or dead? Had she willingly left with her companion, or had she been forced?

Police were inundated with tips and information from the beginning of the case; the more national publicity the abduction got, the more psychics chimed in with information. Officials later complained that well-meaning individuals had been disseminating misinformation about the case, making their investigation much more difficult. Dozens of self-proclaimed psychics offered hundreds of incorrect, vague, and often contradictory tips.

Here's a sampling of information and leads offered by psychics about Bobo: Her abductor might have a scar on his forehead, or a rash on his elbow, or a bite mark on his hand. He might work from home as a graphic designer and long for the 1950s. His hair might be dark brown, or blond, or salt and pepper. He might be clean shaven, or he might have a moustache. He might be a Scorpio. He is either scrawny, or of medium build, or stocky and muscular—possibly ex-military. He might own a black leather wallet, and his name might contain one or more of the following letters: B, A, J, R, W, or M; his last name might be Glenn. Bobo might be (or might have been at one point) in or near a place that has the number 7 associated with it, either an address or a highway number or possibly even seven miles from some landmark or unknown location. One psychic said she believed that the lyrics of the Neil Diamond song "September Morn" contained important clues to finding Bobo because the song had come to her in a vision (Radford 2011a, 2011b).

It's not clear how the police were supposed to use this jumble of random associations, images, numbers, letters, and feelings provided by psychics. This information is so vague, general, and contradictory that it is completely useless; the police need specific, accurate information that leads them to the victim. Immense time and resources would be wasted if the police tried to follow up on even the most credible of these "leads."

Soon after Bobo's disappearance, one psychic confidently stated that she would be found alive, that her abductor was making lots of mistakes and would be captured within five days. Tragically, this information, like all the other information from psychics, turned out to be wrong.

The case even attracted the attention of a prominent psychic, Carla Baron, who said that a friend of the Bobo family had contacted her on their behalf. Baron was part of the show *Haunting Evidence*, in which she and two other investigators tackled real-life unsolved murders. The show was cancelled after twenty-two episodes without a single case having been solved through the efforts of its psychics; two of the cases were later closed through police work.* Baron said that the Bobo family later

* Baron also claimed to have solved the case of Natalee Holloway, an Alabama teenager who went missing on the Caribbean island of Aruba in 2005. Yet the case remains open as of this writing; Holloway's body has not been found, and no one has been charged in her death.

chose not to seek her information on Holly's death on the advice of the police, who, Baron believes, were "terrified to hear what I might have to say" about the abduction.

According to a police spokesman working on the Bobo case, while those who offer random, psychic, and false information "may be pure hearted, [they] do interfere with law enforcement's work" (Radford 2011b). Despite the efforts and information from dozens of psychics, Bobo remains missing as of early 2014.

There are many more cases I could cite, but this sample gives a fair representation of how successful psychics have been in solving crimes and finding missing persons: they have been consistently and remarkably unsuccessful.

Often, psychics will contact the families of missing children and offer their services—for a fee. The parents are usually so desperate for news that they willingly pay, even if they are skeptical. Even those psychics who do not exploit the bereaved for monetary gain are still hurting instead of helping them. Aside from falsely raising the family's hopes, psychic tipsters waste valuable police time and resources, if the police elect to follow up on the information they provide. The police carefully record and investigate each piece of information they receive. But each hour a detective or police officer wastes chasing dreams, visions, and dead ends is an hour that could be deployed trying to find the missing person using proven and effective investigative techniques. And time is especially critical in missing person cases.

Even cases that seem promising for psychic investigation can end up being disappointing in that regard. In 2008 I investigated what has been called the "best case" for psychic detectives, involving the efforts of a New Jersey psychic who gave information to the police about a serial killer in 1982. Despite high hopes and best intentions, the information provided by the psychic, in the end, was of no use to the police. The case is far too detailed to examine here but is described in chapter 6 of my book *Scientific Paranormal Investigation* (Radford 2010).

Even though psychics don't solve crimes or find missing people, what does happen when the police follow up on psychic information? Here's a typical example:

In a chaotic scene in early June 2011 police outside of Houston surrounded a rural farmhouse with guns drawn. They were acting on a tip from a woman who claimed to be psychic; she told them that the property was the scene of a grisly mass murder. Like a scene from the film

The Texas Chainsaw Massacre, dozens of dismembered bodies would be found there, she insisted—including those of children. Helicopters, reporters, and onlookers joined the scene to see what the woman claimed was the state's newest round of serial killing.

Part of the reason that Houston police took the psychic seriously is that they initially found some evidence corroborating her claims, including blood on the ground and the smell of decaying flesh on the property. The psychic also seemed to know the layout of the house without, she claimed, having set foot inside; she had provided amazingly accurate descriptions. Could this be the first case in which psychics accurately alerted police to a genuine crime? It all seemed very mysterious—until the investigators arrived and the mystery was dispelled as quickly as it had arisen.

It was all a waste of time; the police found nothing. "There's no validity to the report," one law enforcement official confirmed. The blood was not from any recently butchered children but instead from an adult who several weeks earlier had cut himself in an unrelated drunken incident. The putrid odor was not from the mass grave that the psychic assured the police they would find but was instead from rotting meat in a broken freezer. But how could the psychic—living far away in Oklahoma—know the layout and details of the Houston-area home? Police determined that the woman had in fact been to the property at least once before; her information came not from psychic abilities but instead from personal experience (Radford 2011c, 2011d).

Even though this case was another high-profile psychic failure, it raises a legitimate question: Do the police take information from psychics seriously?

The answer is no; there's an important difference between police using psychic information in an investigation and police listening to (or following up on) information provided by people claiming to be psychic. To understand the difference, it's important to realize that police investigation procedure requires that detectives follow up on *all* potentially credible tips about crimes, including those from dubious sources. Police investigators routinely deal with liars, hoaxers, jailhouse informants with dubious motives, people with drug habits and mental illnesses, and so on. Why would police ignore information from people claiming to be psychic?

The police cannot simply ignore a lead or tip even if it comes from a psychic—after all, just because a person claims to be psychic doesn't mean that he or she is not involved in a crime or may not have accurate, legitimate information about it. Suspects in criminal cases who have inside knowledge of crimes sometimes pretend that the information they have came from psychics, to avoid incriminating themselves.

Although the police and the FBI don't use psychics, psychics, of course, tell a different story. Most high-profile psychics claim that they have worked closely with police departments to help solve crimes and find missing persons. One of the most famous is Allison DuBois, mentioned earlier. On the website for her NBC television show *Medium*, DuBois claims to have "consulted on a variety of murders or missing persons cases while working with various law enforcement agencies including the Glendale Arizona Police Department [and] the Texas Rangers." Unfortunately for DuBois, I contacted the Glendale police and the Texas Rangers, and both denied having worked with her or any other psychic (Nickell 2007).

Faced with such official denials by law enforcement agencies, psychics often invoke a conspiracy. They insist that the police are lying: they actually *do* use psychics to solve cases but don't want the public to know the truth or share credit with psychics. The police rarely bother to refute this conspiracy theory (they have more important things to do than issue statements refuting that a police conspiracy exists to deny psychics credit in solving crimes), and so many in the public continue to believe that psychics are secretly employed by law enforcement agencies.

Police work is, above all else, a practical profession. The police use whatever works, whatever methods are needed to solve crimes and convict criminals. Police and FBI agents would have no reason not to use psychics—if they really did solve crimes. No hardworking, ethical detective or police officer would fail to enlist psychic abilities if they had been proven to save innocent lives and catch murderers.

PSYCHICS AND THE WEST MESA BONE COLLECTOR MURDERS

But what about psychics in the bone collector case? Just because psychics have consistently failed to solve cases in the past doesn't prove that psychic power does not exist, or that psychics might not finally get it right in this case. It's possible—however improbable—that an Albuquerque psychic might be the first to use psychic powers to help catch a serial killer.

I contacted Albuquerque police detective Ida Lopez, a lead investigator in the serial murders, who told me that she could not comment on those murders specifically because it remains an open, active homicide investigation. Police are notoriously (and understandably) tight lipped about discussing an unsolved case; they have to be careful not to divulge any information that might help the killer (or killers) remain free. In the past serial killers have been known to closely follow news and media coverage of their crimes—knowing (or guessing) what information the police do and do not have can help them elude capture in further crimes. It's even possible that the West Mesa killer, like you, is reading these words at this very moment.

However, Detective Lopez did state for the record that psychics are not used in any investigations. "I have never heard of anyone using psychics. . . . We do not use Albuquerque psychics or any other psychics to help with our cases," she told me in an e-mail. "Yes, we get people calling the tip line claiming to be psychics but we don't actively seek them, nor do we depend on them for our case" (Lopez 2012).

Police acknowledged receiving information from many psychics about the murders, including "a psychic who claimed to have very detailed information about the case" (Proctor 2009d), although none of the tips and information proved accurate or useful. I wanted to find out firsthand what psychics would tell the Albuquerque Police Department if they could—what information they had, or claimed to have, about the worst serial killing in the state's history. Regardless of whether or not police, skeptics, or scientists would believe them, could they offer any real, usable information that might help crack the case and potentially save lives?

In order to find out, I consulted four people in the Albuquerque area who advertise psychic services. I paid for consultations (their charges ranged from $90 to $180 per hour) and asked the psychics what information, if any, they could offer on this unsolved case. Could they determine any useful details about the crime scene, any circumstances of the murders that the police might have overlooked, or any identifying characteristics or details about the killer?*

The first psychic, who charged $90 for a half-hour reading, consulted her tarot deck five times but was unable to provide any information at

* I have not identified the psychics I consulted in this chapter because their identities are not relevant to this investigation. The purpose is not to highlight any given psychic's accuracy or failure but instead to analyze and demonstrate the range and variety of information provided by the psychics overall. Because psychics often claim that skeptics sap or thwart their special abilities (see, for example, Carroll 2003), the sessions were attended by a volunteer.

all about the West Mesa killings. She did offer general information, including that the client (my colleague) had "family concerns"—possibly an argument with a family member—and that there was some unspecified topic of some importance that would require a decision soon. The psychic was pleasant and encouraging but knew nothing about the murders and couldn't help in any way. The second psychic, a man, also consulted his tarot deck but likewise could offer no information about the West Mesa killings, and instead talked at length about himself while offering relationship advice. The third psychic said that she had heard about the murders but rarely followed the news; her psychic powers and tarot deck, also, failed to provide any insight about New Mexico's most notorious unsolved crime.

The fourth and final psychic had more success; she said that she had received some impressions of the West Mesa killer, describing him as a

> rough-looking, kind of bigger, heavyset man. His face is kind of scarred, maybe with old acne or pockmarks, with dark hair, kind of Mexican looking—I don't mean to be racist or anything, but looks like a thug. . . . I'm seeing an orange shirt, like a prison [jumpsuit], maybe he just got out of prison, or ended up in prison I don't know, but it looks like a mug shot and his face is definitely brutal . . . like just stabbing and stabbing. Solid built. I don't see any tattoos on the face. I see someone stout, muscular and strong, but just thug-looking, maybe late thirties or early forties, middle aged. He looks like a hardened criminal, like a raging bull kind of but also methodical in the sense that his energy was predatory, like he knew what he was doing. He was committed, it wasn't a crime of passion, more methodical, almost with a hatred . . . it wasn't personal against the victims . . . he got a kick out of it. There was an element of detachment, but also an element like gloating over what he was doing.

This description of the serial killer may or may not be accurate, although it certainly includes many of the obvious stereotypical characteristics that one would expect from fictional and cinematic portrayals of serial killers. Some of the descriptors are common sense: Is it more likely that a person (probably a man) who was able to kill nearly a dozen women would be "rough-looking," "muscular," and "strong," or meek-looking, thin, and weak? The age is a very likely guess as well: statistically speaking, it's unlikely that the killer is in his teens or elderly, so "thirties" to "middle age" covers a lot of ground and has a very good chance of being correct.

Note also that the characteristics attributed to the killer are rather obvious: of course a person who had successfully murdered so many women would be "predatory," and if he buried them in a place where they would only be found many years later (by accident), he would also be "methodical." If the killer were careless, the victims likely would have been found years earlier. Similarly, it doesn't take an FBI profiler to guess that a serial killer might have acted with hatred and an element of detachment or gloating. Until and unless the killer is captured, there's no way to be certain how many of these adjectives actually fit the bone collector killer, but it's almost certain that at least some of them do, using basic logic and common sense. We can see why this sort of information is of no use to the police. There is, however, one specific fact about the killer that the psychic got completely wrong: she described him "stabbing and stabbing" the victims, but in fact none of them were stabbed. If she got that very specific detail wrong, what else might she have gotten wrong?

From this sampling, it's clear why the police do not (and cannot) use information provided by seers and fortunetellers. In three out of four cases the psychics were unable to come up with any information, and in the fourth case the information was either easily guessed or flat-out wrong. It's important to realize that, as Detective Lopez stated, this sort of information is nothing new; the Albuquerque Police Department has gotten dozens of tips and pieces of information from psychics over the years about the West Mesa murders. If any of this information had been valid and useful in solving the crime and catching the serial killer, that would have been done by now.

If psychics in New Mexico and across the country have the powers they claim, why didn't they alert the police and the public to the killings when they were occurring? Most of the murders are believed to have been committed between 2000 and 2005. Shouldn't psychics have known that something horrific was going on in Albuquerque? Why didn't they do something at the time that could have stopped this killer and saved innocent lives? Why did they wait more than a decade—while the evidence vanished and the trail grew cold—to come forward with information about the killings? Even if their information were completely accurate, it's too little, too late for the victims.

The most indisputable and damning evidence against psychic detectives is that the West Mesa murders, and countless other cases, remain unsolved. This is a fact that even the psychics themselves cannot deny: the results are there for all to see. Either psychic information can solve a case and find a killer, or it can't—and so far the evidence is clear that it can't.

Of course, since the West Mesa crime remains unsolved and the killer remains unidentified, it's possible that one or more details offered by the psychics will turn out to be correct if and when the killer is finally caught. Indeed, if enough psychics chime in with a sufficient variety of details about a killer (or a missing person), sooner or later a few of the details will turn out to be right just by chance. Once you know the answer, it's easy to pick and choose details that seem to match the original predictions, often while ignoring or downplaying those details that turned out to be incorrect. If you only pay attention to the information you got right and ignore the information you got wrong, the overall picture is deceptive and misleading—like an investment banker bragging that a dozen of the stocks he picked far outperformed the market but neglecting to mention that hundreds of other stocks he picked tanked and cost his clients their homes. Looking at just one side of the ledger does not reflect the whole reality. The question is not, "Can psychics accurately predict some elements of a crime scene, killer, or victim?" (because anyone can do that), but instead, "Can psychics provide specific, important, and accurate information about a crime scene, killer, or victim that helps solve the case?"

The bone collector murders remain unsolved. These frustrating and horrific crimes continue to haunt the city of Albuquerque and indeed the whole state of New Mexico. The uncertainty is agonizing: Is the killer still alive, or did he die months or years ago? If he's long since dead, will the police ever solve the case? Or did he leave clues—or perhaps even accomplices—that will one day bring closure (if not justice)? If he's alive, will he be caught and put on trial one day? Even more chilling, could there be more murders and more burial grounds yet to be discovered, either elsewhere in Albuquerque or even in another city or state? Just as the dead, dry bones of the killer's victims were finally unearthed to tell their tale—revealed not by psychics but by a curious dog named Ruca—perhaps one day more clues will be unearthed that will close the case and let New Mexicans remove the stain of fear and uncertainty left by this killer.

Anyone with information about the West Mesa bone collector murders is asked to contact the 118th Street Task Force in Albuquerque at 1-877-765-8273, or Crime Stoppers at 505-843-STOP.

REFERENCES

Carroll, Robert Todd. 2003. "Experimenter Effect." In *The Skeptics Dictionary: A Collection of Strange Beliefs, Amusing Deceptions, and Dangerous Delusions*, 129. Hoboken, NJ: John Wiley and Sons. http://www.skepdic.com/experimentereffect.html.

Lancaster, Robert. 2008. "The People vs. Sylvia Brown(e)." http://www.stopsylvia.com/articles/peoplevsbrown.shtml.

Levitt, Steven, and Stephen Dubner. 2011. *SuperFreakonomics: Global Cooling, Patriotic Prostitutes, and Why Suicide Bombers Should Buy Life Insurance*. New York: William Morrow.

Lopez, Ida. 2012. Personal e-mail correspondence, February 27.

Ng, Christina. 2012. "Trucker with Traveling Torture Chamber Admits to More Murders." *ABC News*, March 30. http://abcnews.go.com/US/texas-trucker-traveling-torture-chamber-admits-murders/story?id=16037743#.T3h8ipgeSkQ.

Nickell, Joe. 2007. *Adventures in Paranormal Investigation*. Lexington: University Press of Kentucky.

Posner, Gary P. 2003. "Noreen Renier and the Laci Peterson Case." *Tampa Bay Skeptics Report* 16, no. 1 (Summer). http://www.tampabayskeptics.org/v16n1rpt.html.

Proctor, Jeff. 2009a. "Police ID 2 More Women." *Albuquerque Journal*, April 4, A1.

———. 2009b. "West Mesa Victims Buried Naked." *Albuquerque Journal*, June 13, A1.

———. 2009c. "W. Mesa Suspect List Narrows." *Albuquerque Journal*, July 31, A1.

———. 2009d. "Closing In on a Killer." *Albuquerque Journal*, October 17, A1.

Radford, Benjamin. 2010. *Scientific Paranormal Investigation: How to Solve Unexplained Mysteries*. Corrales, NM: Rhombus Publishing.

———. 2011a. "Psychics Offer Tips in Search for Missing Woman Holly Bobo." LiveScience, April 19. http://www.livescience.com/13781-psychic-powers-holly-bobo-abduction.html.

———. 2011b. "Holly Bobo Still Missing: Rumors, Psychics Hurt Investigation." *Skeptical Inquirer* 35, no. 5 (September–October): 9.

———. 2011c. "Psychic Fiasco: Texas Mass Murder Raid a Hoax." Discovery News, June 9. http://news.discovery.com/human/psychic-fiasco-texas-mass-murder-raid-a-hoax-110609.html.

———. 2011d. "Texas Mass Grave Hoax: Do Police Really Use Psychics?"

LiveScience, June 8. http://www.livescience.com/14506-psychics-police-investigation-mass-murder.html.

———. 2013. "Sylvia Browne Blunders Again, Telling Mother of Kidnap Victim Amanda Berry She Was Dead." *Skeptical Inquirer* 37, no. 4 (July–August): 7.

CHAPTER 13

SANTA FE'S HAUNTED LA POSADA HOTEL

The historic La Posada Hotel in Santa Fe lies only a short distance from the state capitol. A leisurely stroll in one direction will take you to the city's central plaza, bustling with shops selling fine art and jewelry. A meandering twenty minutes in another direction might bring you to the Georgia O'Keeffe Museum, a miraculous staircase (see chapter 6), or even to the haunted Santa Fe Courthouse, where a ghost was captured on video in 2007 (see chapter 5).

Ghost stories and ghost tours are as common as turquoise, chile ristras, and bandanna-bound coyotes in the "City Different," which was established in 1607 and draws upon four centuries of history. The La Posada Hotel, set back from the characteristically (and proudly) irregular intersection of Palace Avenue and Paseo de Peralta, has a stately entrance, complete with vigas and traditional stucco. The place was originally built by a man named Abraham Staab well over a century ago, and some say that his wife remains there to this day.

HISTORY OF THE LA POSADA

Abraham Staab was born in Germany in 1839 and immigrated to the United States as a strapping lad of fifteen. He spent two years working at trades in Virginia before joining the steady stream of settlers headed west on the Santa Fe Trail. He stayed in Santa Fe and was soon joined by his brother Zadoc, with whom he would soon build one of the largest wholesale and trading companies in New Mexico Territory. A few months after

Abraham Lincoln was assassinated in 1865, Staab returned to the land of his birth to wed his beloved Julia Schuster. Together they returned to Santa Fe, where they would permanently reside.

The official guide to the La Posada Hotel conveys the building's history: "The house [Staab] built on East Palace Avenue in 1882, then the fashionable residential area of Santa Fe, was constructed in the French Second Empire style, with three stories, a Mansard roof, and a widow's walk. It was indeed grand, and while not in the Santa Fe tradition of adobe dwellings, it was in the company of adjacent fine residences on East Palace Avenue built in the emerging Territorial style, with European influences" (La Posada de Santa Fe Resort and Spa 2012).

Julia Staab died in 1896 at age fifty-two, the circumstances of which will be examined presently. And "Abraham, in failing health, began to curtail his activities in the early 1900s and died in 1913, having survived long enough to see New Mexico achieve statehood in 1912, and Santa Fe assured of remaining its capital. . . . After Abraham Staab's death, the Staab House was sold, as no Staab heirs chose to live in it" (Harrelson 2007).

The home was later bought by Lawrence E. and Edna Rich Elliott,

Figure 13.1. *Santa Fe's La Posada Hotel, said to be home to one of New Mexico's most famous ghosts. Photo by the author.*

who lived in the home for a decade while running a nearby hotel. A fire destroyed the third story, likely after the 1920s. The Elliotts lost their fortune in the stock market crash of 1929 and the Great Depression and sold the place in the 1930s, although the home served as a kind of residence hall for artists and writers of the day throughout the 1930s and 1940s. Old photographs of the Staab house are displayed in the hallway near the main staircase (figure 13.2). The building is now the La Posada de Santa Fe Resort and Spa, an elegant and stately resort and part of the Red Rock Resort Group.

For all its opulence and splendor, however, the Staab family story does not end well. "The Staabs had eight children, one of whom, a daughter, died in infancy, and Julia suffered difficulties with her pregnancies. Despite bouts of depression and illness, with recurring journeys to Germany for recuperation, she found her place in Santa Fe society and was a gracious hostess"—including to Archbishop Jean Baptiste Lamy, who plays a role in several mysteries and miracles in the Land of Enchantment (see chapters 6 and 9). Indeed, "Julia Staab loved her home and Santa Fe life, but never really recovered from the loss of her child and succeeding unsuccessful pregnancies. She died in

Figure 13.2. *The author examining old photographs of Abraham and Julia Staab's home—now the La Posada Hotel. Photo by Rachel Duecaster.*

1896 at age 52. Sightings of her ghost have been reported at the Staab House for years, making her the most famous ghost in Santa Fe" (Harrelson 2007).

Julia Staab's ghost is rarely seen, but when she is, according to the hotel's former general manager Michael Cerletti, "she has always been described the same by those who have witnessed her presence. She wears a dark flowing gown and a hood." La Posada's ghost has most often appeared at the top of the grand staircase in the original building in the main complex of the inn (figure 13.3). However, she has also been seen in the Nason Room, a small alcove built upon the old formal gardens of the original structure. The woman for whom the house was originally built in 1882 has apparently never left it. So why does Julia Staab linger? Some say that ghosts appear when death occurs in a state of turmoil and anxiety, such as the circumstances that seemed to attend Mrs. Staab's final years. Depressed over the loss of a child and her other difficult pregnancies, Julia Staab was rumored to have gone mad, retreating to her bedroom until her death. Karen Walker, a Santa Fe real estate broker, experienced several "Julia encounters" when her office was located at La Posada. The day after the party celebrating the Staab house's hundredth anniversary, Walker lunched at the bar in the old building. "It was February and all the doors and windows were shut tight," she recalls, "when suddenly a cold, shivering wind swept in. I asked if someone forgot to invite Julia to the party. After some nervous laughter, we placed a glass of champagne and some roses on the bar and we apologized to Julia. The wind instantly disappeared."

La Posada's resident haunting has been featured in numerous television shows, including NBC's *Unsolved Mysteries* (season 7, episode 2, airdate October 2, 1994). Although most accounts, such as those cited above, only mention one ghost, those who work at La Posada say there are more—many more.

THE GHOSTS OF LA POSADA

What ghosts roam the La Posada halls and rooms? "It depends on what side of the property you're on," said Pauline Jakob, a longtime employee, as she guided me to the entrance to the Staab home. "We have five different individuals. Three of them are in individual locations, and of two them roam around" (Jakob 2012).

Figure 13.3. *The ghost of Julia Staab is sometimes seen at the top of this staircase in the La Posada Hotel. Photo by the author.*

The Cigar Man

"We have the Cigar Man in the Baca house area. He loves cigars, he loves to have people come into his room because he says, 'Come in!' Quite a few of us have noticed . . . when we go into the room there's a cloud of cigar smoke, and there's nobody there." I noted that the entire property is designated as a smoke-free zone; could this ghost get in trouble for violating state law, I asked Jakob? She chuckled and said no. "But we do get calls from other guests saying that someone's smoking. And when we go over there and check, he says 'Come in,' we open the door, and voilà!"

In addition to the Cigar Man (yes, that's his official name), there's another specter haunting the place . . .

The Moustache Man

Another resident ghost is the Moustache Man; "he's been reported to have one of those handlebar moustaches, kind of like a really weird, late 1800s or early 1900s string-tie type? He goes around knocking on doors and says, 'You need to leave.'"

Perhaps he's just being helpful? While at first he may seem to be of genuine service to hotel management, helping evict guests who have stayed past their checkout time, the Moustache Man doesn't check the La Posada computer system to see who in fact is scheduled to depart. Instead, Jakob says, it can happen at any time of day or night: "Guests call us and say, 'There's someone at the door saying I need to leave.' We send someone over, that's all we can do," but the spectral evictor is gone.

It is of course possible that at least some of these stories could simply be pranks by hotel staff or other guests who have heard the ghostly lore and want a bit of fun. It would take little effort to knock quickly on a door, say "You need to leave," and then slip away down the hall or into a nearby room undetected—especially at night, when the occupants are in bed or can be heard in the bathroom. Researcher Joe Nickell (2007) has encountered several haunted hotels where staff members fake ghostly activity for fun, and although there's no proof that this has occurred at La Posada, it's certainly possible. Moustache Man encounters are fairly rare, so even if such pranks only occurred a few times over the years, that would be enough to keep the story alive.

The Little Boy

If moustaches and cigars aren't your thing, there's a chance you'll encounter the Little Boy at La Posada; according to Jakob, "he's about eight or nine years old, and I've had him in the gift shop. I have the only key to the gift shop, and when I left for lunch or on my break a couple of times I would come back and I'd have the bookcase against the back wall, and I had six books of various sizes taken off the bookcase and placed in front of my desk! Other times I would find candy bars in different areas, I'd find toys in different areas, like up on a shelf or a pen tucked among shirts. I'd get it, place it where it's supposed to go, and a couple of hours later I'd get that little chill saying something's wrong. I'd go through the store and I'd find something out of place."

Another time, Jakob said, she lost one of her earrings shortly after arriving at work; she retraced her steps from the time clock to the gift shop but couldn't find it. "So I sat down near the cash register, and then I walked around the gift shop. I didn't feel anything, but when I sat down again I got goose bumps. So I took everything out of my bag, and at the bottom, there it was!" Jakob's experience is not uncommon in ghost reports, in which people will sometimes smell a particular aroma (perhaps of a perfume or flower). Unfortunately, there is no way to definitively and scientifically test for such aromas (at least not without very sensitive and expensive machines). Her descriptions of the ghost's activities are also common, involving trivial pranks and mischief that might be accounted for by other, non-ghostly factors.

The Shadowy Figure

There's one other ghost that no one seems to know much about; he's referred to simply as the Shadowy Figure, and he (occasionally appearing as a rough outline of a man) can sometimes be seen as a shadow that moves across a room or that is glimpsed out of the corner of one's eye. He has no particular defined characteristics, simply a shadowy form. "There is a shadow figure, which is the one I say is not a nice person; he's mostly in the spa area," Jakob says.

And the final ghost is the star of the spirit show, the most famous ghost in Santa Fe: Julia Staab.

JULIA STAAB: "THE MOST FAMOUS GHOST IN SANTA FE"

Unlike the Moustache Man and the Cigar Man—alternately welcoming and dismissing guests, respectively—the ghost of Julia Staab is generally mute. She doesn't speak but instead makes her presence known in other ways. "There have been instances of blankets put on the bed; they're in the closet, and you'll notice that the closet does take a good tug to open. Some of the curtains will move, just a little a bit, like, 'Did I see it move or did I not see it move?' . . . Sometimes the bathtub water faucet gets turned on, she loved to take hot baths. We've had guests complain about noises coming from the third floor—which we don't have anymore," Jakob said.

What does Julia Staab's ghost look like? It seems there's no real answer—or, rather, a dozen different answers from a dozen different people. One La Posada employee, Alan Day, claimed to have seen her by a fireplace late one night while he was mopping the floor. "She was wearing a long dark gown and was translucent, but I could see her dark eyes looking at me. . . . When I looked back up, she was gone" (White 2008, 3). Often, Julia is not seen at all; instead, some curious or unusual event is attributed to her presence—anything from a cold draft to a strange noise to odd lights or shadows on the wall.

In one famous legend, Julia helped turn on the heat:

> One fall night, when the weather suddenly turned very cold in Santa Fe, several guests at La Posada requested that the heat be turned on. But just the day before, the locks to the boiler room had been changed and through a comedy of errors, no one in the building had a key. Nevertheless, sometime during the night, the heat came on. Eventually, a manager with a key to the boiler room arrived and discovered that the boiler had indeed been lit. "It's a very complicated process," says [former general manager Michael] Cerletti, shaking his head. "There are only a few of us here capable of doing it, and none of us had a key to get in." (White 2008, 3)

Another version of that story has the same ghostly twist at the end but is greatly embellished in many important details:

> There is also the time Julia turned up the heat during one of Santa Fe's cold spells. It happened one evening when the temperature in Santa Fe suddenly and unexpectedly dropped, leaving the residents in La Posada shivering in their rooms. The story goes that the only person who had the key to operate the thermostat had gone fishing, and the clerk at the front desk was being flooded with calls about the cold in their rooms. Sometime between seven and eight o'clock, a call came in from room 256. A woman with a thick German accent told the clerk what he had already heard a dozen times that evening, except for adding that her guests were all half-frozen. When he answered the best he could do was provide some blankets and hot beverages until the maintenance man with the thermostat key arrived, he received a brisk response: "Neveer, mind, I vill take care of eet myself." Moments later, the heater was running, and within the hour the hotel was a comfortable room temperature. The man finished his shift not thinking much of the heater, assuming that the maintenance man had returned and

turned it back on. The clerk ran into the caretaker on his way out of the hotel, and thanked him for turning the heat on. "Pardon me?" the caretaker replied, "I just got back in now. I didn't turn the heat on." (La Posada de Santa Fe Resort and Spa 2012)*

I asked how often people report odd occurrences: every few days, every few months? "Just whenever," Pauline Jakob said. "Because a lot of times they're not sure. . . . There are some folks who are absolutely positive. Some folks hear the furniture move, and they do a sneaky peek [over the sheets]—they cover their eyes, don't want to look. And when they rise in the morning, they notice the chairs are a little kiltered, the towels in the bathroom are a little kiltered."

One time, Jakob continued, "I was closing the door, finishing my inventory, walking down the hallways, and all of a sudden—Boom!—it hits me: orange blossoms and roses. . . . And that is not an up-to-date fragrance. But nearby is Julia's rose garden, and that's why she's seen [in that vicinity]; it's her old stomping grounds. When she's happy sometimes the chandeliers will sway a little; sometimes glasses in the bar will clink . . . just little things. When she's not happy my security cameras will go wacky, and we'll have electrical or computer issues."

It seems that many of the stories about Julia Staab are merely myth, rumors, and folklore. According to historian Mary Lee White, "The official record contained nothing untoward about Mrs. Staab's demise. However, rumors afoot in Santa Fe implied that Julia had gone crazy and was kept in her room the last few years of her life" (quoted in Wheeler 2002).

While some feel that this is harmless fun, others may take a different tack: How would you feel if, decades after your death, strangers created and repeated lies and rumors about how you had gone insane and spent your last years locked up? Or that you may have been murdered by your beloved husband (thereby creating two victims), as some stories suggest? If Julia Staab's ghost truly does haunt La Posada, the revenge she would likely take is on those who carelessly taint her memory and dignity.

* Obviously, one (if not both) of these stories is not true. In one case, "several" guests were complaining, and in the other calls were flooding in; in one story, the boiler is inaccessible because the locks had been changed, while in the other story the heater could not be lit because the man with the key had gone fishing (during one of Santa Fe's worst cold spells, apparently!); in one story, Julia doesn't even appear, while in the other Julia's ghost used the telephone to complain about the cold (in a thick German accent, no less).

I have encountered exactly the same situation in other supposedly haunted locations, including the KiMo Theater in Albuquerque (see chapter 1) and the Rose Hall Mansion in Montego Bay, Jamaica (Radford 2010). In the latter case, a woman named Annie Palmer, whose ghost reportedly haunts Rose Hall, was said to have been a witch and a sadistic murderer when in fact there is no evidence that she was anything but a kind and devoted wife and mother. Ghost hunters hoping for a salacious story fabricated and exaggerated her life, sullying her memory.

The best way to truly honor the dead is to tell their true story as best we can. In the case of Julia Staab, many who work at La Posada speak of the importance of respecting Julia and her memory. Julia is no longer with us to defend her reputation; that task is left to historians (and conscientious ghost researchers who value the truth over a good story).

JULIA AND THE SKEPTICS

Julia, it is said, has a habit of turning skeptics into believers faster than you can say "Boo!" Jakob told me that, about seven or eight months before my conversation with her, "we had one houseman, he was totally a nonbeliever, a skeptic, who was here with a housekeeper, and they went upstairs. He was waiting for her between the two rooms there, and he was picking on her, saying, 'You're a chicken, why do you believe in this stuff, you're scared,' and all that. And the housekeeper is trying to ignore it, just saying, 'Stay there while I go in, do what I have to do, and get out.'"

Little did either of them know that the skeptic was about to get a creepy comeuppance: "The fire extinguisher fixture fell forward on the houseman, the whole fixture. The wall wasn't torn, the screws that were attaching it to the wall weren't pulled. . . . It caused him to run down those stairs and quit, just like that. Like I always tell everyone about Miss Julia, this is her home, and we respect it, and when you show disrespect, disrespect will be shown to you."

I went upstairs to inspect the fire extinguisher (figure 13.4) that Julia was said to have pulled off the wall. What would I find? Poltergeist-like activity such as a hinged door opening and slamming shut? A box ripped from the wall with supernatural strength? I've investigated several haunted houses where objects have fallen off walls—seemingly with ghostly help—including in Carson, California, for the History Channel show *MysteryQuest*. So I had some idea of what to look for and what to expect. In this case, however, there was no evidence that anything unusual had happened—or even that the box had indeed fallen off the wall. I closely examined both the metal housing and the wooden floor directly beneath and found no damage, dents, or scuffing at all. I also examined the mounting on the wall, and there was no indication that the box had fallen or been remounted.

I didn't want to be rude or challenge anyone's veracity or memory, but I could find no evidence that the event had even happened. I also realized that, even if I had seen evidence that the fire extinguisher box had fallen off the wall, it wouldn't have proved anything. Sometimes, objects mounted on walls simply fall off. It might have been Julia Staab showing her displeasure at being disrespected, or it might have simply been loose screws or old drywall.

Pauline Jakob told me that, on another occasion, "we had this big old football linebacker guy, he had to be about six foot seven, three hundred and some pounds. [When he and his wife checked in] his wife is going, 'Do you have any information about the ghost?' And he's like, 'Alright already, let's go . . . ' They got their luggage unloaded, brought their car in, took the luggage up. Something happened because the husband came

Figure 13.4. *A fire extinguisher cabinet near Julia Staab's room that reportedly was pulled from the wall by a ghost, frightening a skeptic who had disrespected "Miss Julia." Photo by the author.*

up here, tipped the bellman, and came back down the stairs and said, 'I'm not going back up there. I want another room. Now!'"

I asked if he had said why—what might have changed his mind? Did he say what had suddenly spooked him about the room? "No," Jakob said. "And we don't ask, we just say okay." Her interpretation seemed to be that something had scared him into changing rooms. And that might be true, but it occurred to me that there might be other, equally plausible explanations. Perhaps it had been the man's wife who had a funny feeling about the room, and the man didn't want to spoil her vacation with ghostly premonitions. Or perhaps the room wasn't to his or her liking for some completely unrelated, mundane reason. I don't know why he didn't take the room, and Jakob doesn't either. Since the guest never mentioned anything about the ghost, we don't know whether their abrupt room change had anything to do with it. The ghostly explanation—correct or not—was Jakob's, not the couple's.

I realized that this was a problem with almost all the ghost encounters I was hearing about: I had no way to confirm or verify any of them. I heard and read dozens of stories about things that were said to have happened at La Posada (some mundane, some extraordinary), but almost all of them were reports by unnamed people, given many months or years earlier.

There were a few firsthand eyewitness accounts, but most of the reports were second- or thirdhand stories and anecdotes. I had no reason to doubt the truthfulness of anyone at La Posada—everyone I spoke with seemed sincere and genuine. However, an investigator cannot accept stories at face value, and I had already encountered much misinformation and myth masquerading as truth at La Posada. Part of the reason there's so much misinformation and misunderstanding about the Staab story is that most people who write about it merely copy (sometimes with attribution, often without) from other, previous writers, who themselves never visited La Posada or did original research but likewise copied from even earlier writers. This lack of scholarship plagues many ghost investigations.

While the most common version of the legend says that Julia's daughter died, another source says that it was not a daughter but "one of her sons [who] died in infancy" (La Posada de Santa Fe Resort and Spa 2012). Mark Miller, a senior sales manager at La Posada, says that both of those stories are wrong; instead, "the child was around five, it wasn't a childbirth [death]" (Rush 2011). One source says that "in 1883, Julia gave birth to an eighth child, named Henriette, who died two days . . .

after she was born" (Budd 2010). Another states that, instead, "Staab's seventh child died soon after being born" (Haunted Houses 2010).

Various sources offer different and contradictory details; although it seems clear that one of Julia Staab's children died, depending on which source you consult, it was either a boy or a girl, a newborn or a preschooler, and either her sixth, seventh, or eighth child. Sources can't even agree on which room she lived and died in, supposedly the most haunted room on the property: was it 100, 101, or 256? Some writers even misspell Staab's name as "Julia Staub."

These points may be dismissed as minor details—it's easy enough for typographical errors to introduce confusion—but what of the larger, more important aspects of the story? Are they true? Ghost stories are notoriously unreliable; legends get embellished, fiction is mistaken for fact, and so on. Many writers are so sloppy with their accounts of ghost stories that they inadvertently spawn new legends. If these writers—some of them appearing in respectable publications—can't even get the most basic and easily checkable facts correct, there's little reason to think that their second- or thirdhand stories of ghostly goings-on are any more accurate or reliable. All this is fine if one merely wants to be entertained by spooky stories. However, if one is an investigator—tasked with trying to sort fact from fiction and determine which stories are bogus, which have a grain of truth to them, and which are verifiable fact—then that's another matter.

FOLKLORE AND GHOSTS

I continued my investigation by reviewing some of the information about La Posada's history and reputed spirits. From my previous research in folklore, I immediately recognized several aspects of the La Posada ghost story as legend and lore.

Take, for example, the claim of Alan Jordan, the founder of a company that offers ghost tours in Santa Fe, that after Julia Staab lost her child shortly after giving birth, "her hair is rumored to have turned white overnight" (Lovato 2007). Many people believe that fright can turn hair white, and the theme is common in ghost stories. As discussed in the chapter on the legends of La Llorona (chapter 11), this is a myth.

Legend also has it that a terrible personal tragedy drove Julia Staab insane: "Mother to six children, Julia was expected to host parties, show off the home and keep up the Staabs' standing in the community. There are several accounts of what happened next, but one version says

Julia lost her seventh child shortly after birth. After more unsuccessful attempts to have more children, Julia began to lose her mind. . . . Julia was confined to a room in the home's second story—known today as Suite 100, or Julia's Room—where she spent her days deteriorating until her death in 1896" (Lovato 2007).

The idea that the death of a child causes insanity is also an ancient myth, and a common theme in countless legends and stories. In reality, of course, the death of children is a tragically common occurrence; mothers (and fathers) lose their children every day to accident, murder, and disease, and they are not driven insane with grief (and certainly not institutionalized). This was even truer in Julia Staab's time: the death of a child in the 1800s (due to high infant morality rates and disease) was much more common than it is today. This of course does not detract from the tragic nature of such events, but it was hardly unusual for those living at the time.

Jordan, a professional teller of ghost stories, goes on: "But [Julia] didn't let go completely. She died with a lot of loose ends and as a result she never really left her home. That's one of the important ingredients in why ghosts exist—they're in a place where they have unfinished business, loose ends or an unhappy-premature departure. Things that prevent a total departure from this earth" (Lovato 2007). This explanation, of course, reveals yet another classic motif of ghost folklore: that spirits haunt certain locations because they died with unfinished business.

Although this canard is widely believed and promoted among ghost enthusiasts, the fact is that we don't know for certain whether ghosts exist, and there is certainly no way to know what their intentions or motivations are. There is no book of "ghost rules" explaining how the Other Side works, outlining which ghosts appear where and why. It's all speculation and guesswork and folklore, not anchored in scientific evidence or reality. Investigators must question assumptions in order to draw a clear line between what is known and what is suspected—between proven fact and idle conjecture.

This explanation about "unfinished business" suggests that the only people whose death would *not* create ghosts are those who have lived a full and tidy life, and whose death is anticipated, happy, and timely.

While a few people in specific circumstances (such as those who are suicidal, in hospice, or otherwise hoping to die) might fit that description, almost all of the rest of us would not.

If ghosts exist, it seems unlikely that simply dying unhappy, or with unfinished business or loose ends, would be the motive force creating them. Are there any deaths that are *not* at least somewhat "unhappy" or "premature," or without some (probably a great many) "loose ends"? Surely almost everyone has some unfinished business when they die: loved ones or dear friends they never said good-bye to, unpaid bills, love unrequited, apologies never expressed, borrowed items never returned, books unfinished, opportunities and potential unfulfilled.

Take, for example, the estimated half of Americans who die without a will; these intestate persons leave it up to (often arbitrary) state laws to decide how their assets should be distributed. Children, girlfriends, common-law spouses, and other potential heirs are often left with no bequest. In other cases, minor children are left as wards of the state (or put in orphanages) instead of being raised by a loved one because the deceased never assigned a legal guardian. Surely there can hardly be more significant "loose ends" or "unfinished business" than the fate of one's children. Yet these people left this world unprepared for death and the consequences it would bring; if mere "unfinished business" creates ghosts, then half of all Americans are coming back from the dead.

There are many other examples we could examine in the ghost lore at La Posada and elsewhere, but in all of them we see the paradox that if the assumption is true—that all that is needed to create a ghost is dying before one's personal affairs are put in order—then surely nearly all deaths fit that bill, and there should be literally billions of ghosts. In fact, recent research demonstrates that the dead outnumber the living; according to Carl Haub, a demographer with the Population Reference Bureau, only about 6.5 percent of the number of people who have ever lived are alive today. Thus, the spirits of the dead should be literally everywhere (Howard 2012).

Of course, they are not; ghosts are a relatively rare phenomenon. This canard of ghost folklore has a widespread, melodramatic, and superficial appeal, but it is nonsensical and illogical upon further reflection.

I soon moved on from the parts of the ghost story that were clearly fiction and folklore to the parts that were more likely to have a basis in the real world. Hair can't really turn white overnight, parents don't really go insane after the death of a child, and so on. But could a spirit move physical objects in plain view of stunned eyewitnesses? Can a ghost really cast creepy shadows along a wall?

I heard stories—but only stories. There was nothing to check, nothing to verify. There was no video of anything unusual or ghostly to examine and analyze. Guests and ex-employees of the hotel who were said to have encountered Miss Julia or La Posada's other four resident ghosts were long gone, with no way to track them down for interviews. And even if I had, at best they would only be able to repeat their stories, which had happened years ago with no corroborating evidence. There was little or nothing to verify, just stories and tales (often contaminated by obvious embellishments). There was only one thing to do: see for myself, accompanied by Rachel Duecaster, a visiting colleague.

OVERNIGHT IN THE ROOM OF DOOM: SUITE 100

As I took the room key—a modern plastic swipe card, not the ornate metal latch key that one might have hoped for—I asked Pauline Jakob what we should expect staying overnight in Julia's room. "I would say to have an open heart," she said. "If it happens it happens." I agreed, but it was the "it" in "it happens" that I was a bit uncertain about.

I climbed the stairs and approached the Julia Staab suite with some unease. As an investigator I want to be there when something unusual happens, to document, or at least experience, the event. I've never understood so-called ghost hunters on television who run scared at the first sign that something weird is going on. After all, what's the point in seeking out a ghostly experience if you don't have the nerves to see it through?

Still, some places give an eerie vibe, and people with vivid imaginations (or those who have seen a few haunted house films) know what to expect: dark, spooky corridors; elevators that open at the end of the hall with blood pouring out; seemingly innocuous portraits of long-dead occupants who come alive when your back is turned—or who at least follow you with their eyes; evil clowns; insects. Any number of things . . .

I paused at the carved plaque designating Julia's room. Like in any hotel in the world, whether a grand palace or a flophouse, the room bears an identifying number, but make no mistake: it is Julia's room. We walked in to see an elegantly appointed room (figure 13.6) with a small entryway, a bathroom on the right, and a multipillowed bed in front of two old photos of the house. The building is, after all, very old, and although some of the furnishing is of the period, very little of the Staabs' personal belongings remain. There's a painting in Julia's room, an image looking across toward the bed (figure 13.7). Several sources claim that it's of Julia, placed there so that she can continue to keep an eye on her room, as it were—or that her eyes follow visitors around the room.

Research has revealed that the portrait was painted by John Young-Hunter, a Scottish portrait, figure, and landscape artist who was born in

Figure 13.5. *The Julia Staab suite at the La Posada Hotel: plaque outside the door. Photo by the author.*

Figure 13.6. *Julia Staab's room at the La Posada Hotel. Photo by the author.*

Figure 13.7. *A portrait said to be of Julia Staab hung over a fireplace facing a bed in her haunted room. Photo by the author.*

1874. The painting was done in 1936, forty years after Julia's death. If indeed, as some have claimed, the woman's piercing eyes follow visitors around the room, those eyes are not Julia Staab's; the woman in the painting is in fact either Julia's granddaughter or her niece (Rush 2011).

As for the portrait's eyes and their tendency to "follow" viewers across the room, this is in fact an optical illusion; as one researcher who has examined ghostly portraits has noted, "any two-dimensional portrait in which the subject's eyes gaze directly at the viewer will produce the same effect. It is the result of a three-dimensional view being 'fixed' in the two-dimensional representation" (Nickell 2007, 8).

Other examples of this illusion can be found in da Vinci's famous *Mona Lisa*, and also on the mysterious busts at the Haunted Mansion at Disneyland in Anaheim, California, whose eyes—and indeed whose entire heads—seem to follow those who pass by. It's not a special effects trick using holograms or special imagery; it is instead a clever optical illusion created by lighting a concave face.

JULIA'S PRESENCE

Rachel and I noted that by far the most common ghost reports from the Staab suite were not dramatic sightings of full-body apparitions but instead the far more minor, subtle, and ambiguous phenomena typical of ghosts: odd sounds, strange shadows and lights, unusual smells, and effects of that nature. What might account for strange sights and sounds in the Staab room and the hallway outside?

I began by carefully surveying and photographing the room, noting any details or phenomena that might be relevant. As I wandered around the room, we heard a low moan that didn't sound natural—but it didn't necessarily sound supernatural, either. At first we thought it was coming from the air vents, but we put our hands near the vent and there was no air flow. The moaning soon became more of a rhythmic rumble, and we realized that it was coming from the corner of the room opposite the bed, in fact just outside the window. We looked out the window to discover an unusually populated rooftop maze of four swamp coolers, refrigerated air units, ductwork, pipes, and open roof vents leading to various parts of the hotel.

As native New Mexicans know—although visiting guests from outside the Southwest likely would not—swamp coolers have moving parts, pumps, flowing water, and spinning wheels that often squeak, clank, and rumble. Because any sound whose source is not immediately evident can be attributed to ghosts (knocks, thumps, hums, moans, etc.), it seems at least possible (and indeed likely) that some of the unexplained noises and sounds reported in room 100 and nearby are actually normal noises from the building's heating, cooling, and venting systems. People who live and work nearby may recognize, and become accustomed to, the routine sounds that emanate from a particular building; however, since most La Posada guests only stay a night or two, they have no way of knowing what's normal and what's not. If a guest hears an odd noise for the first time, he may not realize he's hearing something that happens on a regular basis, as the restaurant's kitchen shuts down, for example.

As I walked out of the bathroom fresh from brushing my teeth (and keeping a careful eye on the bathtub, in case Julia decided to turn on the faucet, as she is said to sometimes do), I heard a strange rattling or clawing sound coming from the dark corner opposite the bed, behind the curtains. Rachel, sitting in a nearby chair reading, heard it too and looked up. I stepped curiously but cautiously toward the sound, and within a few seconds I realized that the windows rattled slightly.

I didn't think much of it until I reflected on how rare a phenomenon this is. In the modern homes and buildings where most of us spend our days (especially in today's eco-friendly climate with its emphasis on insulation), windows rarely rattle. But the windows in the Staab suite use a rope-and-pulley mechanism common a century ago (figure 13.8). Because lower and upper windows must slide past each other on a painted wooden track, they cannot fit snugly; otherwise they would get stuck. There must be at least a crack (often much more than a crack) of wiggle room between the windows. This can cause at least two phenomena often associated with ghosts: rattling and cold spots. The lower window often hangs loosely, and it can rattle when the wind blows against it (or even when a pressure differential is created in the room, caused for example by someone suddenly opening or closing a door). Sometimes the rattle is barely audible; other times it is loud, surprising, and nerve wracking. Because it's caused by the wind, there is no pattern to the sounds: the window might never rattle or it might rattle for a few seconds, then fall silent for hours, then suddenly rattle again—all depending on how and when the wind hits it. I have personally seen this happen in several allegedly haunted rooms, including at the famous Myrtles Plantation in Louisiana. If it's chilly outside, the small gap between the upper and lower windows can also create localized cold spots, at least in the area near the window—and, in Julia's room, the bed isn't far away.

I slipped into the bed and waited in the dark for something to happen. I had a flashlight and a camera handy, ready to leap to my feet to investigate anything odd. We waited and waited, each agreeing to wake the other up if we experienced anything strange. I stayed awake as long as I could, but I finally gave up. It had been a long drive and a long day of interviews, research, and investigation. The bed was too comfortable, and nothing was going on except for the occasional thump or

Figure 13.8. *Could antique windows explain some of the ghostly phenomena at the La Posada Hotel? Photo by the author.*

creak that was clearly coming from downstairs or the hallway outside. This is, after all, an actively used modern hotel room, not a museum exhibit.*

Sunlight greeted me the next morning, and I awoke with a stretch and a yawn in a valley of overstuffed comfy pillows. I wish I could report that

* Ideally, to identify and conclusively rule out all natural sources of contamination (noises, lights, vibrations, and so on) that might be mistaken for ghostly goings-on, I'd need to secure the building and essentially shut down (or badly disrupt) the entire hotel and its restaurant. I'd need dozens of cameras and sensors set up throughout the area, both inside and outside the building, as well as a team of investigators to help. That would not only be impractical (and enormously expensive for me) but would result in the loss of tens of thousands of dollars in revenue for La Posada. They would, quite reasonably, refuse such a request, and even if they accepted it, the results would very likely be negative or ambiguous.

Julia (or any of the other resident La Posada ghosts) had come to us in the night or given some unmistakable sign of their presence. But it wasn't to be. Perhaps Julia was busy elsewhere that night, or she just didn't feel like making herself known. Or maybe she doesn't exist at all, outside of legends and imaginations. Any of these conclusions is possible. It also occurred to me that people come and go in that room almost every day and night; if Julia does indeed haunt her room, it's surprising that she is not seen more often.

SPOOKS AND SHADOWS

Many guests in Julia's room report seeing glimpses of light or shadow out of the corner of their eyes: a faint flash of light here, an odd glow there. Sometimes it's noticed as it happens; on other occasions, people won't discover a curious presence until after they review photographs on their cameras (or get the images developed).

There are subtle, unusual features of both room 100 and the hallway outside that may contribute to its reputation as one of the most haunted areas of the La Posada Hotel. One feature is the ornate wall covering, which contains a reflective surface. While most walls we encounter have a flat luster, patches of the walls in Julia's room have a shiny texture that can catch the eye and make movement around the room's light fixtures more noticeable.

And what of the lights themselves? It's not just the walls that can trick and deceive; as I spent some time in the hallway outside room 100 getting a sense of the place, I discovered that the light fixtures cast strange and arcane shapes and shadows on the ceiling and walls (figure 13.9). It's quite accidental, but the candelabra-style electric lights reflect and cast shadows off each other—as well as off the half-dozen glass or crystal prisms that make up each candelabra. Very few ceiling lights in people's houses create such an illusion, and because the fixture hangs freely and is fairly lightweight, it can sway slightly from the wind and ordinary building vibrations. I saw this effect myself when a slight movement caused a faint but detectable shadow to move out of the corner of my eye. Because we don't ordinarily pay much attention to the shadows that light fixtures cast, it would be easy to notice that something was amiss without realizing exactly what it was. In 2014 this illusion was demonstrated in research published in the online science journal *PLOS ONE* (see Radford 2014).

Of course, roof vents, air conditioners, and rattling windows cannot explain every seemingly mysterious knock, thud, thump, rattle, voice, or bang ever heard in the room, hallway, or nearby. And not every shadow, light, apparition, or ghostly figure can be explained by unusual light patterns and reflections on the walls and ceilings—and I won't pretend otherwise. But most reported phenomena attributed to ghosts are in fact mundane, ordinary lights and sounds that seem extraordinary because of their context. The power of suggestion can be persuasive, and often I've found that people are spooked by nothing more mysterious than their own imaginations.

It's clear that there are plenty of myths, legends, and tall tales about La Posada. But is there a real ghost, some genuine, unexplained specter or entity dwelling there? I didn't see any hard evidence of that, but then again I (like most guests) was only there a short time. Some people who have worked there for years said that they'd never experienced anything obviously paranormal—but other people said that they'd directly experienced strange phenomena, and heard about more.

Figure 13.9. *Strange shadows cast by candelabra lights creep along the ceiling and walls of the La Posada Hotel. Photo by the author.*

Some believe and some doubt; for some, no amount of evidence will be enough to disprove ghosts, while for others no evidence is even needed to disprove them. Visit La Posada and decide for yourself, and as a skeptic's dictum famously advises, "It pays to keep an open mind, but not so open that your brains fall out."

WHAT OF SCIENTIFIC EVIDENCE?

As at most other reputedly haunted locations, it is of course possible—without too much effort or expense—to scientifically verify some of the phenomena reported at La Posada using a series of closed-circuit security cameras. If a resident spirit hides merchandise in unexpected places, such as a pen among a stack of shirts as reported by Pauline Jakob, reviewing surveillance footage should explain how the pen got there—was it a careless gift shop employee who accidentally dropped a pen while folding shirts? A shopper who picked up a souvenir pen, planning to buy it, but changed her mind and just left it wherever—a common and expected occurrence in retail sales? Or was it a ghost who picked up the pen and moved it through the air to place it among the shirts? Unfortunately, there is no video evidence from La Posada that might explain these ghostly goings-on. In the end, perhaps the best explanation comes from New Mexico historian Sandra Lynn (1999): "Stories adhere to houses and to their larger cousins—hotels, inns, resorts—and accumulate over the years because in homes our most intimate dramas occur, and in homes-away-from-homes intimate dramas intersect with public life. Seldom does anyone investigate the truth of these stories; they are simply repeated, with errors and embellishments compounded year after year" (132).

REFERENCES

Botter, Mary Ellen. 2010. "La Posada de Santa Fe Resort and Spa Shares Its Space with Spirits." *Dallas News*, October 31. http://www.dallasnews.com/travel/texas/20101031-La-Posada-de-Santa-Fe-Resort-7039.ece.

Budd, Deena. 2010. "Julia Staab and La Posada." BellaOnline. http://www.bellaonline.com/articles/art68636.asp.

Harrelson, Diana. 2007. "Julia Staab and the Legends of La Posada." In "Stories of La Posada Santa Fe's Art Hotel," La Posada de Santa Fe Resort and Spa.

Haunted Houses. 2010. "La Posada: Haunted Houses.com." http://www.hauntedhouses.com/states/nm/la_posada.

Howard, Jacqueline. 2012. "World Population Explained: Do Dead People Outnumber Living, or Vice Versa?" *Huffington Post*, November 7. http://www.huffingtonpost.com/2012/11/07/world-population-explained_n_2058511.html.

Jakob, Pauline. 2012. Interview by Benjamin Radford, September 12.

La Posada de Santa Fe Resort and Spa. 2012. "Stories of La Posada Santa Fe's Art Hotel." http://www.laposadadesantafe.com/_files/pdf/18425.12-La-Posada-History-Book.final2012pdf.pdf.

Lovato, Todd Eric. 2007. "Ghost Stories Staying Alive in N.M." *Albuquerque Journal*, October 28, E1.

Lynn, Sandra. 1999. *Windows on the Past: Historic Lodgings of New Mexico.* Albuquerque: University of New Mexico Press.

Nickell, Joe. 2007. *Adventures in Paranormal Investigation.* Lexington: University Press of Kentucky.

Radford, Benjamin. 2010. *Scientific Paranormal Investigation: How to Solve Unexplained Mysteries.* Corrales, NM: Rhombus Publishing.

———. 2014. "Study Explains Cognitive Illusion of Psychic Powers." Discovery News, January 17. http://news.discovery.com/human/psychology/study-explains-cognitive-illusion-of-psychic-powers-140117.htm.

Rush, David. 2011. "Julia Staabs [*sic*] Ghost at La Posada." YouTube video, 6:20. Posted May 24. http://www.youtube.com/watch?v=h4Gtyxro-KM.

Thompson, Stith, ed. 2001. *Motif-Index of Folk-Literature: A Classification of Narrative Elements in Folk Tales, Ballads, Myths, Fables, Mediaeval Romances, Exempla, Fabliaux, Jest-Books, and Local Legends.* 7 vols. Bloomington: Indiana University Press.

Wheeler, Liza. 2002. "N.M. Has Its Share of Haunts." *Albuquerque Journal*, October 31, C1.

White, Mary Lee. 2008. La Posada de Santa Fe Resort and Spa. Brochure.

CREDITS

The following chapters are revised, updated, and expanded versions of materials (or include materials) published elsewhere.

"Phantom Performances at the Haunted KiMo Theater" (chapter 1) includes materials from "The Definitive KiMo Ghost" by Mike Smith and myself, published in *Weekly Alibi* 17, no. 43 (October 23–29, 2008); "Stage Fright," published in *Fortean Times* (June 2010); and "Ghosts, Doughnuts, and a Christmas Carol," published in *Skeptical Inquirer* 33, no. 3 (May–June 2009).

"The Santa Fe Courthouse Ghost" (chapter 5) includes material from chapter 9 of my book *Scientific Paranormal Investigation: How to Solve Unexplained Mysteries* (Corrales, NM: Rhombus Publishing, 2010); and "Capturing the 'Santa Fe Courthouse Ghost,'" published in *Fortean Times* 229 (November 2007).

"Labyrinths: Sacred Symbols in the Sand" (chapter 10) includes material from "Labyrinths: Mazes and Myths," published in *Skeptical Inquirer* 28, no. 5 (September–October 2004): 49–52.

INDEX